Lafcadio Hearn's America

LAFCADIO HEARN'S
AMERICA

Ethnographic Sketches and Editorials

EDITED

BY

SIMON J. BRONNER

THE UNIVERSITY PRESS OF KENTUCKY

Publication of this volume was made possible in part by a grant from
the National Endowment for the Humanities.

Scholarly publisher for the Commonwealth,
serving Bellarmine University, Berea College, Centre
College of Kentucky, Eastern Kentucky University,
The Filson Historical Society, Georgetown College,
Kentucky Historical Society, Kentucky State University,
Morehead State University, Murray State University,
Northern Kentucky University, Transylvania University,
University of Kentucky, University of Louisville,
and Western Kentucky University.
All rights reserved.

Editorial and Sales Offices: The University Press of Kentucky
663 South Limestone Street, Lexington, Kentucky 40508-4008

02 03 04 05 06   5 4 3 2 1

Frontispiece: Lafcadio Hearn, Cincinnati, late 1870s. Courtesy
Cincinnati Historical Society Library, Alton Mood Collection.

Library of Congress Cataloging-in-Publication Data

Hearn, Lafcadio, 1850-1904.
Lafcadio Hearn's America : ethnographic sketches and editorials /
edited by Simon J. Bronner.
p. cm.
Includes bibliographical references (p.   ).
ISBN 0-8131-2229-5 (cloth : acid-free paper)
1. United States—Description and travel—Anecdotes. 2. United
States—Social life and customs—1865-1918—Anecdotes. 3. United
States—Social conditions—1865-1918—Anecdotes. 4. Ethnology—
United States—History—19th century—Anecdotes. 5. Social classes—
United States—History—19th century—Anecdotes. 6. Hearn, Lafcadio,
1850-1904—Homes and haunts—Anecdotes. 7. Hearn, Lafcadio,
1850-1904—Political and social views. I. Bronner, Simon J. II. Title.
E168 .H43 2001
814.'4—dc21   2001002585

This book is printed on acid-free recycled paper meeting
the requirements of the American National Standard
for Permanence of Paper for Printed Library Materials.

Manufactured in the United States of America

For Jay and Elizabeth Mechling on this side of the Pacific,
and Hisashi Ishida, Seisaku Kawakami,
Yuichi Morioka, and Akira Tamai on the other

CONTENTS

PART III: OPINIONS OF AMERICA

ACKNOWLEDGMENTS

My study of Lafcadio Hearn is part of a larger project to interpret the struggle between tradition and modernity in American life in the late nineteenth century. Hearn as an often cited antimodernist seeking out endangered traditions and groups is a central part of that story, and I featured him in my book *Following Tradition: Folklore in the Discourse of American Culture* (1998). I was convinced that his American ethnographic sketches deserved more attention as a group, because of their documentation of cultural diversity and expression at a time when urban folk cultures were given little attention. A volume of this "field-collected" material, together with Hearn's overviews of American issues, should provide sources for us today to review life in late-nineteenth-century America. This period, I have argued, was crucial in establishing American modernism while constructing American tradition. Indeed, the era was a crossroads of peoples and ideas in American culture, and Hearn's coverage of American cities and sights emphasized the complex intersections of race, ethnicity, class, language, location, and occupation in the emergence of American cultural identities.

I first became aware of Hearn as a graduate student in folklore and American studies at Indiana University when the late professor Richard Dorson, aware of my historical interests in the Gilded Age, advised me to read him. Among the many literary biographies that I found, I spotted a lonely folkloristic chronicle in an article by fellow Indiana American Studies alumnus Bill McNeil. Down in Louisiana, Frank de Caro, another Indiana product, offered insights into Hearn's special perspective on regional folklore and ethnography. These contacts led me to delve more into Hearn's Japanese material, especially as I prepared for a year under a Fulbright grant in Japan in 1996-1997. I found literary and folkloristic consideration of Hearn especially active in Japan, and I had valuable colleagues to advise my reading. Invited to Osaka University, Japan, I appreciated the reflections on Hearn made by professors Seisaku Kawakami, Hisashi Ishida, Yuichi Morioka, Akira Tamai, Michael Wescoat, and George Hughes. I spent a great deal of time in a remote library room where Osaka kept its American studies collection, which included several rare volumes of Hearn's American essays. One that especially caught my eye was *Children of the Levee*, edited by O.W. Frost, published by the University of Kentucky Press in 1957. It reprinted Hearn's longer, vivid articles on the cultural life of black roustabouts in Cincinnati and suggested the value of Hearn's work for inquiries into race, ethnicity, gender, and class in rising

American cities during the late nineteenth century. Other texts that moved me to push for the contribution to cultural history made by Hearn in America were Edward Tinker's *Lafcadio Hearn's American Days* (1924) and Albert Mordell's edition of *An American Miscellany* (1924).

Going from Japan to teach at Harvard in 1997-1998, I was able to continue the conversation about Hearn with colleagues, including Joseph Harris, Stephen Mitchell, Lawrence Buell, Daniel Aaron, and Werner Sollors, and I had access to a major repository of Hearn papers at Houghton Library. I also consulted the Hearn collection at Tulane University and archives at the Cincinnati Historical Society. Returning to Penn State University in 1998, I discovered an impressive collection of Hearn's publications in Rare Books and Manuscripts, and I was able to take advantage of my location to work with them closely. While at Penn State, I benefited from conversations with fellow professors Michael Barton—a skillful scholar of American ethnography, history, and essays—and Jessica Dorman, who ably teaches journalistic literature. They represent exemplary scholarship in American studies, and while I absolve them from any sins of my opinions, I commend them for their intellectual generosity.

I chose essays by Hearn for inclusion here that show most vividly Hearn's ethnographic approach to writing and his views of America. I strove to represent a range of his sketches of ethnic, urban, and folk cultures. I offer them as they first appeared but made corrections or adjustments when errors or inconsistencies were clearly apparent in the original. One feature of Hearn's style that I retained bears explanation: a line of asterisks separates different versions of songs he collected (see "Levee Life").

I am grateful to my wife, Sally Jo, for understanding my drive to do this project. The book is dedicated to special scholars I value in my work on both sides of the Pacific. In their interdisciplinary union, Jay and Elizabeth Mechling in California (he is in American studies at the University of California at Davis, where I had the pleasure of serving as visiting distinguished professor in 1990, and she is in communications at California State University at Fullerton) have shown me the significance of combining communication studies, ethnography, folklore, and American studies. Across the ocean, I have debts to the wisdom and hospitality of my colleagues in literature, linguistics, and American studies at Osaka University, Japan. Between America and Japan, I feel fortunate to have found a part of Hearn's journey that helped me better explore the workings of tradition and modernity.

INTRODUCTION

Lafcadio Hearn's America

⊷ ≼♦≽ ⊶

Lafcadio Hearn's America reeked with the smells of slaughterhouses and docks. It bustled with the arrival of rural migrants and European immigrants in the growing cities. It creaked with rough-hewn reminders of the old days, and it worriedly acknowledged modern intrusions of Americans busily "building up a world." Out of sight of genteel society and the celebrated representatives of American letters, a swirl of roughneck ethnic, occupational, and racial types filled Hearn's sketchbook. After dark, he listened for vibrant sounds and risqué lyrics that were not being reproduced on sheet music. He watched for lurid entertainments and shady activities, and he sought experiences that he could call at once exotic and spiritual. He saw America from street level and at times lived there as a homeless person. The America he wrote about was tougher, more diverse, and odder than the one portrayed by most writers of his day. His America was unpolished and often inhospitable, hardly the usual stuff of journalism, much less of literature and art, but he strove to blend all three in writing that revealed "inner" life in the United States.

This book features Lafcadio Hearn's revealing ethnographic sketches of late-nineteenth-century American life. They are valuable, I argue, for their rare glimpses of ethnic, occupational, and urban groups and customs in a period that was formative for American culture. Hearn has been called a travel writer, a naturalist, a realist, a gothic writer, a prose impressionist, a short-story artist, and a Japanologist, but an ethnographer? Among literary critics, he is often thought of as graphic rather than ethnographic, but his library and letters avow that he was well read in ethnology and folklore, and that background undoubtedly influenced his special brand of journalism. He wanted to be a participant in the variety of earthy cultural scenes beneath the noses of genteel society and report them as action and dialogue worthy of artistic and social attention. Much of his journalism was ethnographic because he drew symbolic significance from the communicative behavior he directly observed in these cultural scenes.

Hearn's special contribution to ethnographic journalism was to explore what he called the underside of the city. Given assignments to cover the "police beat" of murders and robberies, he filled his notebooks with details on the surroundings as cultural scenes. He walked the streets at night searching for stories of marginalized ethnic groups, neglected alleys and quarters, and undesirable occupations. He listened for stories of ghosts and spiritual signs, curious customs, and gutsy folk expressions in speech, song, and craft as reflections of emotionally and socially bonded communities. In short, he documented, and artistically sketched, a side of American life that lay hidden in the shadows, even if it appeared flourishing, boisterous, and often disturbing when one bothered to get close. Those cultural scenes, those groups, and those customs—so much a part of the rising urban American experience in the late nineteenth century—were barely recorded except by the prolific pen of Lafcadio Hearn. Today his accounts can help bring lives and scenes of that era and milieu back into view. This book draws together a selection of his ethnographic material for historical and folkloristic inquiry into the diversity of American social and cultural life in the late nineteenth century and for journalistic and literary reconsideration of Hearn's often underestimated American period.

In the different places in America where Hearn worked, he became lured to the world that respectable America rarely encountered and hardly understood. He went into prisons and dark alleys to investigate grisly crimes, and in some of those same places he made groundbreaking cultural forays and documented traditional expressions for his readers. In his sketches of Creoles, he confronted the hushed topic of miscegenation and opened for consideration the process of creolization in American culture. In an America grabbing after material wealth and industrial strength, Hearn followed those who did not share in national progress. Aware of powerful engines of change steaming ahead in his time, he philosophized about the value of disfranchised groups and their cultural expressions to the mechanized American future. He offered their traditions as spiritual resources and showed that they had myriad aspirations, complex lives, and long-standing legacies.

At times Hearn made his keen observations as an immigrant writer, at other times from the self-conscious viewpoint of an American artist. He used the stance of an outsider to quizzically refer to the oddity of "you Americans," and he embraced the collective "us" and "we" to boast an exemplary American attitude. He could shift from dispassionate accounts of horror to highly ornamented reflections on the beauty of landscape. He was restless and independent-minded; he quarreled heatedly with detractors and friends alike. Of mixed ethnic background, he called himself a Gypsy, a Francophile, and an orientalist as well as an Americanist. The editor of the *Colored American* was convinced that he was African American after reading his reports on Cincin-nati black life that he thought no white reporter could possibly collect. He was self-deprecating about his small stature, his "grotesque" appearance, his dark complexion, and his visual disability. He was painfully shy, and as a result he avoided formal social engagements and declined speaking opportunities. Yet he expressed himself boldly, not to mention voluminously, in writing.

Lafcadio Hearn was born Patricio Lafcadio Tessima Carlos Hearn in 1850 on an island the colonizing British called Santa Maura, one of the Ionian Islands west of Greece—the Leucadia of ancient Greece. Lafcadio's name comes from the modern Greek name for the island of Levkas or Lefcada. His father was Surgeon-Major Charles Bush Hearn, who came from English settlers in Ireland and was reputed to have Gypsies in the family line. While stationed on the island with the British infantry, he romanced a native of one of the islands by the name of Rosa Antonio Cassimati and married her in 1849. To underscore Hearn's multiethnic roots as a possible source of his wandering and of his dark complexion, some of Hearn's biographers claimed for his mother a mixed ancestry that probably included Moorish and Arab components in addition to Maltese (Gould 1908, 14; Tinker 1924, 2; McWilliams 1946, 6). She spoke Italian and Romaic and followed the Greek Orthodox faith. Ex-plaining some of Hearn's interest in mysticism, one biographer called her reli-gious devotion "theopathic" and her character "passionate and romantic" (Cott 1992, 10). Questions arose about her mental health and emotional state, es-pecially after her first child, born out of wedlock to her and Charles Hearn a year earlier, died two months after Patricio Lafcadio's entrance into the world.

The father was not around for the birth or death in 1850. He was reas-signed to the British West Indies after only three months of marriage, and he kept his union a secret from the British authorities. Shortly after his son's second birthday, mother and child went to Dublin to stay with the major's mother. A clash, based in cultural differences, occurred between Rosa and the family, not the least of which was over the family insistence on the Anglicized name of Patrick or Paddy for the boy. Another feature of the "strange-look-ing" boy that drew disapproving looks from the family resulted from his mother's piercing his ears and placing gold loops in them. Mother and son bolted to the more sympathetic Sarah Holmes Brenane, the major's childless, wealthy aunt, who had rebelled against the Anglican Hearn family by con-verting to Catholicism. Charles returned to join his wife and child in 1853 but left again after a few months for action in Crimea. When the major re-turned from war, he found that Rosa had gone back to the islands and aban-doned his son to the care of Aunt Sarah. Charles secured an annulment of the marriage and sailed for India with a new wife and without his son. His outraged aunt disinherited her nephew and, caring for his son, vowed to leave the boy an inheritance.

Patricio Lafcadio was the son and heir that Sarah Brenane and her deceased husband had always wished for but never managed to have. She gave him private tutors who taught him in the ways of Catholicism, but Gothic churches raised images of goblins for him. He recalled being afraid of ghosts, which he claimed to see everywhere. Aunt Sarah had little tolerance for his supernatural beliefs, but her servants came to comfort him and told him mystical stories of their own. He later wrote, "For the best of possible reasons I then believed in ghosts and in goblins,—because I saw them, both by day and night. Before going to sleep I would always cover up my head to prevent them from looking at me; and I used to scream when I felt them pulling at my bedclothes. And I could not understand why I had been forbidden to talk about these experiences" (Bisland 1906, 1:16). His curiosity unabated, he wandered at the age of eight or nine into the household library, where he made what he called "his greatest find," books on mythology and folklore. In an autobiographical essay called "Idolatry," he reminisced about his discovery of an art folio on mythology: "How my heart leaped and fluttered on that happy day! Breathless I gazed; and the longer that I gazed the more unspeakably lovely those faces and forms appeared. Figure after figure dazzled, astounded, bewitched me. And this new delight was in itself a wonder,—also a fear. Something seemed to be thrilling out of those pictured pages,—something invisible that made me afraid. I remembered stories of the infernal magic that informed the work of the pagan statuaries. But this superstitious fear presently yielded to a conviction, or rather intuition—which I could not possibly have explained—that the gods had been belied *because* they were beautiful" (1:27).

Hearn's tutors became alarmed at his pagan interest and heavily censored the nude illustrations and texts describing magic and mythological gods. Instead of repressing Hearn's inquiry by this means, the tutors had excited his enthusiasm for such material. In his recollections, he notes how this attraction in his youth led him to a new understanding of the world around him and a commitment to pantheism in adolescence: "I remember when a boy lying on my back in the grass, gazing into the summer blue above me, and wishing that I could melt into it,—become a part of it. For these fancies I believe that a religious tutor was innocently responsible: he had tried to explain to me, because of certain dreamy questions, what he termed the folly and wickedness of pantheism,—with the result that I immediately became a pantheist, at the tender age of fifteen. And my imaginings presently led me not only to want the sky for a playground, but also to become the sky" (Temple 1931, 39). In

"Idolatry" he elaborated on this supernatural theme that both haunted and exhilarated him.

> Now after I had learned to know and to love the elder gods, the world again began to glow about me. Glooms that had brooded over it slowly thinned away. The terror was not yet gone; but I now wanted only reasons to disbelieve all that I feared and hated. In the sunshine, in the green of the fields, in the blue of the sky, I found a gladness before unknown. Within myself new thoughts, new imaginings, dim longing for I knew not what were quickening and thrilling. I looked for beauty, and everywhere found it: in passing faces—in attitudes and motions,—in the poise of plants and trees,—in long white clouds,—in faint-blue lines of far-off hills. At moments the simple pleasure of life would quicken to a joy so large, so deep, that it frightened me. But at other times there would come to me a new and strange sadness,—a shadowy and inexplicable pain. I had entered into my Renaissance. (Bisland 1906, 1:31-32)

Hearn's "Renaissance" included consuming legends and tales from elderly villagers and recounting them for family members who would listen. During the summers of the late 1850s, Aunt Sarah took him for a vacation to Bangor, Wales, where he sought stories from local fishermen. Hearn biographer Vera McWilliams elaborated on his obsession with oral tradition: "While sharp winds blew in from the distant breakers and familiar patches of shoreweed were washed by the gleaming swells, lusty fishermen fascinated him with recitals of their prowess. (For family consumption he would garnish these stories with deft footnotes of his own which no amount of reproval or punishment could make more accurate.) Or he would sit beside an old Wexford boatman and listen to legendary tales of shipwreck and Irish warfare. Occasionally the old man would halt his rambling narrative to point out its proof on some distant cliff where a crumbling watch-tower lifted stark against the sky. At such times the present fell away and Lafcadio lived in the excitement of a valorous past, time's door swinging backward at the slightest touch" (1946, 37). Hearn apparently preferred the legends of village and sea to the lessons of the Church.

Aunt Sarah's ideal hopes for Lafcadio to become a priest or at least a faithful Roman Catholic were severely challenged by the boy's troubling behavior and pantheistic beliefs. She began turning her maternal feelings, and promises of inheritance, toward Henry Hearn Molyneux, a distant relative of her husband. Thirteen years older than Lafcadio, Henry had attended a Catholic commercial college and was either ostentatiously devout or deviously fanatical, depending on which biography you read (Cott 1992, 23; Tinker 1924, 10; Stevenson 1961, 18). She allowed him to become her financial adviser and eventually lived with him and his wife in Surrey, England. Several biographers argue that Henry Molyneux schemed against Lafcadio, including convincing Aunt Sarah to assign to Henry's family a large estate intended for Lafcadio (Cott 1992, 24; Stevenson 1961, 26). Whether to turn the boy around or get rid of him, Henry persuaded her to send Lafcadio in 1862 to a Catholic boarding school in France, the Institution Ecclésiastique at Yvetot.

Guy de Maupassant also attended the Yvetot school around the same time, and both future writers detested the place. Whether the cause of Lafcadio's distress was the administrator he called a "hateful, venomous-hearted old maid" or the strict religious routines and dreary surroundings, he was able to return to England the following year, this time placed in St. Cuthbert's College in Ushaw. He came away from Yvetot with a command of French, and in his new school he displayed an advanced ability in English composition. The English school did no better than the French in dissuading Lafcadio from his religious challenges. One event at the English school more than any other stands out in his recollections. At the age of sixteen, while attending St. Cuthbert's, he seriously injured one eye. Most accounts blame a game he was playing called "Giant's Stride," which involved a knotted end of a rope that hit him, either accidentally or otherwise. Lafcadio also mentioned being punched by one of his classmates (Gould 1908, 148-49; Cott 1992, 28). The injured left eye became infected and inflamed. Hearn recalled that he left school and "had two years of sickness in bed" as a result (Bisland 1906, 1:36). He lost sight in the eye, and it became covered with a milky film. His nearsighted right eye became enlarged and protruded from the socket as he relied on it more. He was self-conscious about his facial "disfigurement," later labeling himself "the Raven" for his embodiment of Edgar Allan Poe's scary figure. As a result of his embarrassment about his looks and his alienation from his active classmates, Hearn turned to reading more in seclusion and grew increasingly introspective. His friend and frequent correspondent Elizabeth Bisland observed that, actually, his "slight disfigurement . . . was never great," but she recognized that it provided him "a source of perpetual distress." She wrote that "he imagined that others, more particularly women, found him disgusting and repugnant in consequence of the film that clouded the iris." He wore large, floppy hats to cover his face, and he resisted being photographed on his left side. Bisland recalled the lengths to which he went to take in sights despite his handicap: "In writing and reading he used a glass so large

Lafcadio Hearn, 1889.

and heavy as to oblige him to have it mounted in a handle and to hold it to his eye like a lorgnette, and for distant observation he carried a small folding telescope" (1:35).

His holding a magnifying glass to the printed page and small objects to better observe them gave him a sharp sensitivity to each individual word and the tiniest of creatures. He would write of observations at the "insect-level" and reflect on the hidden busy lives he noticed there. He came to see in words "colour, form, character"; he claimed for them "faces, ports, manners, gesticulations." He attributed to them "moods, humours, eccentricities;—they have tints, tones, personalities." He was affected by "the whispering of words, the rustling of the procession of letters . . . the pouting of words, the frowning and fuming of words, the weeping, the raging and racketing and rioting of words, the noisomeness of words, the tenderness or hardness, the dryness or juiciness of words,—the interchange of values, in the gold, the silver, the brass and the copper of words" (Cowley 1949, 12). If his magnifying glass let him imagine all kinds of details, his telescope, he said, enlarged art.

Although Lafcadio was understandably disturbed by his injury, he later credited it with his writer's impressionistic "eye" for the "enormous and lurid" and his keen appreciation for beauty in ordinary things. With a desire to zoom in on the details of "small things" as well as to look off to the sky and the mountain to imagine supernatural experience, his challenge as a writer was to reconcile realism with mysticism. In an editorial on the "Artistic Value of Myopia" written in New Orleans in 1887, he opined that good eyesight "may be a hindrance to those feelings of sublimity that exalt the poetic imagination." He explained that "the more visible the details of a large object—a mountain, a tower, a forest-wall—the less grand and impressive that object. The more apparently uniform the mass, the larger it seems to loom; the vaguer a shadow space, the deeper it appears. An impression of weirdness—such as that obtainable in a Louisiana or Florida swamp-forest, or, much more, in those primeval and impenetrable forest-deeps described so powerfully by Humboldt—is stronger in proportion to the spectator's indifference to lesser detail" (Hutson 1926, 344).

Lafcadio would have a formidable odyssey before he published his first word. With Lafcadio out of school because of his injury, Aunt Sarah arranged to have him stay with her former parlor maid and the maid's dockworker husband in London's East End. After Lafcadio was ready to resume his studies, his aging aunt could no longer afford to put him through school because Henry Molyneux's bad investments for her had driven him and her to bankruptcy. Sudden poverty tumbled Hearn into a wretched workhouse (Bisland 1906, 1:37). Feeling alien to these surroundings, Hearn spent most of his time reading and wandering through the streets of London, where he confronted social scenes of squalor and violence unlike any he had known before. Recalling the city after he arrived in America, he portrayed its "dreariness" and "vast gloom." Discerning the rise of an urban folk culture, he found Londoners "distinct . . . with marked peculiarities of dialect and habit" (Tinker 1924, 8). At once compelled and repelled by the city's darker side near the docks, he wrote to a companion from Ushaw about London's "sights and sounds of horror which even then preferred the shade of night—of windows thrown violently open, or shattered to pieces, shrieks of agony, or cries of murder, followed by a heavy plunge in the river" (Bisland 1906, 1:37).

Henry Molyneux recovered some of his finances in 1869 and called Lafcadio to his office. He handed him a one-way ship ticket to New York City and instructed him to go to Cincinnati, where he would find help from Henry's sister and brother-in-law. There is no indication that Hearn had been thinking about going to America, but he grudgingly accepted the ticket. He became embittered at his aunt, Henry, and the Jesuits. He developed the idea that he had been persecuted because of his dark complexion and exotic Mediterranean background, and he felt rootless. America must have seemed as good a place as any to dwell, and he could escape the depression he experienced in London. Most biographers suspect the worst of Henry's motives for shipping "Patrick" off across the Atlantic. Edward Tinker wrote, "The credulous woman had become a pensioner in the house of her despoiler and he, because he wished to rid himself of Hearn and the possibility of embarrassing future questions, found it easy to poison the old lady's mind against her nephew and persuade her he was nothing but an undeserving young infidel" (Tinker 1924, 10). If Aunt Sarah's mind was poisoned against her "Patrick," she nonetheless included a small provision for him in her will. The boy refused to make claims on it or fight Henry for the promises made for him when she died in 1871.

Stepping onto America's shores at the age of nineteen, Hearn left behind his moniker of Patrick and insisted on being called Lafcadio. Whether it was a protest against his British Catholic raising or a public announcement that he was a freethinking individual with something of an exotic tinge, his newly adopted name signaled his independence. Considering Hearn's fascination with the textures of words, the etymology of *Lafcadio* in the meaning of "to wander" was probably not lost on him. America became his opportunity to start anew, but he was uncertain in what occupation to begin his renewal. He resisted Henry Molyneux's directive to go immediately to Cincinnati, staying in New York City for two years to find work. He tried his hand at copying briefs for a lawyer and had an unsuccessful stint as a waiter in a dingy restaurant. What little memory of this period that Hearn later recorded was mostly of loneliness and starvation. Feeling beaten down by the city, he dejectedly boarded a train to Cincinnati.

Cincinnati in 1871 was America's largest inland city, bolstered by being a steamboat marketing center. Travel writers characterized its southern manners and its feeling of a frontier stop on the way west. The "Queen City," as it was known, overlooked the Ohio River in the southwest corner of the state of Ohio. From there, one could cross the river into Kentucky or take a short trip west to Indiana. The city's population exceeded 216,000, and more than a fifth were Germans. They were concentrated in the work of pork-packing, tanning, soap manufacturing, and beer brewing. A large influx of Irish laborers, known for being "pick and shovel men" on railroads, canals, and docks, contributed to the city's growth. Historian Philip Jordan made the claim that the "Irish and Germans influenced Ohio culture and city life as much, if not more, than did any other immigrant group" (1943, 256).

Cincinnati's industries brought prosperity to the city, and annual industrial expositions to encourage further growth invited still more development. City officials pushed industrial development with ownership and construction of the Southern Railroad, which ran from Cincinnati to Chattanooga. The rapid industrialization also resulted in outcries about unsanitary conditions, including a constant pall of sooty smoke over the city. In 1879 Cincinnati's Dudley Ward Rhodes, a reformist clergyman, caused a stir with his declaration in *Creed and Greed* that "we have a city as badly sewered, as badly lighted, as badly cleaned, and as badly governed as any city on the continent" (Jordan 1943, 192). The death rate was high at more than twenty per thousand, mostly from outbreaks of smallpox, scarlet fever, and cholera. The city's elite built up its claim to high culture worthy of New York and Boston through the construction of opera houses, theaters, and art galleries, but at the same time bawdy houses, minstrel shows, and gambling dens serving the underclass did a thriving business (Jordan 1943, 192; Cott 1992, 32).

Bucktown, the subject of some of Hearn's most memorable essays, was home to most of Cincinnati's substantial black population. Located in the vicinity of Sixth and Seventh Streets east of Broadway, it was described as an area of "overcrowded shanties, hovels, and dens of the mud-inundated and crime-beset neighborhood" (Cott 1992, 31). The other African American area was along the waterfront. Known as the Levee, or Rows, the waterfront district housed stevedores, porters, and deckhands who risked frequent floods and outbreaks of disease to live in pitiable warehouse cellars and run-down boarding houses. Most of the blacks came from backgrounds of enslavement in Kentucky, whose image was fixed with the suffering depicted in *Uncle Tom's Cabin* (1851) by Harriet Beecher Stowe. Despite that lasting narrative, Cincinnati's black population was not just a destination for runaways. Some slave masters resettled their children by enslaved women there, and manumitted slaves headed there from other southern states, especially Virginia. On the eve of the Civil War, more than half of the blacks were counted as mulattoes, a percentage considerably higher than in Louisville and Evansville, also on the Ohio River. Five occupations—boatman, barber, cook, laborer, and waiter—claimed 66 percent of the black male workforce; black women mainly took up positions as housekeepers, washerwomen, and seamstresses (Trotter 1998, 29). Between 1860 and 1900, the black population of the city increased dramatically from 3,731 to 14,482. It then constituted over 5 percent of the city's population (66).

In Cincinnati Hearn also encountered concentrations of Jews, Gypsies, Greeks, Italians, and French people. He was especially attracted to the Jewish district of the city, where he reported on kosher regulations, meat slaughtering techniques, and religious customs—mostly the customs brought over by central European immigrants. Considering his own internal struggles between tradition and modernity, the rising conflict in the Jewish community between maintenance of orthodoxy and a nascent reform movement became the the-

Bucktown section of Cincinnati, early twentieth century. Courtesy Cincinnati Historical Society Library, Alton Mood Collection.

matic core of his stories. The reform movement, based nationally in Cincinnati, sought to "modernize" religious practice to allow Jews to conform better to American society and culture and turn away from "superstitious" and regulatory aspects of Jewish tradition. From his position at Congregation B'nai Jeshurun, Rabbi Isaac M. Wise led the American Judaism movement from 1854 until his death in 1900. Hearn wrote about the reform activities of Hebrew Union College and read the *American Israelite*, which Wise established in the city. He was also attracted to Jewish mystical literature and legends in the Talmud, which he retold in *Stray Leaves from Strange Literature* (1884). By most estimates, the Jewish population of the city ranged between 8,000 and 12,000 during the 1870s when Hearn was in the city, jumping to 28,000 in 1912 with an influx of eastern European immigrants (Marcus 1990, 173). Because Jews were restricted from many commercial and professional occupations, before the turn of the century they mostly engaged in clothing-related businesses, general merchandise, and whiskey, boot and shoe, and trunk trades (Jordan 1943, 280).

Hearn learned of the Queen City's ethnic districts and seedy quarters from his first days there. After receiving some money from Molyneux's brother-in-law, he wandered the streets again in search of work. Edward Tinker reported that "at times he had nowhere to go and spent the night in a rusty boiler, junked in a vacant lot, took refuge in packing boxes thrown out at the back of some store, or even slept in haylofts, after having carefully removed and folded his one suit, in order to keep it halfway presentable. Often he was half starved" (1924, 13-14). He stumbled into the public library, where his skills as a copyist enabled him to become private secretary to the head librarian. He quickly fell from the librarian's favor, because he was distracted by reading books in the office and neglected his duties.

By the time Hearn was introduced to Henry Watkin, a printer from England, Hearn had formed an ambition to become a writer, but forty-five-year-old Watkin persuaded the young man that he needed a trade first. Hearn came to live with him and apprenticed in his shop. By most accounts, Watkin became a father figure to Hearn, and he guided Hearn's thinking and reading on utopianism, spiritualism, and literature as the two of them contemplated changes to society brought by industrialization. He directed Hearn to American writers mining local oral tradition for their fiction; at the same time, he kept up with his favorite French writers, such as Gautier, Baudelaire, Loti, and Flaubert. Hearn referred to Watkin as the "Old Man" and "Dad" and called himself "The Raven." With his help, Hearn took up his first steady work typesetting and proofreading for Robert Clarke and Company, a publisher of Americana. His tasks were not purely mechanical for him: through them he tried to change American methods of punctuation to conform more closely to English standards. He favored a comma before a dash to show the effect of a pause, and he often created flow in texts by inserting ellipses and semicolons, thereby earning himself the nickname "Old Semicolon" with his co-workers. This use of punctuation to create rhythm remained in his writing to his last days. As Elizabeth Bisland reported of her friend, "Punctuation and typographical form remained for him always a matter of profound importance, and in one of his letters he declared that he would rather abandon all the royalties to his publisher than be deprived of the privilege of correcting his own proofs; corrections which in their amplitude often devoured in printer's charges the bulk of his profits" (1906, 50).

Hearn moved on to a trade paper called the *Trade List,* and according to Edward Tinker, he "spent all his spare moments writing queer fantastic tales in order not to have his literary ambitions entirely aborted" (1924, 14). He decided to act on his ambition in October 1872. He took a review of Tennyson's *Idylls of the King* to the offices of the *Cincinnati Enquirer.* John Cockerill, the editor he went to see, recalled the exchange they had: "One day there came to the office a quaint, dark-skinned little fellow, strangely diffident, wearing glasses of great magnifying power and bearing with him evidence that Fortune and he were scarce on nodding terms. When admitted, in a soft, shrinking voice he asked if I ever paid for outside contributions. I informed him that I was somewhat restricted in the matter of expenditure, but that I would give consideration to what he had to offer. He drew from under his coat a manuscript, and tremblingly laid it upon my table. Then he stole away like a distorted brownie, leaving behind him an impression that was uncanny and indescribable. . . . Later in the day I looked over the contribution which he had left. I was astonished to find it charmingly written" (Cott 1992, 38).

Cockerill ran the review and invited other contributions from Hearn. Hearn moved from reviews to sketches of local characters. He interviewed local artists and profiled the city's Jewish community in "The Hebrews of Cincinnati." Hearn became attracted to some grisly subjects such as grave digging and animal slaughtering, and Cockerill, editing for a primarily male reading audience, did not wince. For Hearn, these reports combined the sensationalism that the newspaper needed and some of the "curious customs" he had learned of from folklore and ethnology. He reflected in one letter, "I am striving to woo the Muse of the Odd, and hope to succeed in thus attracting some little attention" (Bisland 1906, 1:291). It was not an idle comment. In another letter, he announced, "I think a man must devote himself to one thing in order to succeed: so I have pledged me to the worship of the Odd, the Queer, the Strange, the Exotic, the Monstrous. It quite suits my temperament. . . . Enormous and lurid facts are certainly worthy of more artistic study than they generally receive" (1:328-29).

Hearn expressed in his early writings many interests that he developed throughout his literary career. He explored diverse religious practices, profiled racial and national "character," and chummed with the outcasts of society. He understood the implications of locating ethnic and folk cultures within the rising, bustling American city and its associations with progress, modernism, and mass society. To draw the reader to the questions he wanted to raise, he relied on other senses besides sight to set the reader in the scene. His narratives dwelled on the sounds, smells, and textures of his settings. He tried to give his sentences a rhythm that approximated the action in the scene he described. He could fall into ornamenting his prose and often digressed into philosophical musing, but for the most part, these early writings were reports dispatched on unusual scenes and characters about the city. In "Grave-Digger Baldwin," he floridly tells of John Baldwin, sexton of the Wesleyan Cemetery: "At a time of life when most men are striving to turn back the pages of their experience and clean up for the final scrutiny of the Great Examiner of accounts, for he is pretty well on to sixty, John is not only not making an effort to turn back a single page, but he is turning those of the future over as fast as it lays in his power, and is carefully stowing some extra wickedness on each" (Hearn 1975, 50). In "A Nasty Nest," he declares the need to open the underside of the city for scrutiny: "Cincinnati may brag of having the handsomest this and the largest that in the world, but she is mighty quiet in regard to her possession of some of the most miserable and disgusting features. Her quiet may come, however, from her ignorance, for it is much better and comforting to think that the good men and women of this city who sit with folded hands, and believe themselves to be Christian, have no idea that there are such foul scabs on the city's face as now and then become uncovered to the light of day" (40). In the same piece, he assaults the senses with his journalistic description: "The slime of the drunkard is over every thing. The doors and windows are never closed, the few remaining panes of glass are crusted with dirt, the cupboard is honey-combed with rat-holes, a greasy mold seems to hang about the bed, and the breath of the woman reeks with the fumes of the liquor fermenting inside her" (41).

In 1874 Cockerill offered Hearn a job as staff reporter. He worked fourteen to sixteen hours a day and was given some of the toughest spots to report on. One of Hearn's associates of the time recalled that "he was never known to shirk hardship or danger in filling an assignment. . . . His employers kept him at the most arduous work of a daily morning paper—the night stations—for in that field developed the most sensational events, and he was strongest in the unusual and startling" (Bisland 1906, 1:55). For Hearn's part, he remembered Cockerill as a "hard master, a tremendous worker, and a born journalist" (1:53). Cockerill assigned Hearn to a desk in his own office and featured the writer as he built up circulation of the paper around human-interest stories and bold displays. Cockerill took his ideas for promoting lively prose in journalism to high-profile posts with Joseph Pulitzer's *St. Louis Dispatch* and *New York World*. Remembering Hearn in 1896, Cockerill wrote:

> He sat in the corner of my room and wrote special articles for the Sunday edition as thoroughly excellent as anything that appeared in the magazines of those days. . . . He was poetic, and his whole nature seemed attuned to the beautiful, and he wrote beautifully of things which were neither wholesome nor inspiring. He came to be in time a member of the city staff at a fair compensation, and it was then that his descriptive powers developed. He loved to write of things in humble life. He prowled about the dark corners of the city, and from gruesome places he dug out charming idyllic sto-

ries. The negro stevedores on the steamboat-landings fascinated him. He wrote of their songs, their imitations, their uncouth ways, and he found picturesqueness in their rags, poetry in their juba dances. (Gould 1908, 29-30)

Under Cockerill's watchful eye, Hearn's "ethnographic" style of describing the "things in humble life" emerged. The style involved establishing the boundaries of a scene, detailing the material and social setting of the surroundings, describing the actors and their characteristics, and then giving the actions and dialogues special significance for revealing the meaning of events or narratives. In some pieces, he featured one particularly colorful character who often had a special life history or legend to tell or a passing craft to impart. The style became important for explaining apparently unusual customs and settings in ethnic districts. In short, Hearn's prose strove to engage readers by making them feel as if they were experiencing the scene themselves. He often lured them in with the very scenes that repulsed them. Literary critic Malcolm Cowley thought that Hearn's journalistic experience put him in a class of American writers rebelling against the genteel, romantic tradition:

American daily journalism gave Hearn a chance he would have found in no other field. He had come to this country at a time when many serious writers, after fleeing to Europe, were complaining from a distance that American books had to be written and American magazines edited for a genteel audience composed chiefly of women. They forgot the newspapers, which were written for men and therefore retained more freedom of speech, besides a touch of cynicism. The newspapers of the time discussed dangerous topics like prostitution, adultery and miscegenation, which couldn't even be mentioned in the magazines. When describing crimes of violence, their reporters were advised to copy the methods of the French naturalists. Their critics were permitted to indulge in fine writing and a show of curious learning. Although newspapers overworked their staffs and paid them miserable wages—standard figures in the Middle West were $10 a week for cubs and $30 for star reporters—still they paid those wages every Saturday and thus provided the only sure livelihood for writers in revolt against the genteel tradition. Bierce, Huneker, Harold Frederic, Stephen Crane, David Graham Phillips and Dreiser—almost all the skeptics, the bohemians and the naturalists—started their careers as newspaper men. (1949, 3-4)

Hearn became a star reporter after a series of articles on a gruesome crime known as the Tanyard Murder. It was not that Hearn had a "scoop" or had been first on the scene, but rather that Hearn's account stood out for its vivid description of the crime, in which the murderer had tried to burn the body. Under the headline "Violent Cremation" on November 9, 1874, Hearn gave the details of the case in unsettling, dramatic style: "The night is pitch dark, fit gloom for the dark deed it veils." His attraction to lurid detail was not lost on this case, as any of the juicy passages from the story of a man pushed alive into a furnace will attest: "The brain had all boiled away, save a small wasted lump at the base of the skull about the size of a lemon. It was crisped and still warm to the touch. On pushing the finger through the crisp, the interior felt about the consistency of banana fruit, and the yellow fibers seemed to writhe like worms in the Coroner's hands. The eyes were cooked to bubbled crisps in the blackened sockets, and the bones of the nose were gone, leaving a hideous hole."

In the same Tallow District where the Tanyard Murder occurred, Hearn explored in equal detail outcasts in slaughterhouses and scenes that demonstrated cultural differences between Gentile and Jewish slaughtering. In "Haceldama" (from the New Testament word meaning "field of blood"), Hearn again used senses other than sight to convey the full effect of the setting: "On a boiling summer day it is not, indeed, a pleasant neighborhood to visit; its very gutters seem foul with the fetor of slaughter, and its atmosphere heavy with the odors of death,—impregnated with globules of blood. Its unpleasantness has rendered it an unfamiliar neighborhood to a large portion of the community, who have no interests in those businesses for which it is famous, and who have no desire to linger longer amid its stenches than they can possibly help." In "The Quarter of Shambles," he paints a graphic, disturbing word picture of the area as "peculiar to itself," but he manages to evoke sympathy for its residents. After charting the landscape—"The main streets here lose their width and straightness in tortuous curves and narrow twists and labyrinthine perplexity—so that the stranger who loses his way in this region of nastiness must wander wildly and long ere he may cease to inhale the ghoulish aroma of stink-factories and the sickening smell of hog-pens fouler than the stables of Augeas"—he editorializes:

> Amid these scenes and smells lives and labors a large and strangely
> healthy population of brawny butchers, sinewy coopers, muscular
> tanners—a foreign population, speaking a foreign tongue, and liv-
> ing the life of the Fatherland—broad-shouldered men from
> Pomerania; tall, fair-haired emigrants from Bohemia; dark, brawny

people from Bavaria; rough-featured fellows from the region of
the Hartz Mountains; men speaking the strange dialects of strange
provinces. They are mostly rough of aspect, rude of manner and
ruddy of feature. The greater part of them labor in tanneries, slaughter-houses and soap factories, receiving small salaries upon which
an American workman could not support his family, and doing
work which Americans instinctively shrink from—slaughtering,
quartering, flaying—handling bloody entrails and bloody hides—
making slaughter their daily labor, familiarizing themselves with
death and agony, and diurnally drenching themselves in blood.
Such occupation destroys the finer sensibilities of men, and more
or less brutalizes their natures; while in return it gives them health
and strength and brawn beyond the average. (Hearn 1925, 1:68)

The editorializing and philosophizing that he injected into his stories often
reflected on the tendency of society to turn its back on its less fortunate. He
blamed modernization, or Americanization, or base prejudice, for the
predicament of people in the city's underside. Through the stench and dirt, he
held up their songs, stories, and skills as signs of their artistry. He gave dignity
to their struggle and brought to light their sense of art and spirit.

Hearn confronted prejudice head on when word got out of his romance
with a mulatto named Alethea "Mattie" Foley. He met her when he was living
at a boarding house in a rundown neighborhood where both blacks and whites
lived. She was the cook, and, shy among the other boarders, he preferred to
spend time in the kitchen with her. She had been born a slave in Kentucky
and before moving to Cincinnati had given birth to an illegitimate child by a
Scotsman named Anderson. She introduced him to some of the black hang-
outs he described for the newspaper and, by some accounts, cared for him
through illness. He was fascinated with her claim of "ghost-seeing" and wrote
of her power, without giving her name, in "Some Strange Experience." In the
late spring of 1874, he surprised Mattie with a proposal of marriage. His
fellow reporters tried to dissuade him, and ministers refused him. Stories circulated that even Mattie tried to talk him out of the illegal marriage. Since
miscegenation laws forbid such a union, he obtained a marriage license by
falsely declaring that Mattie was white. After being turned down by several
white ministers, he found a black Episcopalian clergyman willing to officiate
for a June wedding. But the nuptials could not be held in the church, and the
ceremony was privately performed at the home of one of the bride's black
friends. Lafcadio and Mattie lived together after the wedding but separated
after several months. In an epilogue to the wedding story that reads much like

that of Lafcadio's mother, Mattie returned to the country, where reports had her becoming emotionally disturbed. Lafcadio wrote Henry Watkin that "I have been much more troubled about Mattie than you have any idea of; and the prospect of leaving her to ruin herself is something I can scarcely bear. Whatever I may have said or done, I love her,—more I fancy than I will ever love any woman; and somehow the lower she falls, the fonder I feel of her" (Cott 1992, 89). In Japan toward the end of his life, Hearn claimed a youthful innocence about the events, "I resolved to take the part of some people who were much disliked in the place where I lived. I thought that those who disliked them were morally wrong,—so I argued boldly for them and went over to their side. Then all the rest of the people stopped speaking to me, and I hated them for it. But I was too young then to understand. There were other moral questions, much larger than those I had been arguing about, which really caused the whole trouble. . . . I had been opposing a great national and social principle without knowing it" (Bisland 1906, 1:64-65).

From his post as editor, Cockerill felt pressure to defuse the scandal caused by his star reporter's defiance of miscegenation laws. Although he called Hearn his "best writer," he fired him in July 1875. Rumors circulated of Hearn's attempting suicide after he was laid off (McWilliams 1946, 70). The editor of the *Enquirer*'s rival newspaper in the city, the *Commercial,* took a chance that the gossip would die down and hired Hearn. At the *Commercial,* Hearn expanded his reports of black life, undesirable occupations, and the poor sections of the city. Edwin Henderson, his city editor, gave him ample license to write on whatever he wanted and allowed his reports more room. His series on black life in Bucktown and the waterfront district were considerably longer than anything he wrote from the *Enquirer,* and he gave the stories more literary treatment than before. Soon after coming to his new position, he wrote longer-than-two-column pieces titled "Levee Life," "Pariah People," "Some Pictures of Poverty," "Haceldama," "The Restless Dead, concerning Haunted Houses," "Some Strange Experience," and "The Poisoners" (voodoo). Among his more sensational forays were "Gibbeted, Sickening Scenes behind the Scaffold-Screen," "A Day of Conflagrations in Cincinnati, Horrors of the Broadway Disaster," "The Opium Habit, Chinese Opium-Smokers in Cincinnati," and "A Slaughter-House Story, about One Who Drank Three Glasses of Blood, and Went Blind." He did a series of essays on Cincinnati's industries, including "Porcelain Painting," "Boiled Down, Cincinnati Canning Companies," and "The Manufacture of Yellow and Rockingham Ware in Cincinnati." The lengths to which the almost-blind reporter would go to experience his subject were epitomized by his story "Steeple Climbers" in 1876. He agreed to be hoisted to the top of the city cathedral to describe the risks taken by professional climbers who place and remove decorations. Hearn tried to figure out their "indifference to danger." Despite his poor sight, he admired the vistas climbers gained from their lofty place of work, and he described them in colorful, poetic terms: "The mists climbed higher as the sun commenced to sink in a glory of mingled gold and purple, and a long streamer of ruby light flamed over the western hills." With his ethnographic sensitivity, he noted beliefs peculiar to the climbers that acknowledge their dangerous roles. They refused to climb on Fridays and wore talismans with skull-and-crossbones images on them. After a successful climb, they cut their initials into the summit of the cross. Having created a sense of awe for the climbers, Hearn imitated the matter-of-factness of his informant's invitation to go up again, this time at night, to catch the view. Although known for his flowery writing during this period, Hearn closed this essay simply yet expressively with his answer to the invitation: "The reporter shivered and departed."

Although Hearn had made a significant reputation for himself as "the reporter," he still longed for an independent life as a literary artist. He looked to the South as a place to explore for inspiration and a more leisurely life in rustic surroundings, not to mention an escape from Ohio winters, which he considered dreadfully cold. He described himself as a lizard that sought the sun. His opportunity arose after the contested presidential election of 1876 resulted in recounts in South Carolina, Florida, and Louisiana. National attention turned to the political corruption in Louisiana that sent Ohio native Rutherford B. Hayes into the White House by one electoral vote. The *Commercial* had, in fact, carried a regular column on Louisiana politics. Henderson offered Hearn an assignment to follow up with political coverage in New Orleans. Hearn was excited at the prospect. Besides the tropical climate, the city had a pronounced European background and a romantic folk tradition drawn from the mixed-race heritage of its Creoles. Hearn became more enchanted after reading the magazine stories of George Washington Cable about the city and its mixture of French, Spanish, Indian, and African influences.

Established as a colony by the French in 1718, New Orleans was ceded to Spain in 1764 and then back to France before it came into the hands of the United States in 1803. Under Spanish rule, the city gained an unsavory reputation for carousing and eerie voodoo practices. It was a meeting point of many Atlantic cultures and a hangout for pirates, boatmen, and soldiers. The city was known for its discrete sections: the original French Quarter, the American sector, Fauberg Marigny, and the Garden District. It boasted a major port, which handled mass quantities of flour, tobacco, cotton, and sugar, and a river route that was kind to churning steamboats. With commerce booming by the 1840s, the city attracted German and Irish immigrants. At that time,

New Orleans held the distinction of being the largest southern city and one of the nation's most prosperous ports, but after the Civil War it fell behind northern commercial centers that it once had exceeded. Steamboating through the port struggled to compete with the rise of overland railroading and northern industry. Sudden drops in cotton and sugar prices increased the instability of the local economy. With support of black voters, radical Republicans and northern carpetbaggers obtained the reins of city and state politics and held them until amnesty granted to ex-Confederates in 1872 helped restore traditional white southern control. Racial tensions ran high, spilling over into occasional riots. Unsanitary conditions, outbreaks of yellow fever, widespread crime and corruption, and frequent flooding plagued the city. A large debt incurred under carpetbag administrations hampered needed civic improvements to the city, although the population continued to grow to more than 250,000. A flow of immigrants from Italy and Greece offering manual labor added to the already varied mix of the city. The port also offered a collecting station for land-hungry migrants headed west to the Texas prairies and beyond.

Contrary to the expectations of the *Commercial*'s editors, Hearn sent back little about politics. Instead, he offered picturesque travelogues of the new sights along his journey. Once into the city, he devoted himself to the folklore and ethnology of his surroundings. He studied the Creole dialects, took up Spanish, followed newly arrived Sicilians, and collected songs and stories from Creole characters he met on the street. He enjoyed his life as a "correspondent" and the freedom to follow his interests. His literary aspirations led him to work on translations of French literature and to outline magazine essays and novelettes. Still insisting on political news, the *Commercial* finally lost patience with Hearn and hired another correspondent in Louisiana. With no income to draw on, Hearn once again scrambled for survival. His health suffered, and he complained of losing much of his already diminished sight. With reduction of staffs on the city's newspapers during the recession, he was rebuffed by the major dailies when he offered his services. He got a break in 1878 when a small cooperative newspaper called the *Item*, established only the year before, took him on as assistant editor. The post gave him the opportunity to write editorials expressing opinions on art and philosophy in addition to politics. He also wrote articles on foreign affairs and literature.

Hearn collected more folklore from the streets and featured it in stories for the paper, along with cartoons that he drew. His interests in Creole and African American folklore moved him to associate for a time with George Washington Cable. Cable had earned a national reputation for his local-color writing, which was published in popular magazines and novels. Although he drew praise for leading a southern cultural revival, Cable offended some Louisiana elites for his portrayals of scandalous miscegenation among them and his call for black civil rights. Cable's views did not put off Hearn, and the pair worked together among the city's blacks. They collaborated on collecting folk songs: Cable wrote out the music while Hearn recorded the lyrics. After the gentlemanly Cable left the flattering light of New Orleans's main quarter, the rumpled Hearn continued to explore the dingy back streets deep into the night. Following his experience in Cincinnati, Hearn took quickly to the inner life of the black Creole community and became enthralled with the mystery of its traditions. He assiduously studied the language of the black Creoles, and besides gathering songs, he feverishly recorded foodways, beliefs, customs, tales, and proverbs.

At a time when the local press tarred Cable as a despicable traitor to southern tradition, Hearn stood alone in defense of Cable in his columns. Distance grew between the writers, however, as Hearn affronted Cable's puritan sensibilities by making it known that he was a regular customer at the brothels and that he indulged in narcotics. It also must have been shocking for Cable to read of Hearn's deep involvement in the city's voodoo world. It was Hearn's journalism that helped boost the legends of Marie Laveau (the Queen of Voodoo) and Jean Montanet (the King of Hoodoo). He described them as agents of enormous power, proud of their African origins and commercially successful. He wrote, for example, "Jean, in short, possessed the mysterious *obi* power, the existence of which has been recognized in most slave-holding communities, and with which many a West-Indian planter has been compelled by force of circumstances to effect a compromise" (Cott 1992, 142). Collecting "cultural evolution" tracts on international folklore, comparing modern "survivals" of ancient customs, he made comparisons of the voodoo beliefs he found with medieval practices and speculated on the function of magic in modern life. Hearn added his ethnographic touch to Cable's fiction by publishing "The Scenes of Cable's Romances" for *Century Magazine* in 1883. He described in the piece the real-life settings for Cable's stories, but it was not a dry commentary. Hearn provided, as one critic noted, "his iridiscent verbal palette [which] has added the charm and vividness of a different angle of vision to Cable's delightful architectural portraits of the *Vieux Carré*" (Tinker 1943, xviii). At first celebrating Cable, Hearn later became critical of his literature and politics, questioning the older writer's faithful rendering of local traditions and calls for social equity. Cable returned with censure of Hearn's pantheistic beliefs and lifestyle. The rift between Hearn and Cable became irreconcilable when Cable accused him of stealing, for use in his novel *Chita* (1889), a story that Cable had told Hearn.

Hearn increased his literary reputation at the *Item,* but the paper came close to folding several times. When the purchase in 1881 of the *Times* by the large daily *New Orleans Democrat* brought in a new editor-in-chief who sought Hearn's services at higher pay, Hearn eagerly accepted the position of literary editor and translator for the newly formed *Times-Democrat.* Hearn's journalistic exposure grew. He increased his output of translations and in Sunday features wrote articles and editorials. He continued to write on Creole topics and expanded his musings on art and philosophy. He drifted further from the ethnographic sketches of the streets and produced more "poetic prose," or what he called impressionistic "fantastics." Surreal in content, it was unusual reading for the newspapers, and it moved him further to seek magazine and book outlets for his experiments with prose. Biographer Vera McWilliams called this period "his golden years as a journalist." "Locally he had no peer," she opined, "and at the office he was accorded intelligent appreciation and every courtesy" (1946, 138). Her accolade for Hearn's expressiveness within the pages, and the prose structures, of the newspaper is well considered. Given wide editorial license, Hearn challenged his newspaper audience with artistic essays and forays into comparative culture. He had grown out of the habit in his Cincinnati days to dwell on revolting details, and he overcame his tendency to jarringly shift, sometimes condescendingly, from the vernacular to lofty vocabulary. His profiles of tradition-bearers and customs were more nuanced, with questions about the relations of modernization to community life. He felt more connected to his subjects, as he attests in a letter in 1878 to Henry Krehbiel, a Cincinnati journalist colleague with whom he shared a fascination with folklore: "My new journalistic life may interest you,—it is so different from anything in the North. I have at last succeeded getting right into the fantastic heart of the French quarter, where I hear the antiquated dialect all day long" (Bisland 1906, 1:176). The cultural themes framing his ethnographic explorations of the city's ethnic quarters were more informed by scholarship, although the argument could be made that he also could be more dogmatic about evolutionary principles in that scholarship. In connection with his work on the newspaper, he was reading more international periodicals, and his post as translator was unique among New Orleans newspapers. His reputation as an accomplished translator led to the publication of his first book, *One of Cleopatra's Nights* (1882), a translation of Théophile Gautier's romantic stories for the New York house of R. Worthington.

He envisioned a book featuring his ethnographic project on the Creoles. As he continued to wander among them, he understood the enormity of the task and became as much frustrated as exhilarated. He excitedly wrote Krehbiel in 1878, "I have undertaken a project which I hardly hope to succeed in, but which I feel some zeal regarding, viz., to collect the Creole legends, traditions, and songs of Louisiana" (Bisland 1906, 1:193). He did not have to go far for sources. Living in the "Creole quarter," he solicited songs and stories from landlords, waiters, and nurses in his daily encounters. He wrote Krehbiel in 1881, "I am living in a ruined Creole house; damp brick walls green with age, zig-zag cracks running down the facade, a great yard with plants and cacti in it; a quixotic horse, four cats, two rabbits, three dogs, five geese, and a seraglio of hens,—all living together in harmony. A fortune-teller occupies the lower floor. She has a fantastic apartment kept dark all day, except for the light of two little tapers burning before two human skulls in one corner of the room" (1:222) He requestioned his identity, considering it neither Creole nor American but somewhere between the two: "I am growing weary of the Creole quarter, and I think I shall pull up stakes and fly to the garden district where the orange-trees are, but where Latin tongues are not spoken. It is very hard to accustom one's self to live with Americans, however, after one has lived for three years among these strange types. I am swindled all the time and I know it, and still I find it hard to summon up resolution to forsake these antiquated streets for the commonplace and practical American districts" (1:223).

He left the city for one of his more memorable ethnographic sketches in the reedy wastelands of the Gulf of Mexico. At the urging of George Washington Cable, Hearn used the national magazine *Harper's Weekly* as an outlet in 1883 for his account of a village of Filipino fishermen and alligator hunters hidden in the bayous. In "Saint Malo," he offered a study of the dark side of the community that came out in the quest for harmony. He described accord among the villagers until a woman brought from the outside world caused dissension. He raised eyebrows among his readers with his telling of the subsequent events. The elders gathered to restore peace. Their judgment was that the woman should be hacked up and the pieces thrown to the alligators in the bayou. He followed the notice he received for this piece with contributions to *Lippincott's, Cosmopolitan, Atlantic Monthly,* and *Harper's Bazaar.* Despite the opportunities afforded him for national exposure, he limited his contributions because of his resentment of the limits that popular taste in the magazines put on his poetic prose and because of heavier-handed editing than he was used to in his newspaper work.

During the *Times-Democrat* period, his folklore research and book collecting extended beyond Creoles to West Indian, Arabian, African, Jewish, and Oriental studies. He subscribed to "a library of folk-lore and folk-lore music of all nations, of which only 17 volumes are published so far" (Bisland 1906, 1:277). He began thinking more globally and applying evolutionary ideas to traditional oral literature. He proposed to Krehbiel a "little volume on the musical legends of all nations, introducing each legend by appropriate music," and he had already rewritten legends from Buddhist, Talmudic, Persian, Polynesian, and Finnish sources that fed into his *Stray Leaves from Strange Literature* (1884). Anticipating interest in local culture with the opening of a world's fair in New Orleans, Hearn returned to his Creole project a year later with the publication of *Gombo Zhèbes,* a forty-two-page dictionary of Creole proverbs, and *La Cuisine Creole.* He looked to African sources and sighed as he realized the need for ethnography on the continent of origin. He wrote Krehbiel in 1884, "My *Senegal* books have thrown a torrent of light on the whole history of American slave-songs and superstitions and folk-lore. I was utterly astounded at the revelation. All that had previously seemed obscure is now lucid as day. Of course, you know the slaves were chiefly drawn from the *West Coast;* and the study of ethnography and ethnology of the West Coast races is absolutely essential to a knowledge of Africanism in America" (1:332).

At the fair, he was moved by the Oriental exhibits to study in Chinese and Japanese bibliography. In 1887 he retold Chinese folklore as *Some Chinese Ghosts* and enjoyed his greatest publishing success up to that time. With this work, Hearn shifted his ethnographic stance from that of observer of contemporary practice to storyteller from ancient sources. Hearn confessed that he was more attracted to library sources for his folklore because he felt, of late, inadequate as an ethnographer. Whether because of his strained eyesight or his literary aspirations, he worried in a letter to his friend Ellwood Hendrick, "I find myself unable to create for want of a knowledge of every-day life,— that life which is the only life the general reader understands or cares about." His hope was to eventually produce a library of "philosophical fairy-tales [that] might deal with personal experiences common to all men,—impulse and sorrow and hope and discovery of the hollowness of things" (Bisland 1906, 2:340). In a letter to another crony, Mitchell McDonald, he offered that writers like him had "little knowledge of life, little *savoir-vivre,* to help them in the study of the artificial and complex growth of modern society." Contemplating his role as outsider, he wrote, "unless very exceptionally situated, they are debarred, by this very want of knowledge and skill, from mixing with that life which alone can furnish the material. Society everywhere suspects them; common life repels them" (2:341).

Hearn felt haunted again by ghosts of restlessness. He wrote Henry Krehbiel in 1878, "My eyes are eternally played out, and I shall have to abandon newspaper work altogether before long. . . . What is eternally rising up before me now like a spectre is the ?—'Where shall I go?—what shall I do?' Sometimes I think of Europe, sometimes of the West Indies,—of Florida, France, or the wilderness of London. The time is not far off when I must go somewhere,—if it is not to join the 'Innumerable Caravan.' Whenever I go down to the wharves, I look at the white-winged ships. O ye messengers, swift Hermae of Traffic, ghosts of the infinite ocean, whither will ye bear me?— what destiny will ye bring me,— what hopes, what despairs?" (Bisland 1906, 1:183). He had two sometimes conflicting longings. He wanted to be lost in a more primitive place, and at the same time he wanted to be enmeshed in an intellectual literary circle. "No literary circle here," he concluded to Krehbiel in 1881, and further jabbed, "no associates save those vampire ones of which the less said the better." He closed his letter with the foreboding words, "And the thought—Where must all this end?—may be laughed off in the daytime, but always returns to haunt me like a ghost in the night" (1:225).

A vacation to Grand Isle in the Gulf whetted his appetite for a life of writing in the West Indies. Amid primitive surroundings, the island had its share of vacationers from whom he wanted to get away. He hoped for a more remote island paradise where he could work on his prose undisturbed. The ethnic diversity on Grand Isle prompted in him the desire to be among "mixed races" and native customs and natural sights untainted by modernity. He wrote W.D. O'Connor in 1887, "In Trinidad I can see South American flora in all their splendour; in Jamaica, and especially Martinique, I can get good chances to study those Creole types which are so closely allied to our own. I want to finish a tiny volume of notes of travel—Impressionist-work,—always keeping to my dream of a *poetical prose*" (Bisland 1906, 1:383). After almost a decade in New Orleans, he ventured north to New York with the idea of catching a steamer to the Antilles. In New York he had reunions with Henry Krehbiel and fellow New Orleans newspaper editor Elizabeth Bisland. He also arranged with editor Henry Alden at the Harper offices to write for the magazine while he was in the West Indies. Friends and literary admirers wanted Hearn to make social rounds in the city's intellectual circles, but he became more agitated by the metropolis as time wore on. He complained to Joseph Tunison, "The moment I get into all this beastly machinery called 'New York,' I get caught in some belt and whirled around madly in all directions until I have no sense left. This city drives me crazy, or, if you prefer, crazier; and I have no peace of mind or rest of body till I get out of it" (1:444). He exclaimed, "Civilization is a hideous thing. Blessed is savagery!"

After more than a month in New York City, he sailed for Martinique in July 1887. He immediately became enchanted with the island. He wrote Bisland shortly after arriving, "The effect upon me has been such that I think the North will always look torpid to me,—as a benumbed and livid part of our planet" (Bisland 1906, 1:412). In addition to working on a novel about slave life set in the islands, he wrote a travel narrative describing his attraction to the sources of Creole life in the Indies. *Two Years in the French West Indies*

(1890) glowingly offered the sights and smells of Martinique and Barbados in exotic terms and recorded stories, arts, and songs of the black population. Comparing the spiritual sensations of the islands to those of cold, mechanized America, he felt closer to the heavens in the tropics. "Tropical nights have a splendor that seems strange to northern eyes. The sky does not look so high—so far away as in the North; but the stars are larger, and luminously greater" (Hearn [1890] 2001, 42). Although he would return to the United States, the trip to Martinique marked a sharp split from an American identity that he had earlier begun to cultivate. Writing from the island in 1888, he added: "It appears to me impossible to resign myself to living again in a great city and in a cold climate. Of course I shall have to return to the States for a while,—a short while probably;—but I do not think I will ever settle there. I am apt to become tired of places,—or at least of the disagreeable facts attaching more or less to all places and becoming more and more marked and unendurable the longer one stays. So that ultimately I am sure to wander off somewhere else" (Bisland 1906, 1:424).

Upon reflection, America became for Hearn the epitome of the clamor of modernization. In "Follow the Donkey-Path," written for the *Times-Demo-crat* in 1886, he reflected, "Here, on the west of the Atlantic, there are possibilities of unparalleled magnificence; there are colossal prospects; there are wonderful hopes for all." In his view, Europe was inherently pessimistic, because "there is no more national expansion possible; there is no grandiose future in view; and human anxieties are largely aroused by the mere prospective difficulty of conserving existent conditions." Maybe the philosophy bred by "a world already old" would spread to the United States, he thought. "But for the time being, the wind of the vast whirl and striving of the American life, prevents a general settling down of pessimistic germs." As a result of being "busy building up a world," he concluded, Americans are unreflective, insensitive to national traditions, and lacking in a philosophy of meaning (Hearn 1925, 125). He explained to George Gould, a physician in Philadelphia, "Such is exactly my present feeling,—an unutterable weariness of the aggressive characteristics of existence in a highly organized society. The higher the social development, the sharper the struggle. One feels this especially in America,—in the nervous centres of the world's activity" (Bisland 1906, 1:425). America's optimism, its orientation toward the future, he mused, prevented it from comprehending the problems of growth.

Hearn maintained his correspondence with Gould during his time in the West Indies. Gould initiated the letters as an admirer of his literature, and as an "oculist," he offered to help improve Hearn's eye condition. After returning to New York to read proofs on his novels *Chita: A Memory of Last*

Island (1889) and *Youma: The Story of a West-Indian Slave* (1890), Hearn bitterly complained, "Nobody can find anybody, nothing seems to be anywhere, everything seems to be mathematics and geometry and enigmatics and riddles and confusion worse confounded: architecture and mechanics run mad. One has to live by intuition and move by steam. I think an earthquake might produce some improvement. The so-called improvements in civilization have apparently resulted in making it impossible to see, hear, or find anything out. You are improving yourselves out of the natural world. I want to get back among the monkeys and the parrots, under a violet sky among green peaks and an eternally lilac and luke-warm sea,—where clothing is superfluous and reading too much of an exertion,—where everybody sleeps 14 hours out of the 24" (Bisland 1906, 1:444). The trouble with the tropics, he feared, was that the heat and bucolic surroundings drove out his motivation to work on his prose. Although he reveled in the peace of the islands, he found it intellectually lonely, even enervating. So he impetuously took a train to Philadelphia and showed up on Dr. Gould's doorstep, unannounced. He stayed with the doctor for six months and became to the doctor both patient and literary associate. Hearn reacted more positively to Philadelphia than to New York, but his time there was spent working on his "poetic prose" rather than engaging in new ethnography. Gould claimed to give Hearn his first taste of a normal home life. Sensing a moral failing in Hearn, Gould sermonized to the artist he thought of as an erotic pagan. He argued with him about the need for obedience to conscience and duty to others. In Gould's words, he tried to "give him a soul." When Hearn's relationship with the Gould household became strained, he came across Percival Lowell's *Soul of the Far East,* which reignited his thinking about the mysticism and fidelity to tradition in China and Japan. He considered escaping the approaching eastern winter by shipping off to Japan, but he was short of cash. With his novel *Chita* drawing some notice in New York's literary circles, Elizabeth Bisland persuaded Hearn to give New York City another try.

Returning to Manhattan, he worked on the publication of *Two Years in the French West Indies* with *Harper's* art editor William Patten. The editor was a student of Oriental art, and Hearn borrowed material from him to fire his excitement about experiencing Japan. The pair worked out a plan to follow the kind of ethnographic travel writing in *Two Years* in a narrative about Japan. *Harper's* editor Henry Alden approved the project with the comment that Hearn was the most capable "of fully appreciating and of adequately portraying with the utmost charm and felicity every shade, however quaint and subtle, of the life of strange people" (McWilliams 1946, 256). To raise money for the trip, Hearn penned some translations for *Harper's.* On March

Sketch by C.D. Weldon from memory, of how Hearn
looked as he was leaving New York for Japan, 1890.

6, 1890, Hearn boarded a train with one suitcase and a satchel, accompanied
by *Harper's* artist C.D. Weldon. The pair headed across Canada and boarded
a ship for Japan in Vancouver. The trip was a risky venture, since the *Harper's*
editors never guaranteed that they would accept anything he wrote.

Hearn anticipated staying in Japan for a year but ended up staying the
rest of his life. He thought that with the income from a narrative about Japan,
he would establish a home in the West Indies. After arriving in Yokohama, he
became enraged by the paltry sum given him by *Harper's* for his work, compared to what the artist was paid. He cursed at Alden and broke off relations.
His essays on Japan began appearing in *Atlantic Monthly* in 1891, and he
subsequently collected them in several memorable volumes, including *Glimpses
of Unfamiliar Japan* (1894), *Out of the East* (1895), and *Kokoro* (1896). He
expanded his fascination with folklife and ghostly narratives. The theme of
tradition, in the form of "Old Japan," confronting the "whirlwind" of west-
ernization and modernization ran through much of this writing. Immersed in
Japan, he became a citizen and took on yet another symbolic name change,
this time to Koizumi Yakumo. Koizumi is the family name of the Japanese

woman he married in Matsue, and Yakumo, in keeping with Hearn's skyward yearning, means "many clouds."

Although celebrated for his narratives and folklore collections in Japan, Hearn never left America completely behind. In October 1894, he took a full-time job as editorial writer for the English-language newspaper *Kobe Chronicle*. He offered opinions on social and political events in America, including "The Labour Problem in America," "The Race Problem in America," and "The Growth of Population in America." Taking the voice of an outsider who had lived inside both Japan and the United States, he gave comparative views of Japanese-American relations and foretold the growing conflict between the two nations. He even expressed homesickness for the West and complained that Japan, too, was becoming too modern for his tastes. He wrote, "My conclusion is that the charm of Japanese life is largely the charm of childhood, and that the most beautiful of all race childhoods is passing into an adolescence which threatens to prove repulsive" (Cott 1992, 329). Depressed by new inflammation in his right eye, he fantasized about pulling up roots again, this time for the "savage lands" of the South Pacific, but he remained with his wife and children. As chair of English literature at the University of Tokyo from September 1896 to March 1903, he lectured on American as well as British literature. Amid growing antiforeign tension, he was forced out of his university position and prepared for a short trip back to America to lecture at Cornell. Cornell withdrew its offer, but Hearn gathered the lectures he was supposed to deliver into his best-known book on Japan, *Japan: An Attempt at Interpretation*, published in September 1904. He died in the same month that the book was published. At least twenty-one posthumous collections of his essays appeared in the next thirty years.

The critical themes that underlay the organization of these collections helped fix Hearn's reputation as a Japanese interpreter and literary artist. Most of the volumes featured his literary criticism from the view of someone familiar with the expressions of three continents. The main critical themes explored were those of literary art as emotional expression and Hearn's exploration of the supernatural subject. During the early twentieth century, when the definition of English literature was being expanded to take into account America's coming of age and underestimated literary forms of essays, adapted folktales, travel literature, and short stories, Hearn's perspectives gained attention. Adding to his renown was a literary debate shortly after his death about the value of his art. In 1906 Elizabeth Bisland published two volumes of Hearn's letters with an admiring commentary on his "genius." Her outline of his life gave an evolutionary outline of the development of an artist from "apprentice" in America and the West Indies to "Master Workman" in Japan. A year later, more letters appeared as *Letters from the Raven* under the editorship of Milton Bronner. In his introduction, he unequivocally declared that "the best work of [Hearn's] life was commenced at the age of forty, when he arrived in Japan." Bronner ascribed this mastery to Hearn's ceasing to be a wandering, ethnographic outsider: "When he came to Japan he was weary of wandering, and the courtesy, gentleness and kindliness of the natives soon convinced him that they were the best people in the world among whom to live. A small man physically, he felt at home in a nation of small men. It pleased his shy, sensitive nature to think that he was often mistaken for a Japanese" (Bronner 1907, 11). The "work" worth doing, in Bronner's view, was the literary creativity, not the ethnographic documentation.

George Gould in *Concerning Lafcadio Hearn* (1908) agreed that the Japanese material was his best literary output, but he scathingly attacked Hearn's claim to creativity. He called him an imitator of Flaubert and said he was unworthy of praise for literary innovation. "He was a reflector only," Gould wrote, "plus a colorist—but a colorist of unrivalled excellence and power" (1908, 189). Gould sensed that Hearn's true calling was to folklore, but he criticized his background knowledge of the field. Folklore was to Gould "the one field [with] which his taste, aptitude and function dictated a wide and stimulating acquaintance" (18-19). Gould demeaned Hearn's moral character, complaining of his "heathenish and unrestrained appetites" (7). Following Gould's assault on Hearn's reputation, a number of critics reexamined Hearn's literary contribution. In an admiring biography, Edward Thomas in 1912 lauded the "scientific accuracy of detail" and the "tender and exquisite brilliancy of style" in Hearn's writing. He connected Hearn to French romanticism and saw, as did Arthur Kunst more extensively later, the influence of Hearn's translations from the French on the distinct "coloring" of words in his prose (Thomas 1912, 89; Kunst 1969). Thomas dwelled more than others on the dilemma of race in Hearn's background and the way it came through in Japan as well as in the West Indies and America. In Japan, meanwhile, Hearn's essays gained new life as windows to foreign views of a once-isolated kingdom. He also was respected as a preserver of "Old Japan" and its folktales. Many volumes reprinting his essays under the headings of "Oriental articles," "scientific sketches," and "literary essays" appeared under the editorship of Ichiro Nishizaki.

Probably more than any other criticism, Malcolm Cowley's introduction to *The Selected Writings of Lafcadio Hearn* (1949) fixed the reputation of Hearn as a literary artist whose greatest contribution was an interpretation of Japan. Cowley's word mattered. A major literary historian of the twentieth century, he helped rivet public notice on the likes of William Faulkner, Ernest

Hemingway, and F. Scott Fitzgerald. His concern for Hearn likely came about because Hearn fit into his theme of an artist's alienation from childhood and exile from society contributing to a legend of creativity. While carping about Hearn's "power of construction beyond the limits of a short essay or a folk tale," he honored his gift for collecting and retelling folktales. "Now that so much his work in many fields has been collected into one volume," he concluded, "I think it will be apparent that his folk tales are the most valuable part of it and that he is the writer in our language who can best be compared with Hans Christian Andersen and the brothers Grimm" (Cowley 1949, 15).

To folklorists, Hearn comes under the heading of an amateur ably contributing to the knowledge of folk culture, or a literary artist incorporating folk material into his prose. He is given credit for the earliest documentation of secular African American songs in urban settings and valuable records of Creole folk tradition in the nineteenth century. But it is the Japanese material by which he is mainly judged. W.K. McNeil labeled him an "American folklorist" in an article for the *Journal of American Folklore* but concluded, "He became known as an interpreter of Japanese life, but he was really a cultural historian who kept seeking the old Nippon traditions that could serve as positive values in a rapidly emerging modern industrial nation" (McNeil 1978, 967). For Cowley, Hearn was not literary enough in his ethnography, and for McNeil he was not sufficiently ethnographic. Both note, however, that he was uncovering unusual material and rendering it in a distinctive prose style before other writers or ethnographers found his urban cultural scenes compelling. Their perspectives may be emblematic of the biases that diminished the availability of Hearn's American work in the United States for the last fifty years.

The argument here for American studies is that the mesh of ethnography and art in Hearn's prose is worthy of cultural analysis rather than artistic hand-wringing. Besides illuminating the development of the essay and the sketch as literary forms, his "golden era of journalism" provides rare glimpses of nineteenth-century American urban ethnic and occupational life that are needed to inform a fuller, if darker, picture of American social development. It is hard to separate Hearn's subjects from his experience, for the scenes he wrote up in often purple prose answer to his experience of race, class, and ethnicity. His prose is also steeped in conventions of the day that demand understanding reading today. His use of *Hebrews, colored,* and *Negro* did not indicate lack of sympathy. His constant references to racial "blood" and to national characters were in keeping with evolutionary references of the day and with his particular devotion to the philosophy of evolutionist Herbert Spencer. But whereas most evolutionists were attracted to native "savages"— Indians and aborigines far from civilization—he examined ethnic traditions in the bustling city and dared to consider "mixed breeds" and the hybridization of culture from the tropics into the United States. For devotees of song and story, he offers valuable kernels of cultural expression, much of which could not be documented by the time recording devices came along. Further, he took notice of ethnic groups that escaped the notice of most historians of his period.

Hearn made a name himself with his features in the Sunday edition of the *Enquirer* that wandered from the police beat of murder to the scenes of hardscrabble lives. *Life* was a keyword in many of his sketches. "Levee Life" portrayed the scene around the steamboat market; "Les Chiffonniers" gave ethnographic details on "How They [ragpickers] Live, Work and Have Their Being"; "Within the Bars" told "How Prisoners Look, Live, and Conduct Themselves." These were ethnographic sketches more than studies, as Hearn admitted. He distinguished between his essays, often on literary or artistic topics, and his sketches, which set readers in a contemporary cultural scene. In the sketch, the detail, especially what we would now think of as the ethnographic detail, encapsulated many actions of life swirling about it. Whether it was boiling crabs or drinking blood, the custom brought to light cultural systems of belief and ritual. Reflecting on his writing later in life, he called it "the prose of small things." In a lecture at the University of Tokyo, he explained that "by the word sketch I mean any brief study in prose which is either an actual picture of life as seen with the eyes, or of life as felt with the mind." With his sensitivity to the ability to observe, he cautioned, "It might be only a record of something seen, but so well seen that, when recorded, it is like a water-colour." The sketch combined the journalist's nose for the facts of the case with the artist's eye for emotion. The sketch was typically a brief story, narrated dramatically "within the world of fact and sincere feeling" (Hearn 1969 [1917], 113).

The ethnographic sketch is a type of story that I identify in Hearn's oeuvre that grows out of a description of an unusual custom, speech, craft, song, story, group, or setting. I find three approaches to the ethnographic sketch. One is to profile a "quarter," a "district," a "village," or a "group." Within these categories of social space, Hearn documents distinctive manners and customs. He may editorialize on the inevitable passing of the culture or fret about the conditions that the group is forced to live in. In "The Last of the New Orleans Fencing-Masters," for example, Hearn characterizes the Spanish "element" of the city and sees symbolism of change in the passing of fencing as a ritual component of the ethnic culture. Another approach is to profile individual masters of traditional practices, as he does in "The Last of the Voudoos." Third, he surveys genres of folk expression such as music, craft, or speech as a way to show the vitality of an ethnic urban culture. An example of this latter approach is "New Orleans Superstitions."

As these themes indicate, his reading in "folklore and ethnology" likely had an influence on his idea of the ethnographic sketch. He published reviews of the American folkloristic studies of Alceé Fortier, and he eagerly promoted the French folklore journal *Mélusine,* edited by Henri Gaidoz. In "Some Notes on Creole Literature," he reviews "a tiny work just published by the well-known folklorists, MM Gaidoz and Sebillot at Paris, entitled *Bibliographie des Traditions et de la Litterature popolaire des Frances d'outre-mer*" (Hearn 1924, 2:154). He makes a plea in the essay that "our local folklorists might do much to aid the labors of their brethren abroad" (158). Hearn's reading in the field is evident from his criticism of omissions in the bibliography despite his praising words, "It certainly opens the eyes of the student to the importance, linguistic and anthropological, of the literature considered, and reveals the recent development of that literature in a decidedly surprising manner" (154). That surprise is the shift from ancient mythology studies to more ethnographic descriptions of songs, speech, and legends in the present day. A frequent correspondent with Hearn was his "folklorist" friend Henry E. Krehbiel, who wrote studies of folk songs. Hearn wrote him in October 1883 to discuss writing companion pieces for an American popular magazine like *Harper's* or *Scribners.* He suggested consulting his copy of *Mélusine* and told him of other works on folklore in his collection. He closed the letter with an anecdote of confronting a Creole musician about the value of a roustabout song. To the musician's claim that it was an "abomination," Hearn wrote, "'Nay!' said I, 'It hath a most sweet sound to me; and to the ethnologist a most fascinating interest. Verily, I would rather listen to it, than hear a symphony of Beethoven!'" (Bisland 1906, 1:284).

The America that Lafcadio Hearn heard singing during the 1870s and 1880s was raunchier than the "blithe and strong" of Walt Whitman's nation around the same time. Hearn's ethnographic sense led him to comment on the line in *Leaves of Grass* "I hear America singing, the varied carols I hear" in this way: "What most charms me, however, is that which is most earthy and of the earth" (Cott 1992, 161). From the grounding of folklore found among diverse ethnic societies in gritty cities, Hearn located America's earthiness. Whatever its scientific and artistic limitations, Hearn's ethnographic sketch of America still has strength to lead today's readers to interrogate the muse of the odd and the impression of life as usual. It questions the American struggle between tradition and modernity, between the isolation and the integration of folk cultures, and ultimately, in Hearn's words, it questions America's "vast whirl and striving."

Part I

Communities and the "Under Side" of America

1

LEVEE LIFE

Haunts and Pastimes of the Roustabouts

—◦—◦—

Along the river-banks on either side of the levee slope, where the brown water year after year climbs up to the ruined sidewalks, and pours into the warehouse cellars, and paints their grimy walls with streaks of water-weed green, may be studied a most curious and interesting phase of life—the life of a community within a community,—a society of wanderers who have haunts but not homes, and who are only connected with the static society surrounding them by the common bond of State and municipal law. It is a very primitive kind of life; its lights and shadows are alike characterized by a half savage simplicity; its happiness or misery is almost purely animal; its pleasures are wholly of the hour, neither enhanced nor lessened by anticipation of the morrow. It is always pitiful rather than shocking; and it is not without some little charm of its own—the charm of a thoughtless existence, whose virtues are all original, and whose vices are for the most part foreign to it. A great portion of this levee-life haunts also the subterranean hovels and ancient frame buildings of the district lying east of Broadway to Culvert street, between Sixth and Seventh streets. But, on a cool spring evening, when the levee is bathed in moonlight, and the torch-basket lights dance redly upon the water, and the clear air vibrates to the sonorous music of the deep-toned steam-whistle, and the sound of wild banjo-thrumming floats out through the open doors of the levee dance-houses, then it is perhaps that one can best observe the peculiarities of this grotesquely-picturesque roustabout life.

Probably less than one-third of the stevedores and 'longshoremen employed in our river traffic are white, but the calling now really belongs by right to the negroes, who are by far the best roustabouts and are unrivaled as firemen. The white stevedores are generally tramps, willing to work only through fear of the Work-house; or, some times laborers unable to obtain other employment, and glad to earn money for the time being at any employment. On board the boats, the whites and blacks mess separately and work under different mates, there being on an average about twenty-five roustabouts to every boat which unloads at the Cincinnati levee. Cotton boats running on the

Lower Mississippi, will often carry sixty or seventy deck hands, who can some seasons earn from forty-five dollars to sixty dollars per month. On the Ohio boats the average wages paid to roustabouts will not exceed $30 per month. 'Longshoremen earn fifteen and twenty cents per hour, according to the season. These are frequently hired by Irish contractors, who undertake to unload a boat at so much per package; but the first-class boats generally contract with the 'longshoremen directly through the mate, and sometimes pay twenty-five cents per hour for such labor. "Before Freedom," as the colored folks say, white laborers performed most of the roustabout labor on the steamboats; the negroes are now gradually monopolizing the calling, chiefly by reason of their peculiar fitness for it. Generally speaking, they are the best porters in the world; and in the cotton States, it is not uncommon, we are told, to see negro levee hands for a wager, carry five-hundred-pound cotton-bales on their backs to the wharfboat. River men, to-day, are recognizing the superior value of negro labor in steamboat traffic, and the colored roustabouts are now better treated, probably, than they have been since the war. Under the present laws, too, they are better protected. It used at one time to be a common thing for some ruffianly mate to ship sixty or seventy stevedores, and, after the boat had taken in all her freight, to hand the poor fellows their money and land them at some small town, or even in the woods, hundreds of miles from their home. This can be done no longer with legal impunity.

Roustabout life in the truest sense is, then, the life of the colored population of the Rows, and, partly, of Bucktown—blacks and mulattoes from all parts of the States, but chiefly from Kentucky and Eastern Virginia, where most of them appear to have toiled on the plantations before Freedom; and echoes of the old plantation life still live in their songs and their pastimes. You may hear old Kentucky slave songs chanted nightly on the steamboats, in that wild, half-melancholy key peculiar to the natural music of the African race; and you may see the old slave dances nightly performed to the air of some ancient Virginia-reel in the dance-houses of Sausage Row, or the "ball-rooms" of Bucktown. There is an intense uniqueness about all this pariah existence; its boundaries are most definitely fixed; its enjoyments are wholly sensual, and many of them are marked by peculiarities of a strictly local character. Many of their songs, which have never appeared in print, treat of levee life in Cincinnati, of all the popular steamboats running on the "Muddy Water," and of the favorite roustabout haunts on the river bank and in Bucktown. To collect these curious songs, or even all the most popular of them, would be a labor of months, and even then a difficult one, for the colored roustabouts are in the highest degree suspicious of a man who approaches them with a notebook and pencil. Occasionally, however, one can induce an intelligent steamboatman to sing a few river songs by an innocent bribe in the shape of a cigar or a drink, and this we attempted to do with considerable success during a few spare evenings last week, first, in a popular roustabout haunt on Broadway, near Sixth, and afterward in a dingy frame cottage near the corner of Sixth and Culvert streets. Unfortunately some of the most curious of these songs are not of a character to admit of publication in the columns of a daily newspaper; but others which we can present to our readers may prove interesting. Of these the following song, "Number Ninety-Nine," was at one time immensely popular with the steamboatmen. The original resort referred to was situated on Sixth and Culvert street, where Kirk's building now stands. We present the song with some necessary emendations:

"You may talk about yer railroads,
    Yer steamboats and can-*el*
If 't hadn't been for Liza Jane
    There wouldn't a bin no hell.
    Chorus—Oh, ain't I gone, gone, gone,
    Oh, ain't I gone, gone, gone,
    Oh, ain't I gone, gone, gone,
            Way down de ribber road.

"Whar do you get yer whisky?
    Whar do you get yer rum?
I got it down in Bucktown,
    At Number Ninety-nine.
    Chorus—"Oh, ain't I gone, gone, gone, &c.

"I went down to Bucktown,
    Nebber was dar before,
Great big niggah knocked me down,
    But Katy barred the door.
    Chorus—"Oh, ain't I gone, gone, gone, &c.

"She hugged me, she kissed me,
    She tole me not to cry;
She said I was de sweetest thing
    Dat ebber libbed or died.
    Chorus—"Oh, ain't I gone, gone, gone, &c.
*   *   *
"Yonder goes the Wildwood.

She's loaded to the guards,
But yonder comes the Fleetwood,
   An' she's the boat for me.
   Chorus—Oh, ain't I gone, gone, gone, &c."

The words, "'Way down to Rockingham," are sometime substituted in the chorus, for "'way down de ribber road."

One of the most popular roustabout songs now sung on the Ohio is the following. The air is low, and melancholy, and when sung in unison by the colored crew of a vessel leaving or approaching port, has a strange, sad sweetness about it which is very pleasing. The two-fold character of poor Molly, at once good and bad, is somewhat typical of the stevedore's sweetheart:

Molly was a good gal and a bad gal, too.
   Oh Molly, row, gal.
Molly was a good gal and a bad gal, too.
   Oh Molly, row, gal.

I'll row dis boat and I'll row no more,
   Row, Molly, row, gal.
I'll row dis boat, and I'll go on shore,
   Row, Molly, row, gal.

Captain on the biler deck a-heaving of the lead,
   Oh Molly, row, gal.
Calling to the pilot to give her, "Turn ahead,"
   Row, Molly, row, gal.

Here is another to a slow and sweet air. The chorus, when well sung, is extremely pretty:

Shawneetown is burnin' down,
   Who tole you so?
Shawneetown is burnin' down,
   Who tole you so?

Cythie, my darlin' gal,
   Who tole you so?
Cythie, my darlin' gal,
   How do you know?
   Chorus—Shawneetown is burnin', &c.

How the h—l d'ye 'spect me to hold her,
    Way down below?
I've got no skin on either shoulder,
    Who tole you so?
  Chorus—Shawneetown is burnin', &c.

De houses dey is all on fire,
    Way down below.
De houses dey is all on fire,
    Who tole you so?
  Chorus—Shawneetown is burnin', &c.

My old missus tole me so,
    Way down below.
An' I b'lieve what ole missus says,
    Way down below.
  Chorus—Shawneetown is burnin', &c.

The most melancholy of all these plaintive airs is that to which the song "Let her go by" is commonly sung. It is generally sung on leaving port, and sometimes with an affecting pathos inspired of the hour, while the sweethearts of the singers watch the vessel gliding down stream.

I'm going away to New Orleans!
  Good-bye, my lover, good-bye!
I'm going away to New Orleans!
  Good-bye, my lover, good-bye!
    Oh, let her go by!

She's on her way to New Orleans!
  Good-bye, my lover, good-bye!
She bound to pass the Robert E. Lee,
  Good-bye, my lover, good-bye!
    Oh, let her go by!

I'll make dis trip and I'll make no more!
  Good-bye, my lover, good-bye!
I'll roll dese barrels, I'll roll no more!
  Good-bye, my lover, good-bye!
    Oh, let her go by!

An' if you are not true to me,
    Farewell, my lover, farewell!
An' if you are not true to me,
    Farewell, my lover, farewell!
        Oh, let her go by!

The next we give is of a somewhat livelier description. It has, we believe, been printed in a somewhat different form in certain song books. We give it as it was sung to us in a Broadway saloon:

I come down the mountain,
    An' she come down the lane,
An' all that I could say to her
    Was, "Good bye, 'Liza Jane."

Chorus—Farewell, 'Liza Jane!
        Farewell, 'Liza Jane!
    Don't throw yourself away, for I
        Am coming back again.

I got up on a house-top,
    An' give my horn a blow;
Thought I heerd Miss Dinah say,
    "Yonder comes your beau."
        [Chorus.]

Ef I'd a few more boards,
    To build my chimney higher,
I'd keep aroun' the country gals,
    Chunkin' up the fire.
        [Chorus.]

The following are fragments of rather lengthy chants, the words being almost similar in both, but the choruses and airs being very different. The air of the first is sonorous and regularly slow, like a sailor's chant when heaving anchor; the air of the next is quick and lively.

"Belle-a-Lee's got no time,
    Oh, Belle! oh, Belle!

Robert E. Lee's got railroad time,
   Oh, Belle! oh, Belle!

"Wish I was in Mobile Bay,
   Oh, Belle! oh, Belle!
Rollin' cotton by de day,
   Oh, Belle! oh, Belle!

*   *   *

"I wish I was in Mobile Bay,
Rollin' cotton by de day,
       Stow'n' sugar in de hull below,
         Below, belo-ow,
     Stow'n' sugar in de hull below!

"De Natchez is a new boat; she's just in her prime,
Beats any oder boat on de New Orleans line.
       Stow'n' sugar in de hull below, &c.

"Engineer, t'rough de trumpet, gives de firemen news,
Couldn' make steam for de fire in de flues.
       Stow'n' sugar in de hull below, &c.

"Cap'n on de biler deck, a scratchin' of his head,
Hollers to de deck hand to heave de larbo'rd lead.
       Stow'n' sugar in de hull below, &c.

*   *   *

Perhaps the prettiest of all these songs is "The Wandering Steamboatman," which, like many other roustabout songs, rather frankly illustrates the somewhat loose morality of the calling:

I am a wandering steamboatman,
   And far away from home;
I fell in love with a pretty gal,
   And she in love with me.

She took me to her parlor,
   And cooled me with her fan;
She whispered in her mother's ear:
   "I love the steamboatman."

The mother entreats her daughter not to become engaged to the stevedore. "You know," she says, "that he is a steamboatman, and has a wife at New
Orleans." But the steamboatman replies, with great nonchalance:

> If I've a wife at New Orleans
>   I'm neither tied nor bound;
> And I'll forsake my New Orleans wife
>   If you'll be truly mine.

Another very curious and decidedly immoral song is popular with the
loose women of the "Rows." We can only give one stanza:

> I hev a roustabout for my man—
> Livin' with a white man for a sham,
>   Oh, leave me alone,
>   Leave me alone,
> I'd like you much better if you'd leave me alone.

But the most famous song in vogue among the roustabouts is "Limber
Jim," or "Shiloh." Very few know it all by heart, which is not wonderful when
we consider that it requires something like twenty minutes to sing "Limber
Jim" from beginning to end, and that the whole song, if printed in full, would
fill two columns of the Commercial. The only person in the city who can sing
the song through, we believe, is a colored laborer living near Sixth and Culvert
streets, who "run on the river" for years, and acquired so much of a reputation
by singing "Limber Jim," that he has been nicknamed after the mythical individual aforesaid, and is now known by no other name. He keeps a little resort
in Bucktown, which is known as "Limber Jim's," and has a fair reputation for
one dwelling in that locality. Jim very good-naturedly sang the song for us a
few nights ago, and we took down some of the most striking verses for the
benefit of our readers. The air is wonderfully quick and lively, and the chorus
is quite exciting. The leading singer sings the whole song, excepting the chorus, "Shiloh," which dissyllable is generally chanted by twenty or thirty voices
of abysmal depth at the same time with a sound like the roar of twenty Chinese gongs struck with tremendous force and precision. A great part of "Limber Jim" is very profane, and some of it not quite fit to print. We can give only
about one-tenth part of it. The chorus is frequently accompanied with that
wonderfully rapid slapping of thighs and hips known as "patting Juba."

> Nigger an' a white man playing seven-up,
> White man played an ace; an' nigger feared to take it up,

White man played ace an' nigger played a nine,
White man died, an' nigger went blind.

> Limber Jim,
>   [All.] Shiloh!
> Talk it agin,
>   [All.] Shiloh!
> Walk back in love,
>   [All.] Shiloh!
> You turtle-dove,
>   [All.] Shiloh!

Went down the ribber, couldn't get across;
Hopped on a rebel louse; thought 'twas a hoss,
Oh lor', gals, 't ain't no lie,
Lice in Camp Chase big enough to cry,—
> Limber Jim, &c.

Bridle up a rat, sir; saddle up a cat,
Please han' me down my Leghorn hat,
Went to see widow; widow warn't home;
Saw to her daughter,—she gave me honeycomb.
> Limber Jim, &c.

Jay-bird sittin' on a swinging limb,
Winked at me an' I winked at him,
Up with a rock an' struck him on the shin,
G—d d—n yer soul, don't wink agin.
> Limber Jim, &c.

Some folks say that a rebel can't steal,
I found twenty in my corn-fiel',
Sich pullin' of shucks an' tearin' of corn!—
Nebber saw the like since I was born.
> Limber Jim, &c.

John Morgan come to Danville and cut a mighty dash,
Las' time I saw him, he was under whip an' lash;
'Long come a rebel at a sweepin' pace,
Whar 're ye goin', Mr. Rebel? "I'm going to Camp Chase."
> Limber Jim, &c.

Way beyond de sun and de moon,
White gal tole me I were too soon,
White gal tole me I come too soon,
An' nigger gal called me an ole d—d fool.
            Limber Jim, &c.

Eighteen pennies hidden in a fence,
Cynthiana gals ain't got no sense;
Every time they go from home
Comb thar heads wid an ole jaw bone.
            Limber Jim, &c.

Had a little wife an' didn' inten' to keep her;
Showed her a flatboat an' sent her down de ribber;
Head like a fodder-shock, mout like a shovel,
Put yerself wid yaller gal, put yerself in trouble.
            Limber Jim, &c.

I went down to Dinah's house, Dinah was in bed,
Hoisted de window an' poked out her head;
T'rowed, an' I hit in her de eyeball,—bim;
"Walk back, Mr. Nigger; don't do dat agin."
            Limber Jim, &c.

Gambling man in de railroad line,
Saved my ace an' played my nine;
If you want to know my name,
My name's High-low-jack-in-the-game.
            Limber Jim,
                Shiloh!
            Talk it agin,
                Shiloh!
            You dancing girl,
                Shiloh!
            Sure's you're born,
                Shiloh!

Grease my heel with butter in the fat,
I can talk to Limber Jim better'n dat.
            Limber Jim,

Shiloh!
Limber Jim,
Shiloh!
Walk back in love,
Shiloh!
My turtle dove,
Shiloh!

Patting Juba—And you can't go yonder,
Limber Jim!
And you can't go yonder,
Limber Jim!
And you can't go-oo-o!

One fact worth mentioning about these negro singers is, that they can
mimic the Irish accent to a degree of perfection which an American, English-
man or German could not hope to acquire. At the request of Patrolman Tighe
and his partner, the same evening that we interviewed Limber Jim, a very dark
mulatto, named Jim Delaney, sang for us in capital style that famous Irish
ditty known as "The hat me fahther wor-re." Yet Jim, notwithstanding his
name, has little or no Irish blood in his veins; nor has his companion, Jim
Harris, who joined in the rollicking chorus:

"'Tis the raylics of ould dacency,
The hat me fahther wor-r-re."

Jim Delaney would certainly make a reputation for Irish specialties in a
minstrel troupe; his mimicry of Irish character is absolutely perfect, and he
possesses a voice of great flexibility, depth and volume. He "runs" on the river.
On the southeast corner of Culvert and Sixth streets, opposite to the
house in which we were thus entertained by Limber Jim and his friends, stands
Kirk's building, now occupied jointly by Kirk and Ryan. Two stories beneath
this building is now the most popular dance-house of the colored steamboatmen
and their "girls." The building and lot belong to Kirk; but Ryan holds a lease
on the basement and half of the upper building. Recently the landlord and
the leaseholder had a falling out, and are at bitter enmity; but Ryan seems to
have the upper hand in the matter, and is making considerable money from
the roustabouts. He has closed up the old side entrance, admission to the ball-
room being now obtainable only through the bar-room, and the payment of
ten cents. A special policeman has been wisely hired by the proprietor to pre-

serve order below, and the establishment is, generally speaking, well conducted for an establishment of the kind. The amount of patronage it receives depends almost wholly upon the condition of the river traffic; during the greater part of the week the attendance is somewhat slim, but when the New Orleans boats come in the place is crowded to overflowing. Beside the admittance fee of ten cents, an additional dime is charged to all the men for every set danced—the said dime to be expended in "treating partners." When the times are hard and money scarce, the girls often pay the fees for their men in order to make up sets.

With its unplastered and windowless limestone walls; sanded floor; ruined ceiling, half plank, half cracked plaster; a dingy black counter in one corner, and rude benches ranged along the walls, this dancing-room presented rather an outlandish aspect when we visited it. At the corner of the room opposite "the bar," a long bench was placed, with its face to the wall; and upon the back of this bench, with their feet inwardly reclining upon the seat, sat the musicians. A well-dressed, neatly-built mulatto picked the banjo, and a somewhat lighter colored musician led the music with a fiddle, which he played remarkably well and with great spirit. A short, stout negress, illy dressed, with a rather good-natured face and a bed shawl tied about her head, played the bass viol, and that with no inexperienced hand. This woman is known to the police as Anna Nun.

The dancers were in sooth a motley crew; the neat dresses of the girls strongly contrasting with the rags of the poorer roustabouts, some of whom were clad only in shirt, pants and shocking hats. Several wickedly handsome women were smoking stogies. Bill Williams, a good-natured black giant, who keeps a Bucktown saloon, acted for a while as Master of Ceremonies. George Moore, the colored Democrat who killed, last election day, the leader of a party who attacked his house, figured to advantage in the dance, possessing wonderful activity in spite of his heavy bulk. The best performer on the floor was a stumpy little roustabout named Jem Scott, who is a marvelous jig-dancer, and can waltz with a tumbler full of water on his head without spilling a drop. One-fourth of the women present were white, including two girls only about seventeen years old, but bearing physiognomical evidence of precocious vice. The best-looking girl in the room was a tall, lithe quadroon named Mary Brown, with auburn hair, gray eyes, a very fair skin, and an air of quiet innocence wholly at variance with her reputation. A short, supple mulatto girl, with a blue ribbon in her hair, who attracted considerable admiration, and was famous for dancing "breakdowns," had but recently served a term in the penitentiary for grand larceny. Another woman present, a gigantic negress, wearing a red plaid shawl, and remarkable for an immense head of frizzly hair, was, we were informed, one of the most adroit thieves known to the police. It was a favorite trick of hers to pick a pocket while dancing, and hide the stolen money in her hair.

"How many of those present do you suppose carry knives?" we asked Patrolman Tighe.

"All of them," was the reply. "All the men, and women, too, carry knives or razors; and many of them pistols as well. But they seldom quarrel, except about a girl. Their great vice is thieving; and the fights down here are generally brought about by white roughs who have no business in this part of town except crime."

The musicians struck up that weird, wild, lively air, known perhaps to many of our readers as the "Devil's Dream," and in which "the musical ghost of a cat chasing the spectral ghost of a rat" is represented by a succession of "miauls" and "squeaks" on the fiddle. The dancers danced a double quadrille, at first, silently and rapidly; but warming with the wild spirit of the music, leaped and shouted, swinging each other off the floor, and keeping time with a precision which shook the building in time to the music. The women, we noticed, almost invariably embraced the men about the neck in swinging, the men clasping them about the waist. Sometimes the men advancing leaped and crossed legs with a double shuffle, and with almost sightless rapidity. Then the music changed to an old Virginia reel, and the dancing changing likewise, presented the most grotesque spectacle imaginable. The dancing became wild; men patted juba and shouted, the negro women danced with the most fantastic grace, their bodies describing almost incredible curves forward and backward; limbs intertwined rapidly in a wrestle with each other and with the music; the room presented a tide of swaying bodies and tossing arms, and flying hair. The white female dancers seemed heavy, cumbersome, ungainly by contrast with their dark companions; the spirit of the music was not upon them; they were abnormal to the life about them. Once more the music changed—to some popular negro air, with the chorus—

"Don't get weary,
I'm goin' home."

The musicians began to sing; the dancers joined in; and the dance terminated with a roar of song, stamping of feet, "patting juba," shouting, laughing, reeling. Even the curious spectators involuntarily kept time with their feet; it was the very drunkenness of music, the intoxication of the dance. Amid such scenes does the roustabout find his heaven; and this heaven is certainly not to be despised.

The great dancing resort for steamboatmen used to be Pickett's, on Sausage Row; but year after year the river came up and flooded all the grimy saloons on the Rows, and, departing, left behind it alluvial deposits of yellow mud, and the Spirit of Rheumatic Dampness. So, about two months ago, Pickett rented out his old quarters, partly as a barber-shop, partly as a shooting-gallery, and moved into the building, No. 91 Front street, between Ludlow and Lawrence. He has had the whole building renovated throughout, and painted the front very handsomely. The basement on the river side is now used for a dancing-room; but the room is very small, and will not accommodate half of the dancers who used to congregate in the old building. The upper part of the building the old man rents out to river men and their wives or mistresses, using the second floor for a restaurant and dining-rooms, which are very neatly fitted up. Whatever may have been the old man's sins, Pickett has a heart full of unselfish charity sufficient to cover them all. Year after year, through good or ill-fortune, he has daily fed and maintained fifty or sixty homeless and needy steamboatmen. Sometimes when the river trade "looks up," and all the boats are running on full time, some grateful levee hand repays his benefactor, but it is very seldom. And the old man never asks for it or expects it; he only says: "Boys, when you want to spend your money, spend it here." Although now very old, and almost helpless from a rupture, Pickett has yet but to rap on the counter of his saloon to enforce instantaneous quiet. The roustabouts will miss the old man when he is gone—the warm corner to sleep in, the simple but plentiful meal when out of a berth, and the rough kindness of his customary answer to a worthless, hungry, and shivering applicant for food and lodging. "G—d d—m you, you don't deserve it; but come in and behave yourself." The day is not far off when there will be great mourning along the levee.

With the exception of Ryan's dance-house, and one or two Bucktown lodging-houses, the roustabouts generally haunt the Rows, principally Sausage Row, from Broadway to Ludlow street. Rat Row, from Walnut to Main, is more especially the home of the white tramps and roustabouts. Here is situated the celebrated "Blazing Stump," otherwise called St. James Restaurant, which is kept by a Hollander, named Venneman. Venneman accommodates only white men, and endeavors to keep an orderly house; but the "Blazing Stump" must always remain a resort for thieves, burglars, and criminals of every description. The "Stump" is No. 13 Rat Row. No. 16 is a lodging house for colored roustabouts, kept by James Madison. No. 12 is a policy shop, although it pretends to be a saloon; and the business is so cunningly conducted that the police can not, without special privilege, succeed in closing up the business. No. 10, which used to be known as Buckner's, is another haunt for colored roustabouts. They have a pet crow attached to the establishment, which is very plucky, and can whip all the cats and dogs in the neighborhood. It waddles about on the sidewalk of sunny days, pecking fiercely at any stranger who meddles with it, but the moment it sees the patrolmen coming along the levee it runs into the house.

No. 7—Goodman's clothing store—is said to be a "fence." At the west end of the row is Captain Dilg's celebrated hostelry, a popular and hospitable house, frequented by pilots and the most respectable class of river men. At the eastern terminus of the row is the well known Alhambra saloon, a great resort for colored steamboatmen, where large profits are realized on cigars and whisky of the cheapest kind. The contractors who hire roustabouts frequently have a private understanding with the proprietor of some levee coffee-house or saloon, and always go there to pay off their hands. Then the first one treats, then another, and so on until all the money just made by a day's heavy labor is lying in the counter drawer, and the roustabouts are helplessly boozy.

Of the two rows Sausage Row is perhaps the most famous. No. 1 is kept by old Barney Hodke, who has made quite a reputation by keeping a perfectly orderly house in a very disorderly neighborhood. No. 2 is Cottonbrook's clothing store, *alias* the "American Clothing Store," whereof the proprietor is said to have made a fortune by selling cheap clothing to the negro stevedores. No. 3 is Mrs. Sweeney's saloon and boarding-house, an orderly establishment for the entertainment of river men. No. 4 is an eating- and lodging-house for roustabouts, kept by Frank Fortner, a white man. No. 6 is a barber-shop for colored folks, with a clothing-store next to it. No. 7 is a house of ill-fame, kept by a white woman, Mary Pearl, who boards several unfortunate white girls. This is a great resort for colored men.

No. 8 is Maggie Sperlock's. Maggie has another saloon in Bucktown. She is a very fat and kind-hearted old mulatto woman, who is bringing up half a dozen illegitimate children, abandoned by their parents. One of these, a very pretty boy, is said to be the son of a white lady, who moves in good society, by a colored man.

No. 9 is now Chris. Meyer's; it was known as "Schwabe Kate's" when Meyer's wife lived. This is the great resort for German tramps.

Next in order comes a barber-shop and shooting-gallery—"Long Branch" and "Saratoga." These used to be occupied by Pickett.

A few doors east of this is Chas. Redman's saloon, kept by a crippled soldier. This is another great roustabout haunt, where robberies are occasionally committed. And a little further east is Pickett's new hotel. On these two rows Officers Brazil and Knox have made no less than two hundred and fifty-six arrests during the past two years. The most troublesome element is, of course, among the white tramps.

A number of the colored river men are adroit thieves; these will work two or three months and then "lay off" until all their money has found its way to whisky-shops and brothels. The little clothing and shoe stores along the levee are almost daily robbed of some articles by such fellows, who excel in ingenious confidence dodges. A levee hand with extinct cigar will, for example, walk into a shoe shop with a "Say, bohss, giv a fellah a light." While the "bohss" is giving a light to the visitor, who always takes care to stand between the proprietor and the doorway, a confederate sneaks off with a pair of shoes. A fellow called "China Robinson," who hangs about Madison's, is said to be famous at such tricks. The police officers, however, will not allow any known sluggard or thief to loaf about the levee for more than thirty days without employment. There is always something to do for those who wish to do it, and roustabouts who persist in idleness and dirt, after one or two friendly warnings, get sent to the Work-house.

Half of the colored 'longshoremen used at one time to wear only a coat and pants, winter and summer; but now they are a little more careful of themselves, and fearful of being sent to the Work-house to be cleaned up. Consequently, when Officer Brazil finds a very ragged and dirty specimen of levee life on the row, he has seldom occasion to warn him more than once to buy himself a shirt and a change of garments.

Generally speaking, the women give very little trouble. Some of the white girls now living in Pickett's barracks or in Bucktown brothels are of respectable parentage. Two of the most notorious are sisters, who have a sad history. They are yet rather handsome. All these women are morphine eaters, and their greatest dread is to be sent to the Work-house, and being thus deprived of this stimulant. Some who were sent to the Work-house, we were told, had died there from want of it. The white girls of the Row soon die, however, under any circumstances; their lives are often fairly burnt out with poisonous whisky and reckless dissipation before they have haunted the levee more than two or three years. After a fashion, the roustabouts treat their women kindly, with a rough good nature that is peculiar to them; many of the women are really married. But faithfulness to a roustabout husband is considered quite an impossible virtue on the levee. The stevedores are mostly too improvident and too lazy to support their "gals." While the men are off on a trip, a girl will always talk about what she will be able to buy "when my man comes back—if he has any money." When the lover does come back, sometimes after a month's absence, he will perhaps present his "gal" with fifty cents, or at most a dollar, and thinks he has done generously by her. We are speaking in general terms, of course, and alluding to the mass of the colored roustabouts who "run on the river" all their lives, and have no other calling. It is needless to say that there are thrifty and industrious stevedores who support their families well, and will finally leave the river for some more lucrative employment.

Such is a glimpse of roustabout life. They know of no other life; they can understand no other pleasures. Their whole existence is one vision of anticipated animal pleasure or of animal misery; of giant toil under the fervid summer sun; of toil under the icy glare of the winter moon; of fiery drinks and drunken dreams; of the madness of music and the intoxication of fantastic dances; of white and dark mistresses awaiting their coming at the levees, with waving of brightly colored garments; of the deep music of the great steam whistles; of the torch-basket fires redly dancing upon the purple water, the white stars sailing overhead, the passing lights of well known cabins along the dark river banks, and the mighty panting of the iron heart of the great vessel, bearing them day after day and night after night to fresh scenes of human frailty, and nearer to that Dim Levee slope, where weird boats ever discharge ghostly freight, and depart empty.

2

SAINT MALO

A Lacustrine Village in Louisiana

⊷ ⊷

For nearly fifty years there has existed in the southeastern swamp lands of Louisiana a certain strange settlement of Malay fishermen—Tagalas from the Philippine Islands. The place of their lacustrine village is not precisely mentioned upon maps, and the world in general ignored until a few days ago the bare fact of their amphibious existence. Even the United States mail service has never found its way thither, and even in the great city of New Orleans, less than a hundred miles distant, the people were far better informed about the Carboniferous Era than concerning the swampy affairs of this Manila village. Occasionally vague echoes of its mysterious life were borne to the civilized center, but these were scarcely of a character to tempt investigation or encourage belief. Some voluble Italian luggermen once came to town with a short cargo of oysters, and a long story regarding a ghastly "Chinese" colony in the reedy swamps south of Lake Borgne. For many years the inhabitants of the Oriental settlement had lived in peace and harmony without the presence of a single woman, but finally had managed to import an oblique-eyed beauty from beyond the Yellow Sea. Thereupon arose the first dissensions, provoking much shedding of blood. And at last the elders of the people had restored calm and fraternal feeling by sentencing the woman to be hewn in pieces and flung to the alligators of the bayou.

Possible the story is; probable it is not. Partly for the purpose of investigating it, but principally in order to offer *Harper's* artist a totally novel subject of artistic study, the *Times-Democrat* of New Orleans chartered and fitted out an Italian lugger for a trip to the unexplored region in question—to the fishing station of Saint Malo. And a strange voyage it was. Even the Italian sailors knew not whither they were going, none of them had ever beheld the Manila village, or were aware of its location.

Starting from Spanish Fort northeastwardly across Lake Pontchartrain, after the first few miles sailed one already observes a change in the vegetation of the receding banks. The shore itself sinks, the lowland bristles with rushes and marsh grasses waving in the wind. A little further on and the water becomes deeply clouded with sap green—the myriad floating seeds of swamp vegetation. Banks dwindle away into thin lines; the greenish-yellow of the reeds changes into misty blue. Then it is all water and sky, motionless blue and heaving lazulite, until the reedy waste of Point-aux-Herbes thrusts its picturesque lighthouse far out into the lake. Above the wilderness of swamp grass and bulrushes this graceful building rises upon an open-work of wooden piles. Seven miles of absolute desolation separate the lighthouse keeper from his nearest neighbor. Nevertheless, there is a good piano there for the girls to play upon, comfortably furnished rooms, a good library. The pet cat has lost an eye in fighting with a moccasin, and it is prudent before descending from the balcony into the swamp about the house to reconnoiter for snakes. Still northeast. The sun is sinking above the rushy bank line; the west is crimsoning like iron losing its white heat. Against the ruddy light a cross is visible. There is a cemetery in the swamp. Those are the forgotten graves of lighthouse keepers. Our boat is spreading her pinions for flight through the Rigolets, that sinuous waterway leading to lake Borgne. We pass by the defenseless walls of Fort Pike, a stronghold without a history, picturesque enough, but almost worthless against modern artillery. There is a solitary sergeant in charge, and a dog. Perhaps the taciturnity of the man is due to his long solitude, the vast silence of the land weighing down upon him. At last appears the twinkling light of the United States custom-house, and the enormous skeleton of the Rigolets bridge. The custom-house rises on stilts out of the sedge-grass. The pretty daughter of the inspector can manage a skiff as well as most expert oarsmen. Here let us listen a while in the moonless night. From the south a deep sound is steadily rolling up like the surging of a thousand waves, like the long roaring of breakers. But the huge blind lake is scarcely agitated; the distant glare of a prairie fire illuminates no spurring of "white horses." What, then, is that roar, as of thunder muffled by distance, as of the moaning that seamen hear far inland while dreaming at home of phantom seas? It is only a mighty chorus of frogs, innumerable millions of frogs, chanting in the darkness over unnumbered leagues of swamp and lagoon.

On the eastern side of the Rigolets Lake Borgne has scalloped out its grass-fringed bed in the form of a gigantic clover leaf—a shallow and treacherous sea, from which all fishing-vessels scurry in wild terror when a storm begins to darken. No lugger can live in those short chopping waves when Gulf winds are mad. To reach the Manila settlement one must steer due south until the waving bulrushes again appear, this time behind muddy shoals of immense breadth. The chart announces depths varying from six inches to three and a half feet. For a while we grope about blindly along the banks. Suddenly the mouth of a bayou appears—"Saint Malo Pass." With the aid of poles the vessel manages to shamble over a mud-bar, and forthwith rocks in forty feet of green water. We reached Saint Malo upon a leaden-colored day, and the scenery in its gray ghastliness recalled to us the weird landscape painted with words by Edgar Poe—*Silence: a Fragment.*

Out of the shuddering reeds and banneretted grass on either side rise the fantastic houses of the Malay fishermen, poised upon slender supports above the marsh, like cranes or bitterns watching for scaly prey. Hard by the slimy mouth of the bayou extends a strange wharf, as ruined and rotted and unearthly as the timbers of the spectral ship in the *Rime of the Ancient Mariner.* Odd craft huddle together beside it, fishing-nets make cobwebby drapery about the skeleton timber-work. Green are the banks, green the water is, green also with fungi every beam and plank and board and shingle of the houses upon stilts. All are built in true Manila style, with immense hat-shaped eaves and balconies, but in wood; for it has been found that palmetto and woven cane could not withstand the violence of the climate. Nevertheless, all this wood had to be shipped to the bayou from a considerable distance, for large trees do not grow in the salty swamp. The highest point of land as far as the "Devil's Elbow," three or four miles away, and even beyond it, is only six inches above low-water mark, and the men who built those houses were compelled to stand upon ladders, or other wood frame-work, while driving down the piles, lest the quagmire should swallow them up.

Below the houses are patches of grass and pools of water and stretches of gray mud, pitted with the hoof-prints of hogs. Sometimes these hoof-prints are crossed with the tracks of the alligator, and a pig is missing. Chickens there are too—sorry-looking creatures; many have but one leg, others have but one foot: the crabs have bitten them off. All these domestic creatures of the place live upon fish.

Here is the home of the mosquito, and every window throughout all the marsh country must be closed with wire netting. At sundown the insects rise like a thick fog over the lowland; in the darkness their presence is signaled by a sound like the boiling of innumerable caldrons. Worse than these are the great green-headed *tappanoes,* dreaded by the fishermen. Sand-flies attack the colonists in warm weather; fleas are insolent at all hours; spiders of immense growth rival the net-weavers of Saint Malo, and hang their webs from the timbers side by side with seines and fishing-tackle. Wood-worms are busy undermining the supports of the dwellings, and wood-ticks attack the beams and joistings. A marvelous variety of creatures haunt the surrounding swamp—reptiles, insects, and birds. The *prie-dieu*—"pray-god"—utters its soprano note; water-hens and plovers call across the marsh. Numberless snakes hide among the reeds, having little to fear save from the wildcats, which attack them with savage recklessness. Rarely a bear or a deer finds its way near the bayou. There are many otters and musk-rats, minks and raccoons and rabbits. Buzzards float in the sky, and occasionally a bald-eagle sails before the sun.

Such is the land: its human inhabitants are not less strange, wild, pictur-esque. Most of them are cinnamon-colored men; a few are glossily yellow, like that bronze into which a small portion of gold is worked by the molder. Their features are irregular without being actually repulsive; some have the cheek-bones very prominent, and the eyes of several are set slightly aslant. The hair is generally intensely black and straight, but with some individuals it is curly and browner. In Manila there are several varieties of the Malay race, and these Louisiana settlers represent more than one type. None of them appeared tall; the greater number were undersized, but all well knit, and supple as fresh-water eels. Their hands and feet were small; their movements quick and easy, but sailorly likewise, as of men accustomed to walk upon rocking decks in rough weather. They speak the Spanish language; and a Malay dialect is also used among them. There is only one white man in the settlement—the ship-carpenter, whom all the Malays address as "Maestro." He has learned to speak their Oriental dialect, and has conferred upon several the sacrament of bap-tism according to the Catholic rite; for some of these men were not Christians at the time of their advent into Louisiana. There is but one black man in this lake village—a Portuguese negro, perhaps a Brazilian maroon. The Maestro told us that communication is still kept up with Manila, and money often sent there to aid friends in emigrating. Such emigrants usually ship as seamen on board some Spanish vessel bound for American ports, and desert at the first opportunity. It is said that the colony was founded by deserters—perhaps also by desperate refugees from Spanish justice.

Justice within the colony itself, however, is of a curiously primitive kind; for there are neither magistrates nor sheriffs, neither prisons nor police. Al-though the region is included within the parish of St. Bernard, no Louisiana official has ever visited it; never has the tax-gatherer attempted to wend thither his unwelcome way. In the busy season a hundred fierce men are gathered together in this waste and watery place, and they must be a law unto them-selves. If a really grave quarrel arises, the trouble is submitted to the arbitra-tion of the oldest Malay in the colony, Padre Carpio, and his decisions are usually accepted without a murmur. Should a man, on the other hand, need-lessly seek to provoke a difficulty, he is liable to be imprisoned within a fish-car, and left there until cold and hunger have tamed his rage, or the rising tide forces him to terms. Naturally all these men are Catholics; but a priest rarely visits them, for it costs a considerable sum to bring the ghostly father into the heart of the swamp that he may celebrate mass under the smoky rafters of Hilario's house—under the strings of dry fish.

There is no woman in the settlement, nor has the treble of a female voice been heard along the bayou for many a long year. Men who have families keep them at New Orleans, or at Proctorville, or at La Chinche; it would seem cruel to ask any woman to dwell in such a desolation, without comfort and without protection, during the long absence of the fishing-boats. Only two instances of a woman dwelling there are preserved, like beloved traditions, in the memory of the inhabitants. The first of these departed upon her husband's death; the second left the village after a desperate attempt had been made to murder her spouse. In the dead of night the man was unexpectedly assailed; his wife and little boy helped to defend him. The assailant was overcome, tied hand and foot with fish-lines, and fastened to a stake deep driven into the swamp. Next morning they found him dead: the mosquitoes and tappanoes had filled the office of executioner. No excitement was manifested; the Maestro dug a grave deep in the soft gray mud, and fixed above it a rude wooden cross, which still shows its silhouette against the sky just above the reeds.

Such was the narrative which El Maestro related to us with a strange mixture of religious compassion for the unabsolved soul, and marvelous profanity expressed in four different languages. "Only mosquitoes live there now," he added, indicating the decaying edifice where the dead man had dwelt.

But for the possession of modern fire-arms and one most ancient clock, the lake-dwellers of Saint Malo would seem to have as little in common with the civilization of the nineteenth century as had the inhabitants of the Swiss lacustrine settlements of the Bronze Epoch. Here time is measured rather by the number of alligator-skins sent to market, or the most striking incidents of successive fishing seasons, than by ordinary reckoning; and did not the Maestro keep a chalk record of the days of the week, none might know Sunday from Monday. There is absolutely no furniture in the place; not a chair, a table, or a bed can be found in all the dwellings of this aquatic village. Mattresses there are, filled with dry "Spanish beard"; but these are laid upon tiers of enormous shelves braced against the walls, where the weary fishermen slumber at night among barrels of flour and folded sails and smoked fish. Even the clothes (purchased at New Orleans or Proctorville) become as quaint and curiously tinted in that moist atmosphere as the houses of the village, and the broad hats take a greenish and grotesque aspect in odd harmony with the appearance of the ancient roofs. All the art treasures of the colony consist of a circus poster immemorially old, which is preserved with much reverence, and two photographs guarded in the Maestro's sea-chest. These represent a sturdy young woman with creole eyes, and a grim-looking Frenchman with wintry beard—the wife and father of the ship-carpenter. He pointed to them with a display of feeling made strongly pathetic by contrast with the wild character of the man, and his eyes, keen and hard as those of an eagle, softened a little as he kissed the old man's portrait, and murmured, "Mon cher vieux père."

And nevertheless this life in the wilderness of reeds is connected mysteriously with New Orleans, where the headquarters of the Manila men's benevolent society are—*La Union Philippina.* A fisherman dies; he is buried under the rustling reeds, and a pine cross planted above his grave; but when the flesh has rotted from the bones, these are taken up and carried by some lugger to the metropolis, where they are shelved away in those curious niche tombs which recall the Roman *columbaria.*

How, then, comes it that in spite of this connection with civilized life the Malay settlement of Lake Borgne has been so long unknown? Perhaps because of the natural reticence of the people. There is still in the oldest portion of the oldest quarter of New Orleans a certain Manila restaurant hidden away in a court, and supported almost wholly by the patronage of Spanish West Indian sailors. Few people belonging to the business circles of New Orleans know of its existence. The *menu* is printed in Spanish and English; the fare is cheap and good. Now it is kept by Chinese, for the Manila man and his oblique-eyed wife, comely as any figure upon a Japanese vase, have gone away. Doubtless his ears, like sea-shells, were haunted by the moaning of the sea, and the Gulf winds called to him by night, so that he could not remain.

The most intelligent person in Saint Malo is a Malay half-breed, Valentine. He is an attractive figure, a supple dwarfish lad almost as broad as tall, brown as old copper, with a singularly bright eye. He was educated in the great city, but actually abandoned a fine situation in the office of a judge to return to his swarthy father in the weird swamps. The old man is still there— Thomas de los Santos. He married a white woman, by whom he had two children, this boy and a daughter, Winnie, who is dead. Valentine is the best pirogue oarsman in the settlement, and a boat bears his name. But opposite the house of Thomas de los Santos rides another graceful boat, rarely used, and whitely christened with the name of the dead Winnie. Latin names prevail in the nomenclature of boats and men: Marcellino, Francesco, Serafino, Florenzo, Victorio, Paosto, Hilario, Marcetto, are common baptismal names. The solitary creole appellation Aristide offers an anomaly. There are luggers and sloops bearing equally romantic names: *Manrico de Aragon, Maravilla, Joven Imperatriz.* Spanish piety has baptized several other with sacred words and names of martyrs.

Of the thirteen or fourteen large edifices on piles, the most picturesque is perhaps that of Carpio—old Carpio, who deserts the place once a year to play monte in Mexico. His home consists of three wooden edifices so arranged that the outer two advance like wings, and the wharf is placed in front of the central structure. Smoked fish black with age hang from the roof, chickens squawk upon the floor, pigs grunt under the planking. Small, squat, swart, dry, and grimy as his smoked fish is old Carpio, but his eye is bright and quick as a lizard's.

It is at Hilario's great *casa* that the Manila men pass stormy evenings, playing monte or a species of Spanish kemo. When the *cantador,* (the caller) sings out the numbers, he always accompanies the annunciation with some rude poetry characteristic of fisher life or Catholic faith;

> Pareja de uno;
> Dos piquetes de rivero—

a pair of one (11); the *two stakes* to which the fish-car is fastened.

> Número cuatro;
> La casa del gato—

number 4; the cat's house.

> Seís con su nuéve;
> Arriba y abajo—

six with its nine (69); *up and down.*

> De dos pareja;
> Dos paticos en laguna—

pair of two (22); two *ducklings* in the lagoon or marsh—the Arabic numerals conveying by their shape this idea to the minds of fishermen. Picturesque? The numbers 77 suggest an almost similar ideas—*dos gansos en laguna* (two geese in the lagoon):

> Tres y parejo
> Edad de Cristo—

thirty-three; the age of Christ.

Dos con su cinco;
Buena noche pasado—

twenty-five (Christmas-eve); the "Good-night" past.

Nuéve y parejo;
El mas viejo—

ninety, "the oldest one." Fifty-five is called the "two boats moored" together, as the figures placed thus 55 convey that idea to the mind—*dos galibos amarrados.* Very musical is the voice of the *cantador* as he continues, shaking up the numbers in a calabash:

Dos y nuéve:
Veinte y nuéve—29.
Seís con su cuatro;
Sesenta y cuatro—64.
Ocho y seís:
Borrachenta y seís—86 (*drunken* eighty-six).
Nina de quince (a girl of fifteen);
Uno y cinco—15.

Polite, too, these sinister-eyed men; there was not a single person in the room who did not greet us with a hearty *buenas noches.* The artist made his sketch of that grotesque scene upon the rude plank-work which served as a gambling table by the yellow flickering of lamps fed with fish-oil.

There is no liquor in the settlement, and these hardy fishers and alligator-hunters seem none the worse therefor. Their flesh is as hard as oak-wood and sickness rarely affects them, although they know little of comfort, and live largely upon raw fish, seasoned with vinegar and oil. There is but one chimney—a wooden structure—in the village, fires are hardly ever lighted, and in the winter the cold and the damp would soon undermine feeble constitutions.

A sunset viewed from the balcony of the Maestro's house seemed to us enchantment. The steel blue of the western horizon heated into furnace yellow, then cooled off into red splendors of astounding warmth and transparency. The bayou blushed crimson, the green of the marsh pools, of the shivering reeds, of the decaying timber-work, took fairy bronze tints, and then, immense with marsh mist, the orange-vermilion face of the sun peered luridly for the last time through the tall grasses upon the bank. Night came with marvelous choruses of frogs; the whole lowland throbbed and laughed with the wild music—a swamp-hymn deeper and mightier than even the surge sounds heard from the Rigolets bank: the world seemed to shake with it!

We sailed away just as the east began to flame again, and saw the sun arise with reeds sharply outlined against the vivid vermilion of his face. Long fish-formed clouds sailed above him through the blue, green-backed and iridescent-bellied, like the denizens of the green water below. Valentine hailed us from the opposite bank, holding up a struggling *poule-d'eau* which he had just rescued from a wild-cat. A few pirogues were already flashing over the bayou, ribbing the water with wavelets half emerald, half orange gold. Brighter and brighter the eastern fires grew; oranges and vermilions faded out into fierce yellow, and against the blaze all the ragged ribs of Hilario's elfish wharf stood out in black. Somebody fired a farewell shot as we reached the mouth of the bayou; there was a waving of picturesque hands and hats; and far in our wake an alligator plashed his scaly body, making for the whispering line of reeds upon the opposite bank.

3

SICILIANS IN NEW ORLEANS

Among the dark-eyed sailors from the Mediterranean who have anchored their fortunes at the port of New Orleans, there are swarthy hundreds in whose veins throbs the mingled blood of Roman, Carthaginian, Moor and Norman; and perhaps, too, of those antique colonists who brought into the volcanic lands of Sicily the civilization of Athens. This strange blending of Nations seems always productive of strange results. One would suppose, from comparing those results in various lands, that the more good blood is mixed, the more savage it becomes. From whom are the Greek brigands? From whom are the Italian and Sicilian banditti descended? What blood flows in the veins of the Spanish *matador* or the Spanish *contrabandista*?

I do not think that these Sicilians of New Orleans—these descendants of those who gave to history the terrible memory of the "Sicilian Vespers," and who live here side by side with descendants, no doubt, of French citizens slaughtered in Palermo—are readily distinguishable from Neapolitans, or other Italians, by any outward characteristics. They are, indeed, volcanic-hearted, like the land whence they came, but the eruption of a Sicilian's hatred always bursts forth without premonition. It is the Sicilian of all men who may naturally smile and smile and be a villain still. He masters his passion only for the more complete gratification of it at some judicious moment. But the satisfaction of a wrong by the use of the knife can not be indulged under ordinary circumstances in such a community as this. The spirit of healthier laws than the laws of Sicily prevails against the natural instinct of vengeance for a personal injury. There are, however, circumstances that are extraordinary and injuries that are not strictly personal, under which circumstances and for which injuries the Sicilian seeks vengeance as best he may, without regard to any law save the law of *vendetta*.

Under the code of the vendetta, the civil code is ignored. The avenger never seeks the aid of the State or the municipal law. He is a law unto himself. He feels assured of the sympathy and silence of his compatriots; and he is never betrayed. Even the dying victim will never utter the name of his assassin,—except to his *compadre* or to his nearest male relatives as natural avenger. Even the priest who bears the *viaticum* and hears the last confession may seek in vain, as "ghostly father" of the victim, to learn that name. The shrewdest detective may follow the surest clues only to a certain point where all is deafness and blindness,—shruggings of shoulders and multiplied gestures of ignorance. *"Eet ees vendetta;* I know nothing!" The assassin may even be arrested and imprisoned; none will appear against him; the relatives of the murdered man refuse to testify in the case or accuse the prisoner; the very man whose duty it has become to murder the murderer in *vendetta* will feign utter ignorance of all circumstances connected with the case.

The son avenges his father, the brother his brother, the cousin his cousin, the friend his friend; and the vendetta only dies when the last victim is friendless. The Sicilian who has killed a Sicilian feels safe only when he feels assured that the family of the dead died with him, and that the slain had no *compadre.* But it is rarely indeed that he can feel thus assured.

It is only the Spaniard or the Italian who really knows how to use the knife, and the Italian uses it as naturally as a wild beast uses its claws and teeth, or the serpent its fangs. The knife is the fittest weapon for the vendetta. The pistol speaks, the knife is silent. The pistol leaves a leaden record of circumstantial evidence; the knife leaves none. Consequently the victim of the vendetta is usually a victim of the knife; but sometimes the pistol has been used with equally mysterious secrecy even in the vicinity of the French Market.

West of the Market many of the squares contain huge courts, entered by narrow passages which end on opening into the square, and which are faced by no corresponding passages on the other side. These courts swarm with Sicilians, and these narrow archways have shadowed the perpetration of more than one vendetta. It was in such a narrow passage bearing the rather ghastly-sounding name of Oudade Alley, that one of the most memorable and mysterious acts of vengeance was perpetrated. At either corner of the alley, at its opening on Front Levee street, were stores, and at the time of the assassination the proprietors of these stores were seated at their doors, watching the passers-by. They saw a man enter the alley shortly after dark, and suddenly rush out again, staggering as though drunk. He reeled into the middle of the street and fell dead as stone. There were three poniard wounds in his breast and back, all evidently delivered by a strong and dexterous hand, for they had reached the heart, and the man died without a cry. It had been all the work of an instant, silent and invisible, save to the victim. No one had heard anything; no person, except the dead man, had seen anything. But the assassin who had shadowed this victim of vendetta, and whose hand must have been red with fresh blood, had not followed the dying Sicilian into the light. He had gone back into the darkness, and beyond the darkness into the great court, where hundreds of his compatriots must have seen him, for it was then quite early in the evening. Yet all the efforts of the police were fruitless, the cunning of the detectives availed nothing, and the murder still remains, as it will probably continue to remain, a mystery. The perpetrator of a vendetta is never brought to justice.

Nevertheless, there is something viperine in this sultry Sicilian blood. The dangerous quality in the character of the strong hater who shadows his intended victim year after year awaiting a certain chance for unwitnessed vengeance, is the dangerous quality of the ophidian, which never misses its victim, but gladly glides away from the face of its enemy, if permitted to do so, unharmed. The Sicilian is utterly incapable of comprehending that icy courage of Northern character that enables a strong man to grin back into the grinning face of death. The Sicilian is dangerous only as the snake is dangerous. Those who incur his hate must watch him, not for a day or a week, but for years.

Let me relate an incident illustrative of Sicilian nature. The Sicilians have their clubs here—clubs strong enough to wield considerable influence in local politics. They are a people to whom leaders are a necessity, and will follow their leaders as sheep follow the shepherds. It is of importance, therefore, for either political party to win over the leaders of the Sicilian clubs. On one occasion it was supposed that Warmoth had succeeded in gaining their support, and the White League determined to interfere. At that time the Sicilian Clubs were having great torch-light parades, and had already exhibited some symptoms of ferocity. A drunken negro had fired into one of their processions, and not satisfied with the almost instant death of the negro, they had killed (by way of vendetta, perhaps), thirty or more other negroes, who unfortunately happened to be watching the parade. However, only about forty or fifty White Leaguers undertook one evening to break up a large out-door meeting of these clubs. They formed beside the speaker's stand in a solid body, and hooted off the scene the first speaker who attempted to address the meeting. Then the Sicilian procession wheeled and marched four deep along the side-walk in order to clear it. The White Leaguers made no demonstration until the foremost torches arrived within fifteen yards of them, when somebody called out: "Let them have it, boys," and every man "went for his hip-pocket," the procession instantly broke up; and the meeting scattered in all directions. Yet the Sicilians were all well armed.

4

THE LAST OF THE NEW ORLEANS
FENCING-MASTERS

✦ ✦

I

Perhaps there is no class of citizens of New Orleans—the Marseilles of the western world—about whom so little is generally known as our Spanish element. I do not refer to those numerous West Indian and foreign residents who speak Spanish—Cubans, Manila-men, Mexicans, Venezuelans, natives of Honduras, etc.—or even to our original Spanish Creoles, descendants of those colonists who have left us few traces of the ancient Spanish domination besides a few solid specimens of Latin architecture and a few sonorous names by which certain streets and districts are still known. The old Spanish Creole families exist, indeed, but they have become indistinguishable from the French Creoles, whose language, manners and customs they have adopted. The true Spanish element of modern New Orleans is represented by a community of European immigrants, who preserve among them the various customs and dialects of the mother country, and form an association of about three hundred families. They are more numerous than the Greeks, mostly heavy cotton-buyers and wholesale merchants, who have their own church; more numerous than the Portuguese, who have a large benevolent association; but much fewer than the Italians and Sicilians, who control the whole fruit and fish trade, and own fleets of sailing craft and lines of steamers. Yet, for various reasons, the Spaniards are less publicly visible than the other Latins; they live in the less frequented parts of the city, they pursue special callings, and form special industrial organizations; they have their own trades-unions, their own benevolent associations, their own priests, physicians, and lawyers, and before 1853 they formed an excellent militia corps, the *Cazadores*. This fine body voluntarily disbanded because of the refusal of the governor to permit them to suppress a great anti-Spanish riot, incited by Cuban refugees. The governor wisely preferred to trust the work of suppression to the cooler-blooded and disinterested American militia, justly fearing the consequences of giving rein to the rage of the Spanish soldiery, most Asturians, Catalonians, and Biscayans.

Since the disbandment of its miliary organization the Spanish community, though numerically as strong as ever, has almost disappeared from public view.

Whether Catalonians, Biscayans, Gallegos, Asturians, or men from the Balearic Islands, nearly all these Spaniards are inter-associated as brothers of one order, and Catalan is the prevalent dialect. At their meetings, indeed, Castilian is supposed to be the official tongue; but should any discussion of an exciting nature arise, the speakers involuntarily abandon the precise speech of the *Academia* for the rougher and readier argumentative weapon of dialect.

A great number of these men are in business on their own account; those who are not independent are, for the most part, fresh immigrants or elder sons beginning life; and the trade generally followed is tobacco manufacturing. Many Spaniards own factories. So soon as a young man lays by a certain sum, he marries—usually either a Creole of the poorer class or a European woman, Irish, English, or German—and thus it happens that almost every one of our Spaniards above thirty is the head of a large family.

The New Orleans Spaniard has all the self-reliance, the shrewdness, the economy, and the sobriety of the Italian; he has less patience, perhaps, and is more dangerous to provoke; but strangely enough, crimes of violence are almost unheard of among the Spaniards, while they are fearfully common among our Sicilians, who practice vendetta. Moreover, the Spaniard is rarely found among the criminal classes; if he happens, by some extraordinary chance, to get into trouble, it is because he has used his knife or other weapon, not as a skulking assassin but as an open enemy. Colonel J. A. Fremaux, for many years in command of the second police district, and for many years also captain of the prison, tells me that in all his experience he did not remember a single case of crime among the Spanish immigrants, with the exception of a few assaults made under extreme provocation. In one instance, which appeared at first to form an anomaly, the arrested party proved to be not a Spaniard but a gypsy. Here, as well as elsewhere, the Spaniard is reserved, grave, pacific; but if aroused beyond endurance he becomes a very terrible antagonist. As a rule, he fraternizes with the Creole, but has more or less antipathy for the Cubans and Mexicans, who do not share his patriotism.

There are few Spanish houses in the antiquated portions of the city where a visitor will not observe a certain portrait or photograph—the likeness of a vigorous, keen-eyed, man, with a slightly curved nose, long firm lips, facial muscles singularly developed, and a fair beard having that peculiar curl in it which is said to indicate a powerful constitution. The face is a very positive one, though not harsh, and the more you observe it the more its expression pleases. If you should happen to visit a Spanish home in which the photograph is not visible, it is more than probable that it is treasured away in the *armoire* or somewhere else; it has become one of the Spanish *penates.* But a few years ago it was an even more familiar object in Havana, perhaps also in far Madrid; and the Havanese soldiery, the *voluntarios,* the loyalists, the Spanish ladies, were eagerly purchasing copies at the rate of two *pesos* per copy. Thousands upon thousands were placed in Cuban parlors. Still, the original of that picture, photograph, or engraving (for the likeness of the man has been reproduced in many ways) is not a prince, a diplomat, or a soldier, but a private citizen of New Orleans, a member of our Spanish community. His face is now seldom seen on Canal Street, but he is still a very active and vigorous man, despite his three-score and ten years. He is a hero, and a titled hero who won his fame by sole virtue of those qualities named in enamel upon the golden cross he is privileged to wear: *Virtus et Honore*—"*Virtus,*" of course, with the good old Roman signification of the word, which is valor.

II

Señor Don José Llulla, or Pepe Llulla, as he is more affectionately styled by his admirers, is a person whose name has become legendary even in his life-time. While comparatively few are intimate with him, for he is a reserved man, there is scarcely a citizen who does not know him by name, and hardly a New Orleans urchin who could not tell you that "Pepe Llulla is a great duelist who has a cemetery of his own." Although strictly true, this information is apt to create a false impression of some connection between Pepe's duels and Pepe's necropolis; the fact being that none of his enemies repose in the Louisa Street Cemetery, which he owns, and that he has never killed enough men to fill a solitary vault. There is, in short, no relationship between the present and the past occupations of the cemetery proprietor; but before speaking of the former, I may attempt to give a brief outline of the career of this really extraordinary character who won his way to fortune and to fame by rare energy and intrepidity.

Pepe was born near Port Mahon, capital of Minorca, one of those Balearic Islands whose inhabitants were celebrated in antiquity for their skill in the use of missile-weapons, and have passed under so many dominations— Carthaginian, Roman, Vandal, Moorish, Spanish, French, and English. His own uncommon dexterity in the use of arms, however, does not appear due to any physical inheritance from ancient Balearic forefathers, as he traces back his family to a Moorish origin. This assertion, in view of Pepe's chestnut hair and bluish-gray eyes, would seem untenable unless we reflect that those desert horsemen who first invaded Spain in the cause of Islam were mostly Berbers, kindred of the strange nomads who still preserve their fair skins and blue eyes under the sun of the Sahara—the "Veiled People," who are known afar off by their walk, "long and measured, like the stride of the ostrich." I cannot say that Pepe is really a Berber; but he possesses physical characteristics which harmonize well with the descriptions in Henri Duveyrier's *Les Touareg du Nord;* and Southern Louisiana is full of surprises for the ethnographer. The photograph, which obtained so much celebrity, was taken more than fifteen years ago, and Pepe has but slightly changed since then. He is only a little grayer, and remains very erect, agile, and elastic in his movements; a man about the average height, rather vigorously than powerfully built. He attributes his excellent physical preservation to his life-long abstinence. No liquor has ever passed his lips, and his nerves still retain the steadiness of youth.

Pepe's imagination was greatly impressed during early boyhood by the recitals of sailors who used to visit his father's home at Port Mahon; and his passion for the sea became so strong as he grew older that it required constant vigilance to keep him from joining some ship's crew by stealth. Finally, when an American captain—John Conklin of Baltimore, I believe—made known in Port Mahon that he wanted an intelligent Spanish lad on his vessel, Pepe's parents deemed it best to allow their son to ship as cabin-boy. He remained several years with the Captain, who become attached to him, and attempted to send him to a school to study navigation, in the hope of making a fine sailor of him. But the boy found himself unable to endure the constraints of study, ran away and shipped as a common seaman. He went with whalers to the Antarctic Zone, and with slavers to the West African coast, and, after voyaging in all parts of the world, entered the service of some merchant company whose vessels plied between New Orleans and Havana. At last he resolved to abandon the sea, and to settle in New Orleans in the employ of a Spaniard named Biosca, proprietor of a ballroom and *café*. Being a very sinewy, determined youth, Pepe was intrusted with the hazardous duty of maintaining order; and, after a few unpleasant little experiences, the disorderly element of the time recognized they had found a master, and the peace of Biosca's establishment ceased to be disturbed.

Pepe soon began to visit the popular fencing-schools of New Orleans. He was already a consummate master in the use of the knife (what thorough Spaniard is not?) but he soon astonished the best *tireurs* by his skill with the foils.

At that time fencing was a fashionable amusement. It was the pride of a Creole gentleman to be known as a fine swordsman. Most of the Creole youths educated in Paris had learned the art under great masters; but even these desired to maintain their skill by frequent visits to the *salles d'armes* at home. Indeed, fencing was something more than a mere amusement; it was almost a necessity. In New Orleans, as in Paris, the passions of society were regulated if not restrained by the duel; and the sword was considered the proper weapon with which gentlemen should settle certain disputes. But the custom of dueling prevailed in New Orleans to an extent unparalleled in France since the period of the Revolution. Creole society in Louisiana was an aristocratic and feudal organization based upon slavery. Planters and merchants lived and reigned like princes; the habit of command and the pride of power developed characters of singular inflexibility; passions, tropicalized under this strong sun of ours, assumed a violence unknown in calmer France, and the influence of combined wealth and leisure aided to ferment them. Three or four duels a day were common; this number was often exceeded; and young men seemed anxious to fight for the mere ferocious pleasure of fighting. A friend tells me this queer reminiscence of the old *régime:* "A party of young Creoles, slightly flushed with wine, are returning from an evening entertainment. The night is luminous and warm; the air perfumed with breath of magnolias; the sward is smooth, level, springy as an English turf. Suddenly one of the party stops, feels the sod with his foot, and, leaping nearly to his own height, vociferates, *'Quel lieu pour se battre!'* (What a place for a fight!) His enthusiasm proves contagious; a comrade proposes that the party shall take all possible advantage of the situation. Sword-play begins, at first jestingly; then some fencer loses his temper, and the contest at once becomes terribly earnest, to end only with the death of several participants."

The demand for fencing-masters was amply supplied by foreigners and also by some local experts, *maîtres d'armes* whose names are now remembered only by a very few venerable citizens. the most celebrated were L'Alouette, an Alsatian; Montiasse, also an Alsatian and Napoleonic veteran; Cazères, of Bordeaux; Baudoin, of Paris; the two brothers Rosière, of Marseilles; Dauphin, a famous expert (killed at last in a shot-gun duel which he had recklessly provoked). Behind these fading figures of the past, three darker ghosts appear: Black Austin, a free negro, who taught the small-sword; Robert Séverin, a fine mulatto, afterward killed in Mexico, and Basile Croquère (I am not sure that I spell the name correctly), also a mulatto, and the most remarkable colored swordsman of Louisiana. Those of my readers who have not seen Vigeant's beautiful little book, *Un Maître d'Armes sous la Restauration,* may perhaps be surprised to learn that the founder of the modern French school of swordsmanship, and the greatest swordsman of his century, was a mulatto of San Domingo, that famous Jean Louis, who in one terrible succession of duels, occupying only forty minutes, killed or disabled thirteen master-fencers of that Italian army pressed into service by Napoleon for his Peninsular campaign.

III

It was under L'Alouette that Pepe principally studied; and the fencing-master, finding after a time that his pupil excelled him, appointed him his *prevôt* or assistant. In a succession of subsequent encounters the young man proved that, though he might have one or two rivals with the foils, he had no real superior among the *maîtres d'armes*. Then he began to study the use of other varieties of weapons; the saber, with which he became the most expert perhaps in the South; the broad-sword, with which he afterward worsted more than one accomplished English teacher. With the foil, which is only a training weapon and allows of a closer play, fine fencers have been able to make some good points with him; but with the rapier or small sword he was almost invulnerable. With firearms his skill was not less remarkable. Pepe's friends were accustomed to hold a dollar in their fingers or a pipe between their teeth for him to shoot at. Twenty years ago he would often balance an egg on the head of his little son, and invariably break the shell with a Colt-ball at the distance of thirty paces; with a rifle he seldom failed to hit any small object tossed in the air, such as a ball, a cork, or a coin.

L'Alouette and his pupil became very warm friends; their intimacy was only once chilled by an unfortunate accident. At a time when the bowie-knife was still a novel arm in New Orleans, L'Alouette insisted upon a public contest with Llulla, the weapons to be wooden bowies with hickory blades. Pepe had no equal, however, in the use of a knife of any sort; and L'Alouette, finding himself repeatedly touched and never able to make a point, lost his temper and made a violent assault on the young Spaniard, who, parrying the thrust, countered so heavily that the fencing-master was flung senseless to the floor with two ribs fractured. But the friendship of the two men was renewed before long, and continued until L'Alouette's death several years later. Llulla, in whose arms he died, succeeded him as a teacher, not only of fencing, but also of the use of fire-arms. He did not, indeed, teach the knife, but he has often given surprising proofs of his skill with it. A gentleman who is quite expert with most weapons, told me that after having succeeded in persuading Pepe to have a sham contest with him only a few years ago, he received the point of Pepe's mock weapon directly in the hollow of his throat almost at the very first pass, and was repeatedly struck in the same place during five or six vain efforts to make a point. None of the serious contests in which Pepe has engaged lasted more than a few moments; he generally disabled his adversary at the very outset of the encounter.

Although remunerative in those days, the profession of fencing-master did not suit Llulla's energetic character. He kept his *salle d'armes,* but hired assistants, and only devoted so much of his own time to teaching as could be spared from more practical duties. He had already laid down the foundation of his fortune, had brought out from Minorca his mother and brother, had married, and commenced to do business on his own account. Few men have attempted as many different things as he has with equal success. He built slaughter-houses and speculated in cattle; he bought up whole fleets of flat-boats and sold the material for building purposes (working all day up to his waist in water, and never getting sick in consequence); he bought land on the other side of the river and built cottages upon it; he built a regular Spanish bull-ring and introduced bull-fights; he bought a saw-mill and made it pay, and finally purchased the Louisa street cemeteries, after accumulating a capital of probably several hundred thousand dollars. During the war he remained faithful to the Union, declaring that he could not violate his oath of allegiance to the *United* States. After the war he bought the island of Grande Terre, in the Gulf (excepting, of course, the government reservation on which Fort Livingston and the Barataria Light house are situated) a wild, wind-swept place, to which cattle from neighboring islands sometimes swim in spite of the sharks. In summer it is a fine pleasure resort for sea-bathers, and Pepe could never wholly separate himself from the sea.

During all those years Pepe kept his fencing-school, but rather as a recreation than as a money-making establishment. He is now the last of the old fencing-masters, and although he has practically retired from public life will not refuse to instruct (*gratis*) pupils introduced to him by personal friends. For nearly half a century he was the confidant and trainer of New Orleans duelists, and figured as second in more than a hundred encounters. The duello is now almost obsolete in the South; and Creole New Orleans is yielding in this respect to the influences of Americanization. It is fully three years since Pepe's services were last called into requisition.

While his formidable reputation as an expert often secured him against difficulties and dangers to which another in his position would have been exposed, it did not save him from the necessity of having some twenty or more affairs of his own. In half a score of these affairs his antagonists weakened at the last moment, either apologizing on the field or failing to appear at all, and that only after having attempted to take every advantage attached to their privilege of the choice of weapons. One individual proposed to fight with poniards in a dark room; another with knives inside a sugar hogshead; another wanted a duel with Colt revolvers, each of the principals to hold one end of the same pocket-handkerchief; another proposed that lots should be drawn for two pistols—one empty, the other loaded; and a Cuban, believing no such weapons procurable in New Orleans, proposed to fight with *machétes;*

but, to the horror of the man, Pepe forthwith produced two *machétes,* and proposed to settle the difficulty then and there, a proposal which resulted in the Cuban's sudden disappearance. Only once was Pepe partly thwarted by a proposition of this sort, when some Havanese filibuster proposed that both principals and witnesses should "fight with poisoned pills," lots to be drawn for the pills. Pepe was willing, but the seconds declared they would not take the pills or permit them to be taken. Several of Llulla's duels were undertaken in behalf of friends, while he was actually acting in the *rôle* of second only, and when one of the principals could not fulfill the duties of the moment. On a certain occasion the second of the opposite side, who was a German fencing-master, declared his principal in no condition to fight, and volunteered to take his place. "We accept," replied Llulla instantly, "but in that case you shall deal, not with my principal but with me!" Ten seconds later the German lay on the ground with a severely gashed arm and both lungs transpierced. It was seldom, however, that Pepe cared to wound an antagonist so severely; and although he has had duels or difficulties with men of most European nationalities, only two men died at his hands, after having placed him under the necessity of killing or being killed. In none of his duels, even at the time when the duel regulated society, was he actuated by other motives than friendship or pride; and the only gift he would ever accept from the man whose part he assumed, was a weapon of some sort. But his admirers have treated him so well in this respect that he now possesses a perfect arsenal, including all kinds, not only of swords but of rifles, pistols, revolvers, poniards, cutlasses, etc., which forms quite a curiosity in itself. Since the war Pepe has had no personal difficulties, except those assumed in the cause of Spanish patriotism; but these affairs first made him really famous, and form the most interesting incidents of his singular career.

IV

After having long been the headquarters of the Cuban filibusters, New Orleans was violently convulsed, in 1853, by the fate of the Lopez expedition, and serious outbreaks occurred, for the results of which the Spanish government subsequently demanded and obtained satisfaction from the United States. It was Pepe Llulla who at that time saved the Spanish Consul's life, by getting him out of the city safely to the plantation of a compatriot. Pepe's own life was then menaced; and though none ventured to attack him in broad daylight, his determination and courage alone saved him from several night-attempts at assassination. After the Lopez riots the anti-Spanish fury died down to be revived again in 1869 by another Cuban tragedy. But in 1869 the United

States garrison was strong, and there was no serious rioting. The rage of the Cuban revolutionaries vented itself only in placards, in sanguinary speeches, in cries of *Death to Spain!* and in a few very petty outrages upon defenseless Spaniards. Pepe Llulla challenged one of the authors of the outrages, who, failing to accept, was placarded publicly as a coward.

Then he resolved to take up the cause of Spain in his own person, and covered the city with posters in English, in French, and in Spanish, challenging all Cuban revolutionaries, either in the West Indies or the United States. This challenge was at first accepted by a number, but seemingly by men who did not know the character of Llulla, for these Cuban champions failed to come to time, a few declaring they respected Pepe too much to fight him; yet at the same time a number of efforts were made to assassinate him—some by men who seemed to cross the Gulf for no other purpose. Fortunately for himself Pepe has always proved an uncommonly hard man to kill; moreover, he had become so accustomed to this sort of danger that it was almost impossible to catch him off his guard. Even gangs bold enough to enter his house or place of business had been terribly handled; and a party of seven drunken soldiers who once attempted to wreck his establishment left five of their number *hors de combat,* felled by an iron bar. Again, a Mexican, who had hidden behind a door to attack Llulla with a knife, had his weapon wrested from him and was severely beaten for his pains. The Cuban emissaries and others fared no better in 1869. Two men, who concealed themselves in the cemetery at dusk, were unexpectedly confronted with Pepe's pistols, and ordered to run for their lives, which they proceeded to do most expeditiously, leaping over tombs and climbing over walls in their panic. Another party of ruffians met the Spaniard at his own door in the middle of the night, and were ingloriously routed. Once more, hearing that a crowd of rowdies were collecting in the neighborhood after dark with the intention of proceeding to his house, Llulla went out and attacked them single-handed, scattering them in all directions.

At last the Cubans found a champion to oppose to the redoubtable Pepe, an Austrian ex-officer who had entered the Cuban revolutionary service, a soldier of fortune, but a decidedly brave and resolute man. He was a good swordsman, but considering the formidable reputation of his antagonist, chose the pistol as a weapon more likely to equalize the disparity between the two men. The conditions were thirty paces, to advance and fire at will. When the word of command was given, the Spaniard remained motionless as a statue, his face turned away from his antagonist; while the Austrian, reserving his fire, advanced upon him with measured strides. When within a short distance of Llulla he raised his arm to fire, and at that instant the Spaniard, wheeling suddenly, shot him through both lungs. The Austrian was picked up, still breathing, and lingered some months before he died. His fate probably deterred others from following his example, as the Cubans found no second champion.

The spectacle of a solitary man thus defying the whole Cuban revolution, bidding all enemies of Spain to fight or hold their peace, evoked ardent enthusiasm both among the loyalists of Cuba and the Spaniards of New Orleans. Pepe soon found himself surrounded by strong sympathizers, ready to champion the same cause; and telegrams began to pour in from Spaniards in Cuba and elsewhere, letters of congratulation also, and salutations from grandees. There is something particularly graceful and sympathetic in Spanish praise; and in reading those now faded missives, hung up in pretty frames upon the walls of Pepe's dwelling, I could not help feeling myself some of the generous enthusiasm that breathes in them: *"Felicitamos cordialmente y afectuosamente al pundonoroso y valiente Señor Llulla; ofriciendole, si necessario fuere, nuestras vidas" (Voluntarios de Artilleria)* . . . *"Los Voluntarios de Cardenas admiran y abrazan al valiente Señor Llulla" (El Commandante La Casa)*. . . . *"Felicitamos al Señor Llulla por su noble, generosa, y patriotica conducta, ofriciendole nuestra coöperacion en todos tiempos y lugares."*

Such telegrams came fluttering in daily like Havanese butterflies, and solicitations for Pepe's photograph were made and acceded to, and pictures of him were sold by thousands in the streets of the great West Indian City. Meanwhile the Cubans held their peace, as bidden. And then came from Madrid a letter of affectionate praise, sealed with the royal seal, and signed with the regent's name, Don Francisco Serrano y Dominguez, el Regente del Reino, and with this letter the Golden Cross of the Order of Charles III (*Carlos Tercero*), and a document conferring knighthood, *libre de gastos,* upon the valiant son who had fought so well for Spain in far-away Louisiana.

But I have yet to mention the most exquisite honor of all. Trust the Spanish heart to devise a worthy reward for what it loves and admires! From Havana came one day a dainty portrait of Pepe Llulla worked seemingly in silk, and surrounded by what appeared to be a wreath of laurels in the same black silk, and underneath, in black letters upon a gold ground, the following honorific inscription: "A Don José Llulla, Decidido Sostenedor de la Honra Nacional entre los Traidores de New Orleans." But that woven black silk was the silk of woman's hair, the lustrous hair of Spanish ladies who had cut off their tresses to wreathe his portrait with! It hangs in the old man's parlor near the portrait of his dead son, the handsome boy who graduated at West Point with honors, and when I beheld it and understood it, the delicious grace of that gift touched me like the discovery of some new and unsuspected beauty in human nature.

5

A GYPSY CAMP

A Group of Veritable Bohemians

There were a number of Gypsies encamped in this county during the past week. The few tentfuls who remained at Red Bank, on the Little Miami Road, yesterday, attracted a host of visitors. Most of the callers were profitable ones, for there were few gentlemen who did not willingly give up a dollar to have their "fortune" told, and no ladies who could resist the temptation. "What's the use of going to a gypsy camp unless you do?" pouted one dark-eyed beauty whom we saw holding out her rosy palm to an old haggard woman, who but for her shrewdness, her ample command of correct and musical English, might have been taken for a squaw of an American Indian Tribe.

The encampment was composed of families, each having its stout, well-covered wagon, its horses and its rude tents (God save the mark!) of tattered parti-colored blankets stuck up on hoop-poles, and forming a semi-circular protection from the wind. The tops of these tents are open, and altogether they, as well as the groups around, are as wretched and weather-worn as could be asked by the coldest-blooded photographer or the maddest lover of the picturesque. The contrast between these habitations and the fat, sleek horses and stout wagons tells nearly the whole story. They are wanderers by inheritance, by instinct and by necessity. They can not rest in one place long, because of their fever for "travel"—as one bragged to us—and because one neighborhood will not afford them sustenance for many weeks. When they make a move it must be a long one. Moreover, to account for the contrast, the honest, ostensible employment of the men is that of horse-trading. Women, children and men display more or less of that ragged grace in dress and colors which have, idealized, very much idealized, we may say, given our operas some of their most effective costumes. Yesterday was Sunday, and every gypsy was idle, except those who were catching the evening meal of turtles, small fish, or even mice. The general appearance of things was, though, that if it had been Monday the supply of spare time on hand would have been equally lavish. The women were mostly intelligent. They explained that the large camp of last week was caused by the accidental meeting of families, some of whom had

never met before, and others of whom had been separated for years. Over one
of the tents presided an old woman, all of whose numerous children had been
born on the tramp in this country during the last seventeen years. This old
mother laughed when asked where "The Queen" had gone. "Every body is
her own queen here, unless the children, by way of compliment, point out
some one as queen to romantic young ladies," was the reply. She said she had
lived by "begging, borrowing and stealing," but added that she was joking
about the thieving, as, if the Gypsies stole, they would not be allowed to
encamp by the neighborhood. Indeed, the indications were that their thefts
are of the most trifling character. It is probable, however, that Chickens would
differ from us in this estimate of the honesty of the genuine Bohemian. Other
women were fresh from England, and of the Simon-pure type, speaking a
patois that may be called "Gypsy."

    The women tumble to every one's occupation and position in life al-
most at once. They hear, without seeming to hear, every word said by every
one of a party. On this basis, and backed by a general knowledge of human
nature for which their race has for ages been famous, they make up a pretty
story enough for those who "cross their palms" with dirty green paper instead
of the silvern coin of old.

    Bohemian life is dear to us all in song and in story. Looking, indeed,
upon the wretched beings at Red Bank, and realizing that their life-thirst for
change, change, all the time, makes them, for its sake, undergo every physical
suffering, we can not wonder that the same passion, gratified amid luxury,
flattery and love, has robbed literature and science in every age of the con-
stancy of the brightest minds that have enlisted in their service.

6

SOME PICTURES OF POVERTY

Impressions of a Round with an Overseer of the Poor

―――― ⋇⊹⊵ ――――

"That shattered roof, and this naked floor;
   A table, a broken chair;
And a wall so blank, my shadow I thank
   For sometimes falling there."

West Seventh, Nos. 206, 208, and 210, and the mysterious buildings in the rear, running back to the alley, is a locality of such picturesque wretchedness as, perhaps, may not be found elsewhere within the city limits,—not even in the labyrinthine hollows of the famous negro quarter in the East End. Narrow hallways, from whose irregular sides the plaster has fallen away in shapeless patches, lead through the frame cottages, fronting on Seventh street, into a species of double court-yard in the rear, whose northern end is bounded by a block of three-story frames, usually termed the Barracks, and inhabited by the poorest of the poor. Within the court itself is situated one of the strangest, most irregular, and most outlandish wooden edifices possible to imagine. It might have been a country farm-house in days before the city had crept up north and west from the river; but now inclosed in the heart of a block, its dingy colorlessness and warped deformity suggest a mediaeval rather than a modern haunt of poverty—one of those tottering hovels which crowd humbly and beseechingly about the elder Cathedrals of the old world, like so many Miseries seeking refuge under the shadow of a great Faith. The good planks have warped and bent with age, the building has shrunken and shriveled up paralytically. All its joints are rheumatic, all its features haggard and wretched. It seems to have once undulated throughout its whole gaunt length, as though the solid soil had surged under it in the groundswell of some forgotten earthquake. There is probably no true right angle in its whole composition. The angles of its windows and doors all present extraordinary obliqueness or acuteness, as in the outlines of a child's first attempt to draw a house; and no child ever drew plans more seemingly impossible and out of plumb than the withered front of this building. Molded by the irresistible pressure of the contracting walls, the narrow stairways have been squeezed up at one side, and down on the other, while the feet of dead generations of poor and children of the poor have worn deep hollows in every step. The floors slope like the cabins of vessels riding over a long swell; and one marvels how objects of furniture maintain an upright attitude in the tottering house. Part of the crooked basement appears to have sunk into the ground, as the newer pavement of the courtyard rises nearly two feet above the level of the lower floors. The northern end of this floor has ceased to be inhabitable; the southern end has its dwellers, ancient poor, who dwell with memories and their dead.

Here the Overseer is a frequent and welcome visitor, and here commenced a round of observation at once painful and picturesque. The little rickety door opened into a room small and dark; the plasterless ceiling might easily be touched with the hand, and, excepting the deep gray square of light afforded by one tiny window, the gloom was illumined only by one spot of crimson light which issued from the jaws of a shattered stove, throwing out a broad ray of red across the heavy smoke which floated through the dark.

There was the voice of a child crying in the darkness; and the voices of an aged negro couple, seated on either side of that wavering line of ruddy light across the smoke, came huskily in greeting to the visitor's ears. The husband had beheld his eightieth year and the smiles of his children's children; the wife's years were scarcely fewer. Age had brought with it the helplessness of weakness, and the silent resignation which best befits both. They spoke a little to us of a Virginian plantation, where each had first known the other sixty years ago; of the old master who had given them manumission, and of little memories kindled into life by some kindly questions. We could not see their faces in the night on either side of the thin stream of red light, but their voices, speaking to us through the dimness and the smoke, bore something of a sad poetry with them—the poetry of two lives meeting in the summer and sunlight of strong youth, and knowing little knowledge save that of the tie which bound each to the other faster and firmer, as the summer and sunshine faded out, and the great Shadow, which is the End, approached to draw them nearer to each other in the darkness.

. . . There was light up stairs in a tiny crooked room, which the Overseer entered after cautious gropings along a creaking corridor whose floor had been eaten through in unexpected places by hungry pauper rats. The room—lighted partly by a flaring candle, with "winding-sheet" drippings, and partly by some thin, yellow flames, which wrestled weakly together

within a ruined monkey-stove for the possession of a fresh lump of fuel—
had an eastward slope; the old whitewash upon the walls had turned to the
hue of strong tallow; a quantity of coal had been piled up into one corner
within a foot of the greasy ceiling, and long articles of worn-out raiment,
hung about the chamber, seemed to maintain in their tattered outlines a
certain goblin mockery of withered bodies they might have clothed. Beside
the fire sat two women. In the rounded outline of one figure, draped thinly
in neat garments, spoke the presence of youth and comeliness; but the face
was hooded in shadow and veiled with a veil. The other face stood out in
strong relief under the mingled light from the coal fire and candle flame. It
was the face of an aged woman, with ashen hair,—a face sharply profiled,
with a wreck of great beauty in its outlines, that strong beauty of wild races
which leaves the faces of the aged keenly aquiline when the forms of youth
have withered away.

"This old lady," observed the Overseer, smiling, "is upwards of sev-
enty-two years of age. She has the blood of the Indian races in her veins,
and is quite proud of it, too."

The outlines of the thin, fine face, with its penetrating eyes, bore a
shadowy testimony to the speaker's words, against the fact that such a story
has not unfrequently been offered to conceal the source of a yet darker
tinge in the veins. All her kin were dead and lost to her; but there were poor
friends to aid her, and the city, also, bestowed its charity. Many held her
wise in weird ways, and sought her counsel against unforeseen straits; and
many also, like the silent visitor at her side, loved the pleasure of converse
with her, and talks of the old days. Speaking pleasantly of her earlier years,
with that picturesque minuteness of detail natural to minds which live most
strongly in memories, the aged woman said that as she grew older, the
remembrances of childhood seemed to grow clearer to her. "For within the
last few years," said the good lady, "I can remember the face of my mother,
who died when I was a child."

And there was something so sadly pathetic in this memory of seventy
years—this sudden rekindling of a forgotten recollection in the mind of
that gray woman, sitting alone, with shadows and shadowy thoughts—that
the writer could not but ask:

"Can you describe that recollection to me?"

"I remember her face," slowly came the answer, "only as the face of a
beautiful dead woman, with closed eyelids, and long hair, all dark, and flowing back darkly against a white pillow. And I remember this only because
of a stronger memory. I remember a hired girl, seated on a little plank
bridge lying across a shallow branch of water. She was washing a white cap

and a long white dress. Some one asked her who was dead, pointing to the white things; and when she answered, I knew it was my mother."

. . . Passing from corridor to corridor, and room to room, throughout the buildings on the Groesbeck property, the actual novelty of the experience soon gave place to consciousness of the fact that poverty in Cincinnati is not only marked by precisely the same features characteristic of pauperism in the metropolitan cities, but that its habits and haunts, its garments and furniture, its want and suffering, even the localities wherein it settles, are stamped by a certain recognizable uniformity even here. So strikingly similar were the conditions of tenants in the Groesbeck property, that a description of one apartment would suffice for a dozen; and having passed through many rooms, the recollections of each were so blended together in the mind, by reason of their general resemblance, that only by the aid of some peculiarly painful or eccentric incident could the memory of any one be perfectly disentangled from the mass of impressions. The same rickety room, the same cracked stove, the same dingy walls bearing fantastic tapestry of faded rags and grotesque shadow-silhouettes of sharp profiles; the same pile of city coal in one corner, the same ghastly candle stuck in the same mineral water bottle, and decorated with a winding sheet; the same small, unmade bed and battered cupboard at its foot; the same heavily warm atmosphere and oppressive smell, seemed to greet the visitor everywhere. Even the faces of the aged women gradually impressed one as having nearly all been molded according to one pattern. As the circle of observation widened, however, these resemblances commenced to diverge in various directions; forcing the observer to recognize strongly marked lines between certain classes of city poor. Aged Irish people who need city charity, form, for example, a class by themselves, and rather a large one. They are usually far better housed and more comfortably situated in regard to furniture and household necessaries than are the poorest colored people.

These characteristics and classes began to make themselves manifest ere the Overseer had made his last call in the Seventh street barracks, among some good old women telling their beads, who called down benedictions upon him in their native Erse. Afterward the definition of these features of poverty became clearer and clearer, especially during the last round of visits in the East End.

. . . The Overseer said that there used to be a very wonderful negro woman in the Groesbeck buildings, who was said to be a hundred and seventeen years old, and had been brought to the States from Africa by a slave-trader while a vigorous young woman, so that she remembered many interesting things—the tropical trees and strange animals, the hive-shaped huts of her people, the roar of lions in the night, the customs of the tribe, and some fragments of their wild tongue. But we could not find her; and subsequently learned with dismay that she was accustomed to speak of Washington. Then after a brief round of calls in the frames east of Vicker's Church, which left with us visions of other ancient women with sharp faces and of a young mother with two infants lying upon the framework of a broken bedstead, without mattresses or blankets, we visited a tottering framework on East Eight street, not far from Crippen alley. Its interior presented no novel aspect of decaying wood and fallen plaster and crooked stairs; but one peaked and withered face which peered out upon us from behind a candle, tremblingly held at a creaking door, wore a look so woebegone that for days afterward it haunted the memory like a ghost.

Within the piteous room, by the yellow light of a dip candle, the face seemed to force its misery upon observation involuntarily yet irresistibly. There were shadows about the eyes and long lines about the mouth which betrayed a torpor of hope, a life frozen into apathy by the chill of long-protracted disappointment. She looked at the visitor with a sort of ghastly tremor, like one so accustomed to an atmosphere of wretchedness that the pressure of a cheerful being becomes an actual infliction by contrast.

"How's the old man?" quoth the Overseer, pleasantly.

She shrugged her bony shoulders wearily, and replied in a husky voice, bitter as a winter wind, that he had gone to the Poorhouse. The husband of eighty years had left her in a fit of weak anger; they could not "get along together;" "*he* was too fretful and childish."

"H'm," sympathetically ejaculated the Overseer. "No other relatives living, eh?"

The old woman smiled a weird smile, and taking the candle, approached an old chest of drawers, so rickety that it had been propped against the miserable bed to prevent its falling upon the floor. After a hurried search in the bottom drawers she brought out a letter in a faded envelope, and handed it to the visitors. It had been dated from a mining village in the far West, in years gone by. The papers had a greasy look and a dull hue of age; the writing had turned pale. It told of a happy marriage and prospects of wealth, fair success in the race for fortune and promises of assistance from a strong son.

"That was the last," she muttered, "——, 1849."

How many times that letter had been fondly read and re-read until its paper had become too old to crepitate when the withered hand crushed it in miserable despair, only perhaps to remorsefully stroke it smooth again and press out the obscuring creases. Years came and went wearily; want came and passed not away; winter after winter, each seemingly sharper than the last, whitened the street without, and shrieked in ghostly fashion at the keyhole; the little mining village in the far West had grown to a great city; but the Silence remained forever unbroken, and trust in the hand that had written the faded yellow words, "Dear mother" slowly died out, as the red life of an ember dies out in the gray ash. And when the door closed with a dry groan behind the departing feet of the Overseer, we felt strangely certain that the old letter would be once more read that night by a throbbing candle flame, ere returned to its dusty resting-place in the dusty room.

. . . These wanderings in the haunts of the poor, among shadowy tenement houses and dilapidated cottages, and blind, foul alleys with quaint names suggesting deformity and darkness, somehow compelled a phantasmal retrospect of the experience, which cling[s] to the mind with nightmare tenacity. It came in the form of a grisly and spectral vision—a dream of reeling buildings of black plank, with devious corridors and deformed stairways; with interminable suites of crooked rooms, having sloping floors and curving walls; with crazy stoves and heavy smells; with long rags and ragged gowns haunting the pale walls like phantom visitors or elfish mockeries of the dead; and all the chambers haunted by sharp shadows and sharp faces that made them piteous with the bitterness of withered hopes, or weird by fearful waiting for the coming of the dreamless slumber, as a great Shadow, which, silently falling over lesser darkness, absorbs them into Itself. The fearsome fancy of thus waiting for the end in loneliness—with only the company of memories, and the wild phantasmagory wrought upon the walls by firelight; wondering, possibly, at the grimness of one's own shadow; peering, perhaps, into some clouded fragment of quicksilvered glass to watch the skull-outline slowly wearing its way through the flesh-mask of the face—brought with it a sense of strange chill, such as might follow the voiceless passing of a spirit.

. . . "Sixteen years in bed," said the Overseer with one of those looks which appear to demand a sympathetic expression of commiseration from the person addressed under penalty of feeling that you have committed a breach of etiquette. The scene lay in the second story of a sooty frame, perched on the ragged edge of Eggleston Avenue Hill. The sufferer was an aged man, whose limbs and body were swollen by disease to a monstrous size, and for whom the mercy of death could not have been far distant. The room was similar to other rooms already described, excepting that in the center of the weak floor a yawning, ragged hole had been partly covered by a broken-bottomed washtub; and the conventional figure of the Aged Woman, with weirdly-sharp features, was not absent. The slowly dying man moaned feebly at intervals, and muttered patient prayers in the Irish tongue.

"Betther, is it?" said the Aged Woman, in a husky whisper, casting, with her hands uplifted, a crooked shadow, as of Walpurgis Night, upon the wall: "Shure, honey, the Lord knows there's no more betther fur the likes iv him."

"Trying to get him to sleep, I suppose," nodded the Overseer, lowering his voice to a sympathetic whisper.

"No whisht, honey; it's afeared we are of Her," pointing to the hole in the floor, "The Divil down below."

There came up through the broken planking, even as she spoke, a voice of cursing, the voice of a furious woman, and a sound of heavy blows, mingled with the cry of a beaten child. Some little one was being terribly whipped, and its treble was strained to that hoarse scream which betrays an agony of helpless pain and fear, and pleading to merciless ears. To the listener it seemed that the whipping would never end. The sharp blows descended without regularity in a rapid shower which seemed to promise that the punishment could only be terminated by fatigue on the part of the punisher; the screams gradually grew hoarser and hoarser, with longer intervals between each until they ceased altogether, and only a choking gurgle was audible. Then the sound of whipping ceased; there was a sudden noise as of something flung heavily down, and then another hoarse curse.

"Why, she must be killing her children," muttered the Overseer.

"To be sure she is," whispered the Aged Woman, looking awfully at the hole in the floor as though fearing lest the "Divil" might suddenly rise up through it.

"But how often does this thing go on?"

"How often, is it? Shure there's no ind to it at all, at all. Ah, she bates the childher whinever she takes a dhrap too much, bad cess to her!—an' may God forgive me fur spakin' that word—an' she's dhrunk all the time, so she is, night and day. Thin, if I wor to spake a word to the Divil, she breaks up the flure undher us wid a pole; an' many's the night I've stud over the hole, thryin' to kape the flure down, an' she a-breaking it up betune me feet."

The very grotesqueness of this misery only rendered it all the more hideous, and one felt it impossible to smile at the trembling terror of the poor old creature. After all, it seemed to us there might be a greater horror in store for the helpless poor, than that of awaiting death among the shadows alone. This haggard woman, working and watching by her dying husband, in shivering fear of the horror below; the moans of the poor sufferer, the agonized scream of the tortured child, the savage whipping and violent cursing, the broken floor pried up in drunken fury,—all seemed the sights and sounds of a hideous dream, rather than the closing scene of a poor life's melodrama.

We visited Her—a strong, broad, flamboyant-haired woman, with hard, bloated features, and words haunted by the odor of spirits. Ignorant of what we had already heard, she brought the children forward for the visitor's admiration. They were not hungry-looking or thin, but there were written in their faces little tragedies of another character than hunger or cold can write. They watched with frightened eyes their mother's slightest action. Their little features were molded in the strictest obedience to the varying expression of her own. She smiled in the effort to seem agreeable, and they smiled also, poor little souls; but such smiles! God help them!

. . . Why should gray-haired folk, half palsied by the tightening grasp of the Skeleton's hand, mutually related in the strong kinship of misfortune, themselves the subject of sustaining charity, strive to do each other evil? We received ample evidence that they do. The Overseer daily hears jealous complaints from withered lips about alleged immoral conduct or imposition upon the part of other city poor. Wretched creatures supported by the city's alms in wretched hovels, seem so anxious to deprive other wretched creatures even of the comforts possible to be enjoyed in wretched hovels. It occurred to one, on hearing these whispered stories, that there must be something more than is ordinarily supposed in those quaint proverbs regarding the gossipy and mischief-making tendencies of venerable people. But happily for the unfortunate, the keen Overseer absorbs little of such gossip, though seeming patiently attentive to all who receive charity from his hand. Understanding the poor failings of human nature, he humors them when he can, rather than inflict pain by rebuke.

. . . There was a pretty pathos in the little evidences of aesthetic taste peculiar to the negro people which no degree of misery seems capable of crushing out, and which encounters one in the most unlikely places and in the midst of the uttermost wretchedness. It was nothing short of startling to find that a certain iron railing which guards the opening of a cellar stairway in Bucktown, bore on its lower part that unmistakable Greek border-design which is formed by a single line worked into a beautiful labyrinth of right angles, and which Athenian women embroidered upon their robes three thousand years ago. But it was even more startling to find one's self, in an underground den, face to face with a very faded engraving of the famous face known to art by the name of "Beatrice Cenci," or a pale print after Raphael Morghen. One little picture we noticed on the wall of a miserable frame shanty near Culvert street, which had become little better than an outline under the dimming veil of dinginess and dust, had been carefully fixed into a frame evidently cut out of kindling wood with a penknife. It was an engraving of the head of one of Raphael's Madonnas. In extraordinary contrast hung, nailed to the plank wall beneath it, a ferrotype portrait of some rude-featured white lad; and a frightful chromo, representing one mud-colored child carrying another over a green brook, was pasted close by. Then there was, also, a dusty print of a child feeding two doves, which was decidedly pretty. It was evident that these things, together with other pitiful little articles which adorned the wall, had been picked up at random, without any actual knowledge of their artistic merit, but simply because they seemed pretty to the poor child-minds who love trifles. Probably the frightful chromo was considered by its proprietor as the gem of her little art gallery.

She was slowly dying at the time of our visit; some colored friends were sitting by her bedside; a little brown child, with frizzly hair standing out in a wild, bushy way from its head, was crying in a corner; and an old colored preacher was singing the refrain of a queer hymn which he must have supposed afforded great spiritual consolation:

> "Dese old bones of mine, oh—
> Dese ole bones of mine, oh—
> Dese ole bones of mine
> Will all come togeder in de morning."

The sufferer had her eyes fixed upon that little print, framed so clumsily in bits of kindling-wood; and it seemed to us that she was thinking less of the Great Morning about to dawn upon her, than of the rude, but perhaps kind hand of the dead steamboatman who carved the poor, coarse frame, and whose resting place remains unmarked even by a ripple on the River's breast.

7

PARIAH PEOPLE

Outcast Life by Night in the East End

The Underground Dens of Bucktown and the People Who Live in Them

The district lying east of Broadway, between Sixth and Seventh streets, and extending to Culvert or thereabouts, constitutes now but a small portion of what was known some eight or ten years ago as Bucktown, and was once not less celebrated as a haunt of crime than the Five Points of the Metropolis. Lying in the great noisome hollow, then untraversed by a single fill, the congregation of dingy and dilapidated frames, hideous huts, and shapeless dwellings, often rotten with the moisture of a thousand petty inundations, or filthy with the dirt accumulated by vice-begotten laziness, and inhabited only by the poorest poor or the vilest of the vicious, impressed one with the fancy that Bucktown was striving, through conscious shame, to bury itself under the earth. To-day we find much of the horrible hollow filled up; and the ancient Bucktown is gradually but surely disappearing, not as though by reason of a *fiat* from the Board of Improvements, but as though the earth were devouring, swallowing, engulfing this little Gomorrah. And our modern Bucktown is thus, perhaps, partly divested of its old terrors. Murders have become rare there, and vice tries to hide itself more successfully than of yore. There was a time when it sorely tried a policeman's soul to be ordered on a Bucktown beat, and when highway robbery and assassination were rather common occurrences in that locality. People can still remember how, in a certain low brothel there, masked by a bar, a negro levee hand blew a brother roustabout's brains all over the bar; and how the waiter girl related the occurrence with a smile to divers breathless policemen and reporters, at the same time wiping the blood and white brains off the counter with a cloth—like so much spilt beer. It was said in those days that many a stout man had been decoyed into a Bucktown den, and disappeared forever from public view; for there were scores of eerie-looking frames in the hollow, with a reputation scarcely inferior to that of certain lonely inns in the Hartz Mountains, which we used to read about in childish days with a feeling of nightmare horror. But now the policeman is supreme king in Bucktown; his will is law, his presence terror, and every door opens promptly at his knock at any hour of the night. The fugitive from justice hides there still, but only with the certainty of being arrested; the drunken stranger may be victimized by a panel game, but if he squeals at once his lost property will generally be forthcoming; and, in short, those who live in Bucktown live under a reign of terror, and only because they can find nowhere else to live—no other rest for the soles of their sinful feet.

They are Pariahs, Sudras, outcasts—often outlawed even from common criminal society for the violation of laws held sacred by most criminals, and the outraging of prejudices entertained and respected by the criminal or non-criminal world at large. The inimity [inimicality] ordinarily concomitant with the admixture of race ceases to exist in the confines of Bucktown; whites and blacks are forced into a species of criminal fraternization; all are Ishmaels bound together by fate, by habit, by instinct, and by the iron law and never cooling hate of an outraged society. The harlot's bully, the pimp, the prostitute, the thief, the procuress, the highway robber,—white, tawny, brown and black—constitute the mass of the population. But there are two other classes—very small indeed, yet still well worth notice. The first is composed of those who have lost caste by miscegenation; the second, that of levee hands, who live in a state of concubinage with mistresses who remain faithful to them. Of the former class it is scarcely necessary to say that white women wholly compose it—women who have conceived strange attachments for black laborers, and live with them as mistresses; also, women who boast black pimps for their masters, and support them by prostitution. Of the other class referred to we may observe that it constitutes but a part of the floating population of Bucktown, inasmuch as the levee hands and their women are the most honest portion of this extraordinary community. Consequently, they live there only because their poverty, not their will, consents and whenever opportunity offers, they will seek quarters uptown, in some alley building or tenement-house.

As the violation of nature's laws begets deformity and hideousness, and as the inhabitants of Bucktown are popularly supposed to be great violators of nature's laws, they are vulgarly supposed to be all homely, if not positively ugly or monstrously deformed. "A Bucktown hag," and "an ugly old Bucktown wench," are expressions commonly used in the narration by uninformed gossips of some Bucktown incident. This idea is, however, for the most part fallacious. The really hideous and deformed portion of the Bucktown population is confined to a few crippled or worn out, honest rag-pickers, and perhaps two or more ancient harlots, superannuated in their degrading profession, and compelled at last to resort to the dumps for a living. The majority of the darker colored women are muscular, well-built people, who would have sold at high prices in a Southern slave market before the war; the lighter tinted are, in some instances, remarkably well favored; and among the white girls one occasionally meets with an attractive face, bearing traces of what must have been uncommon beauty. Gigantic negresses, stronger than men, whose immense stature and phenomenal muscularity bear strong witness to the old slave custom of human stock breeding; neatly built mulatto girls, with the supple, pantherish strength peculiar to half-breeds; slender octoroons, willowy and graceful of figure, with a good claim to the qualification pretty,—will all be found among the crowd of cotton-turbaned and ebon-visaged throng, who talk alike and think alike and all live and look alike. To a philosophical or even fair-minded observer the viciousness and harlotry of this class are less shocking than the sins of Sixth street, or even than the fashionable vice of Broadway; when it is considered how many of the former have been begotten in vice, reared in vice, know of none but vicious associations, have never been taught the commonest decencies of life, and are ignorant of the very rudiments of education.

Desiring to see the inner life of Bucktown the writer, some evenings since, accompanied a couple of police offers in the search for a female thief, who had been shortly before observed fleeing to this city of refuge. Bucktown by day is little more than a collection of shaky and soot-begrimed frames, blackened old brick dwellings, windowless and tenantless wooden cottages, all gathered about the great, mouse-colored building where the congregation of Allen Temple once worshiped, but which has long since been unused, as its score of shattered windows attests. But by night this odd district has its picturesque points. Bucktown is nothing if not seen by gaslight. Then it presents a most striking effect of fantastic *chiar'oscuro;* its frames seem to own doresque façades—a mass of many-angled shadows in the background, relieved in front by long gleams of light on some obtruding post or porch or wooden stairway; its doorways yawn in blackness, like entrances to some interminable labyrinth; the jagged outline of its dwellings against the sky seems the part of some mighty wreck; its tortuous ways are filled with long shadows of the weirdest goblin form. The houses with lighted windows appear to possess an animate individuality, a character, a sentient consciousness, a face; and to stare with pale-yellow eyes and hungry door-mouth all agape at the lonely passer-by, as though desiring to devour him. The silent frames with nailed-up entrances, and roof jagged with ruin, seem but long specters of dwelling-places, mockeries in shadow of tenanted houses, ghosts, perhaps, of dwellings long since sacrificed to Progress by the philosophical Board of Improvements. The gurgling gutter-water seems blacker than ink with the filth it is vainly attempting to carry away; the air is foul with the breath of nameless narrow alleys; and the more distant lights seem to own a phosphorescent glow suggesting foul miasmal exhalation and ancient decay.

Following the guide down the sloping sidewalk of broken brick pavement from Broadway on Sixth street east, all along in the shadow figures in white or black are visible, flitting to and fro in a half-ghostly way, or congregated in motley groups at various doorways; and the sounds of gossip and laughter are audible at a great distance, owing to the stillness of the night. The figures vanish and the laughter ceases as the heavy tread of the patrolmen approaches—even the tap of a police-club on the pavement hushes the gossip and scatters the gossips. These are the owls, the night hawks, the Sirens of Bucktown, the wayside phantoms of this Valley of the Shadow of moral Death. They walk abroad at all hours of the tepid summer night, disappearing from view by day into their dens. Dens, indeed, is the only term which can with propriety be applied to many of their dwellings, whereof the roofs are level with the street, and the lower floors are thirty feet under ground, like some of those hideous haunts described in *The Mysteries of Paris*. For while some old rookeries have been raised, others have been fairly covered up by the fills of Culvert, Harrison, and lower Sixth streets; houses that once stood on stilts and to which access was only obtained by ladders, are now under the roadway and can only be entered by crawling on hands and knees. Fancy a lonely policeman struggling with a muscular and desperate murderer, thirty or forty feet under ground, in a worse than Egyptian darkness! There are many reasons, however, why such noisome, darksome, miasmatic dens should be forthwith destroyed, or at least why leasing or renting them to tenants should be prohibited by law. It was found necessary, in Paris, some years since, to wall up certain dark arches under the ramparts, which had been used for dwelling places by the poorest of the poor; nearly all the children born there were deformed, hideous monsters.

"These," observed the patrolman, pointing with his club to the building between the corner drug-store and the first alley east of Broadway, "are occupied by people who claim to be respectable. They never give us trouble. East of this there is scarcely a dwelling that is not occupied by the worst kind of people." Nevertheless, this alley can not be said to mark the boundary between two classes, as it is lined with evil haunts. It is foul with slime, black with slime, and is haunted by odors peculiarly unsavory. Passing by its entrance, and subsequently by some three or four well known "ranches," as the patrolman terms them, we enter the house of Mary Williams, a mongrel building, half brick, half frame.

This place is notorious as a panel den, a hive of thieves, a resort for criminals and roughs of the lowest grade. The door is wide open, and the room within lighted by the rays of a lamp with a very smoky chimney. A bed with a dirty looking comfort, a battered bureau, a very dilapidated rocking chair with a hole in its bottom, a rickety table, and a mirror, constitute all the furniture of the apartment. The walls have not been whitewashed or repaired for years; and the plaster has fallen away here and there, in great leprous patches, baring the lath frame-work beneath. Mary Williams and a black girl, with a red bandana turban, receive the patrolmen with a smile and a nod of recognition. Mary is on her best behavior, having escaped a long sentence but the week before through the failure of a prosecuting witness to appear. A very ordinary looking woman is Mary—bright mulatto, with strongly Irish features, slight form, apparently thirty-five years of age. This blood seems to predominate strongly in the veins of half the mulattoes of Bucktown. The dreamy Sphinx-face with well-moulded pouting lips, and large solemn eyes, and wide brows—the face that recalls old Egyptian paintings, and is not without a charm of its own—is never seen in Bucktown, although not an infrequent type of physiognomy in respectable colored circles. The solemn, calm, intelligent thought, quiet will, dormant strength of the Sphinx-face is never associated with vice.

Mary swore "to her just God" that no one was concealed about the premises; but the policemen lighted their candles and proceeded to examine every nook and corner of the building, under beds and tables, behind doors, and in shadowy places where giant spiders had spun gray webs of appalling size and remarkable tenacity. The rear room of the ground floor was a dark and shaky place—dark even in daylight, being beneath the level of the alley. The creaking of the boards under one's feet suggests unpleasant fancies about the facile disposal of a body beneath. A hundred robberies have taken place there. The fly once fairly in the trap, the lights are blown out, and he is left to make his exit as best he can, while the wily decoys, "thridding tortuous ways," are soon beyond pursuit. Above is the equally notorious establishment of Jennett Stewart, now, indeed, partially robbed of its old terrors by the committal of some half a dozen of its old denizens to the Workhouse. Here Officer Sissmann once narrowly escaped being murdered. There was a tremendous fight going on in the third story, and the patrolman had mounted the creaky staircase to the scene of action, when he was suddenly pounced upon by the belligerent crowd of harlots and ruffians. Out went the candle; the treacherous club split in twain at the first blow; and before he could draw his revolver Sissmann was thrown over the balusters of the top floor, to which he still managed to cling for life. While hanging there the women slashed at him in the dark with razors, and the men kicked at his clinging hands in the endeavor to force him to let go. But the officer's muscles were iron, and he held on bravely, though covered with blood from random razor-slashes, until his partner rushed up in time to turn the tide of warfare. The recollection of this incident conjured up some decidedly unpleasant sensations on the occasion of our visit, while wending our way up the steep ascent of black and rotting stairs, fitfully illumined by gleams from Patrolman Tighe's candle. A double rap with the hickory club on a plank door at the summit, causes its almost instantaneous opening, and shows a group within of three colored women and two men, the former clad only in night-wrapper and chemise, the latter in shirt and pants. A tall, good-looking mulatto girl, with long, black, wavy hair and handsome eyes, but who smokes a very bad stoga and squirts saliva between her teeth like an old to-bacco-chewer, answers the patrolmen's queries:

"What are you doing here, Annie?"

"I was hiding."

"Who are you hiding from at 2 o'clock in the morning?"

"Chestine Clark, Mr. Martin; for Christ's sake don't tell him I'm here—he swears he'll kill me."

Chestine is something of a dandy ruffian in Bucktown—a tall and sinewy mulatto, who always resists officers when opportunity offers; and is altogether a very unpleasant customer. Clark's father is a respectable and well-to-do old man, and has helped his son out of several very ugly scrapes. Annie is "his girl," and the officer evidently puts faith in her statement, for he promises secrecy. Having looked under the beds and examined every corner, the patrolmen descend, to emerge by a door on the second floor out on the noisome alley in the rear. This alley used to be a frightful place of a summer night, being crowded with thieves and harlots like Sausage Row on a June evening. But Anne Russell, Belle Bailey and Rose Lawson having been sent to the penitentiary, for cutting or passing counterfeit money; while Ann Stickley, Annie Moore, Annie Fish, Jennie Scott, Matt. Adams, Addie Stone, Molly Brown, Annie Jordan, Gabriella Wilson, and a hundred other notorious females, have been shipped off to the Workhouse. "I always made it a rule," said Sissmann, "to keep the greater part of these women in the Workhouse during the time I ran that beat. Otherwise the life of a patrolman would not be worth a hill of blue beans there. Where the prostitutes collect the thieves always gather. There are now between one hundred and fifty and two hundred women from Bucktown in the Workhouse."

There were two women in white dresses sitting on doorsteps a little further on down the alley—one a bright quadroon, with curly hair, twisted into ringlets, and a plump, childish face; the other a tall white girl, with black hair and eyes and a surprisingly well cut profile. Both are notorious; the former as a Sausage Row belle; the latter as the mistress of a black loafer, whom she supports by selling herself. Her sister, once quite a pretty woman, leads a similar existence when not in the Workhouse. The patrolmen point them out, and pass into a doorway on the south side of the alley, leading to the upper story of the dwelling tenanted by John Ham, barkeeper. Mrs. Ham, an obese negress, with immensely thick shoulders, comes forward to meet the patrolmen.

"Who's upstairs, Mrs. Ham?"

"Dey's no one only Molly, fo' God."

"Where's Long Nell?"

"In de Wuk-hus."

"And little Dolly?"

"Wuk-hus."

"And crooked-back Jim?'

"Wuk-hus."

"Ah, they've cleaned out these ranches since I used to run this beat before. Come up, gentlemen." Through a dark hall-way, over a creaking floor to a back room, and the patrolman's club plays the devil's tattoo upon the rickety planks. The door is unlocked and "Molly" makes her appearance.

Molly is the colored belle of this district. What her real name is neither her companions nor the police officers know. So far she has never been in the Workhouse. She seemed to be about eighteen years old, of lithe and slender figure; complexion a Gypsy brown; hair long and dark with a slight wave; brows perfectly arched and delicately penciled; dreamy, brown eyes; nose well cut; mouth admirably molded; features generally pleasing. But Molly is said to be a "decoy" and a thief, and her apparent innocence a sham. The room is searched and found empty.

"Where did you get these?" exclaimed Tighe, picking up from the table a handsome pair of jet bracelets with heavy silver setting.

"They were made a present to me."

"That's too thin! Who gave them to you?"

"A man uptown."

"What man?"

[No answer.]

The officer lays down the trinkets with a frown; tells Molly that he has a good mind to lock her up "on suspicion"; and departs, looking unutterable things. "Did she steal them?" we ask.

"Oh, no," is the reply; "I only want to scare her a little for I happen to know who gave them to her. It is a curious fact that business men and people of respectability get decoyed down here occasionally by girls like that, and get infatuated enough to bring them presents. She wouldn't tell, though, even if I locked her up."

Near here, a couple of doors away, is Joe Kite's place, concerning which horrid stories were once told; the old den kept by Addie Stone, a handsome but tigerish woman, now in the Workhouse for cutting; and further on, the noisome underground den of Gilbert Page, who has lived in Bucktown for twenty-two years, and has paid over five thousand dollars for fines to the Clerk of the Police Court. Here fish and bad whisky and pigs'-feet are sold three stories underground; and here a police officer was nearly murdered while trying to arrest a prisoner in the labyrinth below. Over Joe Kite's lives a good-looking white girl, with some outward appearance of refinement, and who still retains that feminine charm soonest lost by a life of dissipation—a sweet voice. This is Dolly West, or "Detroit Dolly," as they call her, a colored man's woman, and one of the princesses of Bucktown. "Indian Maria," a yellow-skinned and hideous little woman from Michigan, with a little red blood in her veins, lives with others in the building once occupied by Addie Stone. Last week Matt. Lee, a mulatto girl, carved Indian Maria's ugly face with a razor, and was sent to the Workhouse therefor. And not far from Culvert, in a two-story building known as Limber Jim's, lives a very peculiar-looking woman, Belle Bailey, just released from the Columbus Penitentiary. Belle is a West Indian, tall and gracefully built, with a complexion of ebony, but with beautiful hair, and features that are more than ordinarily attractive in their aquiline strength. Belle is not considered much of a thief, but she is dangerously quick with the knife. Indian Maria is not the only Indian here. There is also Pocahontas, a tall, hawk-nosed, yellow-skinned, superannuated sinner, who lives on Culvert street, back of the bar-room kept by the white desperado, Kirk, who has served a term in the Penitentiary. Pocahontas claims to be related to John Smith, of Virginia—"you know all about John Smith, of Virginia." Pocahontas, Indian Maria and a ghoulish-looking little woman without any nose, who lives over Greer's grocery, are all dump-pickers. So is Kate Miller, alias Hunnykut, who lives next to Kirk's, on the Sixth street side. We must not forget to mention Kate Hayes' den, the lowest thieves' hole in Bucktown, which is situated next to Pocahontas' and stands at the corner of Harrison and Culvert. Most of these buildings are two or three stories underground. Culvert, between Sixth and Seventh, seems to mark the boundary line, east and west, between ignorant poverty, pure and simple, and ignorant vice of every description. On Culvert the population is about half and half of either sort; but from the fill up Seventh street north as far as Pruden's Barracks—a tenement house—for harlots, or to Mary Herron's den, still further up, wickedness reigns supreme all through the hours of darkness. On the south side of

Seventh street matters are equally bad; and all along the nameless alleys and the tumble-down rookeries about the big factory in the heart of Bucktown, the sublimity of moral abomination abounds. The density of the population here is proportionately greater than in any other part of the city, although it is mostly a floating population—floating between the workhouse or the penitentiary, and the dens in the filthy hollow. Ten, twelve, or even twenty inhabitants in one two-story underground den is common enough. At night even the roofs are occupied by sleepers, the balconies are crowded, and the dumps are frequently the scenes of wholesale debauchery the most degrading. How it is that sickness is not more common among this class, we confess ourselves unable to comprehend. The black hollows are foul, noisome, miasmatic; full of damp corruption, and often under water, or, better expressed, liquid filth. In the alley which runs by the old Allen Church, on Fifth and Culvert, some twenty feet below the fill, is a long, stagnant pool of execrable stench, which has become a horrible nuisance, and which never dries up. Insect life, the foulest and most monstrous, lurks in the dark underground shanties near by; and wriggling things, the most horrible, abound in the mud without. There is here a large field for both the Board of Health and the Board of Improvements to exercise talent. At the corner of Culvert and Sixth is a hole running into the sewer—a hole as deep as a well and as wide as a church door, and only covered with a few broken planks—splendid place to dispose of a body in. Then below the lots opposite Harrison and Culvert, where stand the ruins of Gordon's oil factory and Woods & Carnahan's burnt out establishment, there is an immense well uncovered, save by some charred beams. Here Bucktown thieves congregate in packs at times, and highway robberies, rapes, and brutal fights have been committed time out of mind. That well should be filled up.

The search for the fugitive thief was continued by the officers until the sky became a pale gray in the east—down shaky ladders into cavernous underground dwellings, up rotten stair-cases into shaky frames, into hideous dens hidden away between larger buildings looking out on the alley. The sheepish humiliation of the debauchees, when the light from the officer's bull's-eye fell upon them, was sometimes pitiful. It was not uncommon to find white men of respectable appearance, and well dressed, sleeping in such dens. The police will seldom molest them while they "behave themselves"; but the well known male thief, be he white or black, is allowed no place in Bucktown to hide his head, and if found in any den is at once kicked into the street. The first instance of this which came under our personal observation was in the brothel of a white woman, known as "Fatty Maria," who keeps on Sixth, near Culvert, opposite Kirk's. As a general rule no door is at any time closed against the police; but on this particular occasion, the women evidently knew what was coming, and all feigned slumber as long as they dared. Finally, repeated rappings and terrible threats caused a sudden opening of the door, and a fellow named Collison was found by the officers sleeping between two women, and at once ordered to vacate the premises. He first feigned sleep and drunken insensibility to the "nippers," and a wholesome tapping with a club; finally, he refused to depart. The women took part, and Fatty Maria attacked one of the officers like a wild cat. He received her with a back-handed slap in the face that sounded like the crack of a whip, when she sprang to the mantle-piece and seized a razor. Before she could use it, however, she was disarmed by another patrolman, and held down, powerless, on a chair, while Collison was fairly flung out of the room and kicked into the exterior darkness. "If that woman did not harbor thieves," said the officer, "we could get along well enough with her, as she is generally quiet; but only this morning she pawned one of her beds and a bureau and a clock for $12, because she wanted to bail out a rascal from the Workhouse."

During this episode at Fatty Maria's, a disgusting occurrence, which well illustrates the brutality of the Bucktown rough, occurred almost immediately across the way. There is a young white woman now in Bucktown, who spends the greater part of her existence in the Workhouse for drunkenness, and whose degradation is such that she has even ceased to be known by name. On the day previous to our trip this wretched creature had been discharged from the Workhouse, and returned to her old haunts. Some one had decoyed her into a low den, made her drunk and taken the most cowardly advantage of her condition, afterwards thrusting her into the street. Soon after some roughs half carried, half dragged her into Kirk's bar-room and poured some more poison down the poor creature's throat for similar purposes. When they heard the police approaching they dragged her out upon the sidewalk and propped her up in a sitting position upon some paving stones near the curb. Here she failed to attract attention while the officers passed down the other side, although in her drunken helplessness she fell sideways upon the stones, her hair streaming over the curb to mingle with the filth in the gutter. While the police were expelling Collison from Fatty Maria's a crowd of ruffians, white and black, lifted the unconscious woman, and carried her to a vacant lot in the hollow in rear of Kirk's, where they tore off part of her clothing. Before the police could reach the spot, the fellows fled beyond pursuit. The officers brought the wretched creature to a neighboring shanty, Kate Miller's. Kate agreed to take care of her, but expressed fears that the rowdies would return for their victim! It is comforting to think that in ten years hence Bucktown will have ceased to exist.

8

Les Chiffonniers

Rags, Wretchedness and Rascality

The Gnomes of the Dumps

How They Live, Work and Have Their Being

—◆—≡◆≡—◆—

There is much the same kind of grotesque poetry about the rag business as there is about most of Gustave Doré's pictures—a fantastically dismal and darksome poetry. Its bare mention conjures up visions of ghoulish gropings in the midst of hideous decay—of dilapidated carts with crumbling woodwork, drawn by skeleton horses through unfrequented back alleys—of moldy ash-barrels and uncleaned back yards and foul-smelling dumps. But beyond such vague notions the general public know little about the importance of this immense and profitable branch of traffic, and still less, perhaps, about its business routine. Feeling that the publication of a few facts relative to this queer traffic could not fail to interest a large proportion of our readers, an ENQUIRER reporter yesterday called upon several of the leading rag-merchants of Cincinnati, who kindly consented to furnish him with such information as he desired. From Mr. E. Pollock, of B. Benjamin & Co., the first gentleman visited, we obtained a good many curious facts regarding the business in Cincinnati.

"I suppose," said the reporter, "that the main portion of the rags bought and sold in this city are used in the manufacture of paper?"

"Yes. Cincinnati has become one of the great centers of the rag-trade, owing to the number of paper-mills in the Miami Valley. There are seven alone at Miamisburg; then there are three at Franklin, one at Middletown, three at Hamilton, four at Dayton, and five or six at Lockland. Rags are shipped to this market from North, West and South. Why, we get them even from Galveston, Texas."

"Are all these rags gleaned by rag-pickers?"

"Far the greater portion are. But much is also sold directly to rag ware-houses by large firms such as clothing houses and newspaper offices. The former sell their "clippings," and the latter waste paper in great quantities."

"How are the rags sorted?"

"Well, there are three principal varieties: Cotton Rags, Hard Woolens, and Soft Woolens. The cotton rags are worth about 2½ cents; they go to make white paper. The hard woolens (old clothes, carpets, &c.) are worth about 1 cent per pound, and are only used for wrapping paper. The soft woolens, such as knitted socks and underwear, will sell as high as 5½ cents per pound. They are used in the manufacture of shoddy. Tailors' clippings sell much higher. Old rope is worth from 3 to 3½ cents per pound."

"Some of these rags must come to you in a frightfully filthy condition?"

"No; we won't take foul rags at all, and we won't buy from the dump-pickers. You see rags may be classified into Country Rags—those sold by farmers, &c.; City Rags—such as are collected by those gatherers who drive through the alleys with their carts early every morning; and Dump Rags. Now very few houses will buy Dump Rags; they're almost worthless. But then rags are liable to be adulterated, like any other article of commerce; and there are petty rag-dealers who buy even the dirtiest rags and mix up with those of better quality."

"Well, don't you buy any rags from the dump-pickers?"

"No. You see our specialty is iron; and we do not care to devote such attention to the rag department as dump-rag purchasing would involve. We handle about 1,500 tons of old iron in a year. Cast-iron is now worth three-fourths of a cent per pound, and wrought iron about one and one-eighth cents. Then all old metal is bought up in the same way. Copper is worth from eighteen to twenty cents; brass, ten to fifteen; lead, about five; zinc, four, and pewter about eighteen cents per pound. Washboiler copper sells highest, and old brass coins and medals sell very high. I am giving you dump-pickers' prices now. Then they sell glass and bones, too, which we don't buy, of course. The Hemingray glass-works now buys up all the glass; and bones are bought by Fertilizing Companies, soap-boilers and lamp-black manufacturers. Bones are a very valuable article. Nice white leg-bones, after being boiled and the grease extracted, are sent in shiploads to Europe, where they are used in the manufacture of knife-handles, etc. A great part of this kind of stock comes from Texas, where cattle are just killed by thousands for their hides, and the carcasses left to rot. Enterprising men have realized fortunes by collecting these bones at a very small cost, and shipping them to Europe. I have seen vessels leave a Southern harbor laden with hundreds of tons of bones. One cargo of seven hundred tons I saw being shipped was estimated to be worth $14,000. The rough bones—"kitchen bones," as we term them—are ground up, and made into fertilizer, and the spotted ones burnt to make lampblack. But you could write a two-column article on the trade in bones."

"Can you not give me some information about the dump-pickers here? How they live, and how much they make, etc.?"

"Well, no; I can't tell you much about them, because we do so little

business with them. But I have known some of them to make money at the
business. There is now an old man living on Hamilton road, near Mohawk
bridge, who commenced with a paper sack, and has now become comfortably
independent. And one would suppose that poking in dump-heaps is an un-
healthy business, but it don't seem to be. These dump-pickers seem to be very
healthy people, and live to a great age. They sell a good deal of their stuff on
Central avenue, or along the canal, in the smaller rag-shops. But some of the
gentlemen at the warehouse of McCall, Sutphin & Co., who do the largest rag
business in the city, can tell you a good deal about those people."

Before visiting the Walnut street firm, however, the reporter resolved to
make a pilgrimage to the dumps, in the hope of obtaining an interview with
some of the rag-pickers themselves, and a brisk walk of ten minutes brought
him to the neighborhood of Sixth and Culvert streets.

It is not a locality which people often visit, save when compelled by
circumstances over which they have no control; and those who have once
beheld never wish to behold it again. A wilderness of filthy desolation walled
in by dismal factories; a Golgotha of foul bones and refuse; a great grave-yard
for worn-out pots and kettles and smashed glasses, and rotten vegetables and
animal filth, and shattered household utensils and abominations unutterable.
The broken ground glitters with tin shreds and scrapings; the sunlight falls
luridly on the fetid dump-piles through the noisome veil of thick smoke that
hangs over all; and other sounds are deadened by the dull, never-ceasing roar
of the machines in the huge factories on either hand. Here and there evil-
featured women, children, and hideous old men may be seen toiling and bur-
rowing amid the noisome piles of rottenness—beings frightful as gnomes,
realizing the grotesquely horrible fantasias of some modern French writers.
Victor Hugo must have visited the Dumps ere writing that nightmare tale,
"The Dwarf of Notre-Dame." Clad in rags fouler than those they unearthed
from the decaying filth beneath them, the dump-pickers worked silently side
by side, with a noiseless swiftness that seemed goblin-like to one coming upon
such a scene for the first time. At a greater distance these miserable creatures,
crawling over the dumps on all fours, looked, in their ash-colored garments,
like those insects born of decay, which take the hue of the material they feed
upon.

The reporter clambered over the debris, and addressed the toilers one by
one. Old men, begrimed to hideousness with filth and feeble with disease,
glared weirdly and wildly upon him for a moment, and returned to their foul
labor without replying to his query. Children, gaunt, hungry, dirty—children
that had never had a childhood, looked upon him in a piteously dazed, con-
fused manner, with great dull eyes, and stammered incoherent replies to his

inquiries. Finally, the reporter came to a little group in the most lonesome portion of the little desert, who were quarreling angrily in the German tongue—a woman and two boys. The boys, saucy, half-nude little urchins, were seated on the dump-pile, sorting out such trash as had fallen to their lot. The woman, kneeling crouched, with her back turned to the reporter, had not noticed his approach. He touched her on the arm, and she turned half-round.

It was a goblin-like face, horrible to grotesqueness. A huge vulture nose, great black eyes, deep-set, and glowing with a brilliancy that seemed phosphorescent, a high, bold, frowning forehead, crowned with a filthy turban, long, thin, bloodless lips, and a long, massive chin, all begrimed to deep blackness by the filth of the dumps. The woman had evidently once possessed immense physical strength. She was unusually tall, and huge of limb, grim and gaunt and wolfish in appearance.

"Do you make your living this way?" asked the reporter.

"Yes"—sullenly.

"Please excuse my questions. I'm a newspaper reporter, and would like to know something about your business. Do you make a good living this way?"

"No"—fiercely. "I am out all day, and I can't make more'n two or three dollars a week. And then I have two boys to keep."

"Why don't you try something else—washing for instance? You look strong enough."

"Yes, I've been pretty stout, and I'm stout yet. But I cut the tendons of my right wrist all through about a year ago, and I had to give up washing. I used to do it once."

"Can't you get any other employment—something that will pay you better?"

"I don't want to talk about it. You can't do me any good anyhow, and I'm too busy to bother with you."

"Well, where do you live? I'd like to have a talk with you some other time, when you have leisure."

"Ah!"—with a dangerous look—"I don't want any man 'round me. I can make my living honestly, anyhow."

The disgusted reporter handed his card to the frightful old ghoul by way of argument. She handed it to one of her boys, and the urchin immediately placed it in his waste-paper bag. And the reporter departed, more in sorrow than in anger.

"Say, mister," cried one of the ragged urchins, as the reporter strode away, "there's a big maggot on your coat-tail!"

*　　*　　*

The reporter next called upon Messrs. McCall & Sutphin, of Walnut street, who received him with much cordiality, and furnished him with some curious facts concerning the dump-picking business.

"There isn't much use," said Mr. Sutphin, "in trying to interview the dump-pickers. They are too ignorant to understand the object of your inquiries, and they think that you only want to injure them. But most of them come here to sell their gatherings, and we know them all pretty well. We can tell you a good deal about them. They are mostly very old people, crippled and rheumatic, who can do nothing else for a living."

"Well, how much, on an average, can these rag-pickers make?" asked the reporter.

"From 10 cents to $1.50 per day. But very few can make a dollar and a half. The average is from twenty to fifty cents."

"How many work for your firm?"

"About forty. They are nearly all very old and feeble; some of them cripple, and some have interesting histories."

"Can you give me the names and ages of a few of the best-known?"

"Yes; we can give you a few."

Mr. Sutphin and one of the clerks, after some little delay, gave the following names to the reporter:

DAVY LAWLER.—Davy is a white man by birth, but a black man by habit. He is over seventy years of age, and has been more than fifteen years at the business. He is so terribly filthy by nature that McCall has to send him to the Infirmary once a month to be cleaned up. Whenever he makes a couple of dollars he goes on a spree in Bucktown, and the firm, being aware of his weakness, charitably keeps his wages in arrears.

RICHARD PARKERSON.—Sixty-five years of age (white), engineer by trade; had to abandon his occupation by reason of bad eyesight; has been a rag-picker for twelve years.

GENERAL HARVEY THOMAS.—Colored, one hundred years old. Keeps his person clean and neat. Fought at the Battle of New Orleans; fourteen years at the business; is shrewd, and successful in business.

HARRY KAPT.—Over 75 years old. Has been at the business over eighteen years. Is exceedingly filthy and improvident.

GEORGE GOODWIN.—(Colored), eight years at the business. Clean, tidy and thrifty.

GEORGE NELSON.—Ninety-seven years old, and deaf. He has saved a great deal of money at the business during the last twenty years.

JAMES CLARK.—(White), eleven years rag-picker. Seventy years old. Averages fifteen cents a day.

MARY WINKER.—Fifty years old. Sixteen years at the rag business. Drunk, disorderly and filthy.

MRS. MILLER.—Her husband and grown-up son refuse to support her. Over fifty-five years of age, and fourteen at rag-picking.

MAGGIE MURPHY.—Seventy years old, and seven years at the business. One eye knocked out during a fight in Bucktown.

POLLY GAZZONI.—Has made a great deal of money. Seventy years old, and thirty years at the business.

TONY WOODFALL.—Thirty years old, neat, respectable and successful in business.

THOMAS AVERITTE.—Two years at business, forty-five years old; incapacitated by rheumatism from following any other occupation.

CARL WINKLER.—Unutterably filthy in habits, seventy years old; nine years at business.

W.C. GRIMES.—Forty-five years old, eleven years at the business; (white), clean.

A. SACKENPAPER.—A cleanly, thrifty, energetic little German, sixty years old. Stays up at the Soldiers' Home all the winter. Has only been at the business ten years, but has been very successful.

SEBASTER SELLER.—(White) fifty-five years old, sixteen years at the business. Wife comes up to warehouse hebdomadally for the purpose of appropriating his wages.

"MOLLY."—(White)—Between fifty-five and sixty years old. Steals soft woolens while selling a dime's worth of dirty paper; been at the business fourteen years. Davy Lawler and Molly go habitually together on Bucktown sprees. Lawler is said to be a No. 1 tailor, but fell through a skylight three years ago and cut his hands so terribly as to incapacitate him from any work but rag-picking.

9

WITHIN THE BARS

How Prisoners Look, Live, and Conduct Themselves

Some Glimpses of Life in the County Jail

It is now some three years since the jail on Sycamore street, behind the Court-house, has been used for the imprisonment of persons sentenced for minor offenses. It is that length of time since the Work-house has been built, and instead of now keeping tiers of cells of persons lying idle they have been put into workshops where they may make some return for the bread they eat.

The County Jail

At present is occupied by those who have been sent up from the Police Court charged with crimes for which that Court has no power to punish; also, those arrested on Magistrates' warrants and for violation of laws on the revenue—sellers of whisky without license, cigar-makers who use no stamps on their cigars and counterfeit money handlers. There are two occasions when the jail may be seen to good advantage—at dinner time and on Sundays when there is praying and singing.

The Prisoners

There are in the jail now about thirty-five prisoners, and the number rapidly lessens during the sitting of the Court, an average of three and a half prisoners being tried and sent off daily. The inside of the jail, as no doubt every one knows and has no objection to be told over again, is star-shaped, so that one standing in the center may look down through the different points and have the whole under his eye at once, so to speak. When dinner is cooked, one man goes around with a basketful of tin pannikins, in each of which is some boiled beef, a chunk of bread, and half of a raw onion. He gives the tin a knock against the iron wall of the cell, and a hand is reached out through a small hole, knee-high from the floor, and the tin taken in. Another man follows with a bucket of soup, which he ladles out in similar tins, being taken in in the same way.

Inside the Cells

There is a marked difference between the inmates of prisons where no work is done, where the cells are dark and those where they are kept busy and shut up only at night. In the last they have about the same look they wear outside, perhaps cleaner; in the other they have a weary, listless air, and lounge about with vacant looks upon their faces. Just as one night in the station-house cell will give the most respectable looking person a frowsy and disreputable air in the morning, so will a short residence in these cages make a man a very different looking creature from what he was outside. Be the barley soup ever so nutritious, and the corn-bread healthier even than the jailer believes it to be, jail life, even when lightened up with occasional broom and scrubbing-brush exercise, pulls a man down as nothing but trouble and imprisonment will.

Men Ought to Grow Fat

In jail, think the jailers, but they don't. Not even with rice soup changed with barley soup, and raw onions varied by carrots and turnips; with breakfasts and suppers of black coffee and corn-dodgers; with nothing to do but wait, and with regular visitations from the pious young men and hymn-screeching young women—with all this they are still lean and yellow, and think of little but the day when they will once more tramp the free pave, or hear the clack of the showmaker's hammers in the Work-house.

Individual Habits

Some of the prisoners squat of their cot beds, pulled in the middle of their cells, and with hands under their haunches watch the stray bits of sunlight by the hour, moving only to lie down or to eat. They live this way week after week, moody and gaunt, while others trim their cells up until by comparison they are little palaces. One ingenious young man, who is in for counter-feiting money, has with scolloped and ornamented newspapers festooned the ceiling of his den, and covered the walls with prints, framed with like trimming, until it has lost much of its prison look. There are hanging shelves made from card-board and ends of twine, and match-holders in which matches were never seen, and cigar-holders innocent of cigars, all fashioned from newspapers, and gaudily set off with fringes and rosettes.

Fine Art

There is among the prisoners a great demand for pictures; nothing seems to push back the iron walls and enlarge the breathing space as do plenty of pictures, and every shred of an illustrated paper is carefully pasted up. The ordinary method is to paste them close together, one after the other, but the more artistic way is to put them up according to size, and inclose them in frames of paper. The *Day's Doings* and *Frank Leslie's* contribute the larger number of these adornments, but here and there are more pretentious prints, a steel engraving, and occasionally, next to a picture full of female lower limbs, may be seen a Bible motto in red and gold.

Literature

If Miss Linda Gilbert could but have the handling of the library of this jail, there would very speedily be an addition to the waste paper heap. Books on theology, wormy lives of travelers, lifeless accounts of polar explorations and dead-letter histories form the bulk of a mass of books that the most book-hungry of prisoners never touch. Not that persons locked up for crime are to be tickled with standard literature or furnished with exciting reading; any book is more than they have right to, but, if it is considered good to give them books at all, they might be furnished with those improving books such as they would be likely to read. As it is, their books are treated with little more respect than are Thane Miller's tracts, which are used for drying tobacco cuds on and for holding salt.

Bond, the Tomahawker

Sits in an upper cell, where he has plenty of light and room. Since his throat-cutting he has been kept under continual watch, a man keeping him company all day, and another all night, at a cost of five dollars to the State every twenty-four hours. It is thought that he will again attempt suicide. Every mark of his last effort has healed away, and the handkerchief tied around his neck is kept on from habit. He has grown gray and gaunt, speaking to no one but Dr. Tucker and his mother. He awaits the action of the Supreme Court before which Major Blackburn is working to have the sentence of a year in the Penitentiary reversed. Although Bond has been in the jail fully nine months, he would prefer to stay there twice as many more rather than go to the State Prison, the name of which has such a peculiar effect on him. He has a number of books.

Other Newspaper Familiars

The voice of Henry Mayrose, imprisoned by Judge Halliday for selling unstamped cigars, was heard swearing through the iron bars over what he could see of a pool of barley soup (his share for the dinner) spilled outside on the pavement by an unskillful server. A noted thief with a red head and large freckled face lay stretched out on his bed, where he had lain for days and nights with his eyes wide open, and in a corner sat talking with his wife, an interesting young woman, Cozine, the escaped and recaptured prisoner.

The Health of the Imprisoned

Is good. Although there is a lack of energy and a weakly look generally, there is little call for the doctor or his medicines. Now and then a man complains of looseness of the bowels. "All right," says the doctor, "I'll give you something for that." "I say, doctor, don't you think if you give me wheat bread instead of corn for a while it would cure me?" "We'll try it," returns the doctor, and with the medicine the bread is changed. The doctor grieves to say that the pills and powders are thrown down the waste-pipe. Sickness is feigned in order to be given work and exercise, many prisoners preferring to scrub up the floor and wash dishes, to the confined idleness of the cell.

Keeping Them Clean

There are bath-tubs and although they have a very new and unworn look, it is said that the prisoners are compelled to wash all over twice a month. The practice in some jails of requiring a man on entering to go through a shower-bath and hair-cutting experience, while his clothes are held over burning sulphur, is not here carried out. As the prisoner comes from the station-house cell and the Black Maria he is locked up, and yet the Jailer claims that the cells and bedding are free from vermin. His opinion regarding the plentifulness of lice in beds occupied by a variety of unclean persons is different from that of the young man in charge of the Rev. Thomas Lee's Bethel lodging-house. Pointing to the beds in that institution, one day last week, the youth was asked regarding their freedom from vermin. "Oh! they're full of them." he answered; "do you see those beds there?"—pointing to the upper end of a row yet tumbled from the sleepers of the night before—"I never go near *them*!" He also advanced the opinion that beds promiscuously occupied could not be kept clean; but Jailer Thomas Evitt believes there is not a creeper in his whole establishment.

Air and Water

In each cell, directly under the head of the bed, is a pipe which brings in, from the roof, fresh air besides which the grated door on the one side and the barred window on the other are unglazed, and every cell is provided with a small faucet, supplied with water from a tank in the upper story, kept full by a continually working engine. Each prisoner is also provided with a privy, foul smells from which are avoided by a full supply of water. The cells are so constituted that if it were not for the occasional exercise no prisoner need ever cross his door-sill during his imprisonment.

Outside Friends

(It is a rule in the jail that no friends of the prisoners shall fetch them eatables.) Those who wish to do this may effect the same end by the furnishing of money, the jailer providing extra food at prices not higher than charged outside. Cigars are sold for five cents, and a plug of tobacco for ten, while fried steak may be had for fifteen and twenty cents. It is not, however, to give the jailer the monopoly of furnishing extras that this rule is enforced. As might be supposed, saws and chisels may easily be introduced in a loaf of bread or in a pie, and it will be remembered the recent detection at this jail of a cake of tobacco packed full of fine saws, and a pie stuffed with the same.

Escape

Is not easy from the jail. The mass of cells rest within the thick walls much as a round honey-comb rests in a square box, and even after the cell is sawn through there remain the granite walls and the heavily-barred windows. The most persistent attempts at escape were those made by one of the three young men hung here some time since, who, it will be remembered, sawed off his manacles daily, and no one found out where he hid the saw, although after he was hung a fellow-prisoner declared that he had kept it under his thumb-nail. Among the heavy iron bands used for desperate cases may be seen one on the padlock of which is a deep cut made by the same person in his last and unsuccessful attempt. One of the most clever escapes was that made by the colored boy who was locked up in the dark dungeons. These dungeons, of which there are four, were used for those who broke prison rules. Night itself is light compared to their dense darkness, within the walls of which no count can be kept of the passage of time, no line drawn between day and night. In these cells there is a narrow opening leading from the ceiling to the roof, like a chimney, and up this chimney the colored boy crawled and got away. Iron bars have been placed across the opening since then, but the dungeons have fallen out of use.

10

CINCINNATI SALAMANDERS

A Confederation of Twenty Little Communities

Characteristics and Peculiarities of Our Fire Department

Short Sketches of the Several Companies

━━ ≍♦≍ ━━

Mental and moral, as well as physical, peculiarities impress themselves powerfully upon communities of men associated together for a common purpose or in a common calling. Even the most breadth-giving profession is liable to exert certain narrowing influences upon those who pursue it. Each vocation makes its mark into the character of its followers, often so deeply as to be read with almost unerring certainty by the skilled observer. A practiced eye will, in a miscellaneous crowd of strangers, detect the lawyer, the doctor, the mechanic, the merchant, and more readily than any other, the school-master, from the handwriting on their faces and in their acts. While some occupations develop more harmoniously the whole nature of a man than others, there is not one, perhaps, that does not overpoweringly exert some one expanding influence peculiarly and exclusively its own. The army is the only school in which certain men may develop certain virtues, and the sea, the desert and the wilderness each teach lessons to be learned of no other master. Growth of character seems to be the normal condition of human existence, incident and essential to human activity and human happiness. Character is wrought upon not only by vocation, but by every circumstance and accident of time, location, climate, and social surroundings. The multitude are, therefore, wiser than any man, from the very fact that diverse vocations diversify the gifts and powers of men, and give that variety to character which, securing the world unity in variety, redeems it from the dreariness and desolation of a dead monotony. Cut every leaf on an elm in the same die, and we have unity without variety, but the beauty of the tree is gone. Make all the oaks in a forest *fac similes* of each other, and the grandeur of that forest is lost.

We have probably no better exemplification of the effects of a common vocation and the modifications of the same by situation and surroundings than is exhibited by the varied characteristics of the Companies which compose our Fire Department. They are twenty tribes, with each distinctive traits and yet all with traits in common. Each Company is a little State, as it were, with a character of its own and distinctive tastes and habits, and the Department a confederacy of these little States unified by more general characteristics. From necessity of the case a fireman must be vigorous and hardy physically, and plucky, brave and trustworthy morally. His life trains him to obedience, to discipline, patience, fortitude, and in a measure self-forgetfulness. He acquires, as it were, professional pride more readily and holds to it with more tenacity than the man of most other callings. To an outsider it would seem a matter of no significance to change the number of an old Company from Two to Six, but the fireman, who instinctively presumes and glories in traditions, would be deeply hurt by any such trifling with a number around which cluster precious memories and dear associations. We propose to sketch the various Fire Companies in the city, and put down some of the leading traits of each imprinted upon it by the accidents of situation and local influence.

The "1's," Race and Commerce, Captain Joe Bunker, is near the river, among the business houses and away from dwellings. It has comparatively little society from the neighborhood. Occasionally its members have to go out at night to quell a street disturbance when the police are not by. It is generally known that all firemen are policemen, and clothed with police powers, but not required to go far from their respective stations.

The 1's are not unsocial, but are taciturn and thoughtful, their minds being much occupied in apprehension lest their rivals, the 9's—of whom we shall speak presently—will beat them to the next fire.

The 2's, Ninth and Freeman, Captain Pius Chambers, exhibit the effects of contact with men of ability. Enoch Carson, J. M. Waters, and a host of lawyers who inhabit the West End, make that a place to drop in occasionally and discuss matters of city and State. It was the head-quarters for scenting Millcreek stenches last summer. This Company is one of the best informed in the Department upon the upper class city matters. In the way of recreation it takes to dominoes, and its members are highly accomplished in that game. It still uses a set old as the Department, and so worn that the spots on them are only visible to the practiced eyes of those whose fingers have worn them out.

The "3's," Sixth, near Vine, Captain John Miller, is the head-quarters and telegraphic center of the Department, where the office is located and where the "Bosses" make their headquarters. As is to be expected, the members here know more than anywhere else about the doings and wants of the

Department. It is a dropping-in place for old firemen and for men of all classes from all parts of the city.

The members generally have pretty broad views of Department affairs and of public matters in general. For amusement they take to euchre, whist and cribbage, in which they can furnish men hard to beat. Of course the Phoenix H. and L. Co., which is located here, is included in this sketch, and being exposed to the same influences develop the same characteristics.

The "Fours," Sycamore, above Seventh, Captain Wiedier, is exposed to Church influence and is a reverential sort of a Company. All the members are men of family except one, and there is an immediate prospect that he will be chucked into the matrimonial state by his fellow-members if he does not enter it voluntarily.

Among other things this Company is distinguished for the French boy who drives the hosereel, George Crusoe, a very interesting youth of seventy-five summers. He has all the vivacity of his countrymen, and no man fifty years his junior is more spry and active than he.

The "Fives," Vine, near Court, Captain John Pohlman, has the speediest engine in the city, and until Christmas night the "Sevens," with a longer run, beat them to the corner of Main and Court. The "Fives" get up and off, as a rule, quicker than any other Company in that quarter of the city, and their horses are as beautifully trained as their men. Let a gong ring at midnight, and on the first stroke three or four men, clad and booted, will spring from the floor as if shot up through it by traps. By the time the number is rung out the first time, unless it be a very short one, the Company is whirling away at full speed. The house of this Company is frequented by local politicians in campaign times. The members are waggish, fond of practical jokes, and have scored some good ones upon habitual bores.

The "Sixes," corner of Pearl and Martin, Captain J. C. Donovan, is well versed on Waterworks affairs and in campaigns keeps well up on political subjects. It is composed of cheerful, good-looking fellows who know what courtesy means, especially to strangers. This place is quite a resort in summer evenings on account of the cool breezes which come to it from the river, and the view it commands of the Water-Works Park and its attractions at that season.

The "Sevens," Webster street, Captain Henry Meinze, has among its members the book-worm of the Fire Department, Henry Mehring, who quits reading only to eat, sleep, and run to a fire. This company keeps well up on the subject of fire-engines—improvements in them. This house has splendidly-trained horses, and is about to take the palm for quickness in running to fires. The Captain is an old salt, and experienced a little sea-fighting at Vera Cruz in the Mexican War.)

The "Eights," Captain Leonard, on Cutter, above Laurel, is head-quarters for teamsters of a wet day or in dull times. Its members are solid, solemn-looking men, but they afford some of the best checker players in the city, and some not bad at cribbage. (Old volunteer firemen living near resort there to revive the traditions of the early firemen in the city.)

The "Nines," corner of Rose and Second, is a new company with an old number, Captain John Daniels commanding. It has a big engine but gets out quickly. The Ones watch it, and it watches the Ones, and it is always a matter of interest which is first to reach a fire, the runs being equal. It enjoys the reputation of being very voluble in language, which, by some, is imputed to the sympathetic influence of the Gas-works, which are located not far away, and whose pungent odors are always in the nostrils of the members of that company. It is isolated from society, and does not hear much news before it gets into the papers.

The "Tens," corner of Third and Lawrence, Captain Dick Miller, has many late calls every night from men walking to their up-town homes. Its location at the terminus of a street-car route and on the way to and from the Newport Ferry, make it quite a public place and the most newsy house in town. Outsiders frequently indulge in games of cards and checkers here. The Company contains more adepts in the art of smoking and can display more big pipes than any of its confederates. The members are exceedingly social men, and have the address and polish which frequent contact with men brings.

The "11's," Front and Vance streets, Fulton, Captain Jesse Bennett, is distinguished for the number of Captains it has had in the last year. One after another men were detailed from various other companies to "Captain" this one, and gave up the job, till Jesse Bennett, late of the 3's, a quiet but desperately determined little man, went in and stuck. It is now winning a fine reputation, and in the work of building up a fine character.

The "Twelves," called the "Mohawks," Hamilton road and Vine street, Captain John. Morewood, is properly called "the killers." Two or three years ago the air-chamber of its engine exploded and killed somebody. On one summer evening after that lightning struck the engine-house and pitched Dr. Fishburn, who was sitting at the door, into the middle of the street, at the same time strewing three or four firemen, seated near him, up and down the sidewalk, fortunately inflicting serious injury on no one. At the late Work fire Adam Machle, its pipeman, was hurt, with two or three others, by a falling wall, and hurt again by the later Brighton Station fire.

This Company is a rendezvous for public-spirited German citizens, and is quite German in its sympathies and characteristics.

The "Thirteens," known as the Brightons, Bank street, between Linn and Central avenue, Captain Walter Phares, is the high-toned company of the city. George W. Skaats, Amor Smith, General Hickenlooper, James H. Laws, Ex-Mayor Davis, Hon. W. T. Bishop, and many other Dayton, York and Bank street gentlemen drop in there occasionally, and in times of local excitement frequently. It is often the place of an indignation meeting, and always the center for a little social chat. The company is well versed in the upper class city matters, not given to gossip, readers, good firemen, and gentlemen.

The "Fourteens," Fifth and Smith, Capt. D. W. C. Lee, has been recently called the "Star Company." It is head-quarters for Assistant Engineer Lew Wisby. Always a live set of men, quick movers, it is now breaking its horses to come to their places on full gallop at the sound of an alarm. Next to the Threes it is best up in all the doings of the department. The engine-house is frequented by citizens only less than some of the houses in parts of the city less devoted to business houses. The men here must be very reserved, great readers or great sleepers, for day or evening most of them stay upstairs in their elegant sitting-room or library.

The "15's," Captain Charles Gilman, is on Mt. Adams. Its apparatus consist of a ladder truck to be drawn by hand, and four portable chemical extinguishers. Captain Gilman manages affairs at night and Mrs. Gilman by day, when the Captain, whose principal duty is with the fire-alarm telegraph, is absent at the Central Office, takes charge of the apparatus. In case of fire, citizens draw the truck by hand, and act under the Captain's direction. This is the most domestic, happy and harmonious Company in the Department. Its force varies from time to time, and its strength is never precisely known till the pay-rolls come into the Commission for approval.

The "16's," West Walnut Hills, George Mohl, Captain, is a good young Company. It is the head-quarters of Mr. H. P. Bowman, Trustee of the Water-works, where he meets boon companions to enjoy a game of casino. It is quite a place of resort for Walnut Hills people. Hon. Ben Eggleston drops in occasionally, and Henry Lewis, Dr. A. E. Jones and Irv. Wright have been there.

The "Seventeens," Storrs Township, corner of Neave and German streets, is a recent acquisition; character scarcely formed. Captain Martin Cronin commands. Its members spend much of their time in cleaning their boots, a labor incident to the location.

The "Eighteens," Crawfish road, on the western confines of Columbia, Captain Ed. Evans, is the "disturbed element" in the Fire Department, the place where harmony has not always reigned. It is on the borderline between two ancient civilizations, and border people have always been noted for commotions. It has been fusing down during the past few months into the general mass and will probably soon lose the characteristic which lately distinguished it. This Company has good material, and the way is clear before it to rival any of its compositors [competitors]. More fires and more work will help it amazingly.

The "19's," Vine Street Hill, or Corryville, Captain Dennis Creed, is the half-way house for people riding out on Sunday. As is to be expected, this company stands first in entertaining visitors, as, by much practice, its members have become good talkers. It has an elegant house, and is quite a local center for the interchange of news, occupying, as it does, the middle ground between Mount Auburn and the city on the one, and Clifton on the other hand.

The "Twenties" is without character. Its future is all before it. In fact, it is sans Captain, sans men, sans engine—merely a company in posse, with only a location for an engine-house. Within a few months it will have men, horses and apparatus. The location is Cumminsville.

Of course, the ladder companies are included in the above sketches. They partake of the character of the fire companies in whose houses they are located. An advantage soon to be realized by the Fours, on Sycamore street, is the location of the head-quarters of Assistant Engineer Jakey Hughes, the wag with smiling face and winning ways, at that house.

11

STEEPLE CLIMBERS

Joseph Roderiguez Weston, the daring steeple climber, who recently affixed the green wreaths and tri-colored banner to the cross of the Cathedral spire, called at the *Commercial* office a few days ago and expressed the desire that a reporter should accompany him on his next trip to the giddy summit, when he should remove the temporary decorations there placed in honor of the Archbishop's Golden Jubilee. Such a proposition could not well be accepted without considerable hesitancy—a hesitancy partly consequent upon the consciousness of personal risk, and partly owing to the probable nature of the public verdict upon such undertakings. The novel and rare experiences of such a trip, coupled with the knowledge that a correct description of them could not fail to elicit some public interest, and that the hardy enterprise of the professional climbers themselves could only be done justice to by temporarily sharing their dangers, ultimately proved sufficient inducements to a *Commercial* reporter to attempt the experiment. The ascent was fixed for 4 o'clock yesterday afternoon, at which time Mr. Weston, accompanied by John Klein, of the Globe Slating Company, who is no less daring a climber than his experienced comrade, called at the office with a buggy for a representative of the *Commercial.* Each of the party had previously prepared for the event by changing their ordinary dress for a worn-out suit. Mr. Peter Depretz, also of the firm of John Klein & Co., awaited us at the Cathedral with all the necessary climbing apparatus,—ropes, grappling-ladders, block and tackle, etc.

It is scarcely necessary to observe that the writer, wholly inexperienced in the art of hazardous climbing, did not start out upon such an undertaking without considerable trepidation, notwithstanding the reiterated assurances of his guide that nothing was to be feared in view of the secure arrangements and first-class apparatus; and when we drove under the Cathedral spire itself, towering symmetrically against the clear blue, pillar piled on pillar, and cornice succeeding cornice, up to the last long, bare peak of white stone, it was impossible to quell a little fluttering of the heart. The lightning-rod appeared like a tiny black line, slender as a spider's thread; the lofty flag, floating in the afternoon breeze, seemed from below no larger than a kerchief of colored silk; and the great stone cross itself, wreathed with evergreens, looked far too small to afford foothold on its summit for any human being. The fantastic and shadowy interior of the spire itself was calculated to increase rather than to lighten the novice's weight of anxiety. With the doors of the Cathedral closed, we groped our way up the winding stairs of stone in ebon darkness, passing above the choir, through an iron door, which slides portcullis fashion, and whereof the purpose is to cut off connection between the spire and the main building in case of a conflagration. Here the spiral stairway of stone ceased, and a gas jet being lighted, revealed a seemingly interminable series of octagonal stone chambers above, rising above one another in lessening perspective, separated only by floors of open beam or plank work, and lighted, far up, by a dim gray light struggling through louver windows. The cold, bare walls of rough stone seemed to sweat a chilly sweat under the gas-light, which revealed clinging to them growths of those tiny fungi which thrive even in darkness. The walls at this point are eight feet in thickness, massive as those of a feudal donjon-keep; and flights of grimy wooden stairs, narrow and often unsteady, creep in a long-drawn-out spiral around the interior. Looking down from the balustrade an abyss of gloom alone is visible; the beams of the stair-structure are thickened on their upper surface with inches of colorless dust; the panels of the iron door are edged on the lower groove with a deep layer of detached rust; the wooden steps creak and shriek as the foot falls on them; and far up above, in the deep darkness, the solemn pulsations of the great clock's iron heart are weirdly audible, monotonously awful, as the footfall of Something coming up the stairs of a haunted house. "I have heard the beating of that clock," said the steeple-climber, "on wild, wintry nights, when I had to go aloft to fix something and the goblin sound almost frightened me. It sounds gruesome in the dark."

Again and again gas jets were lighted and stairs climbed, until the light of day struggled faintly in upon us, the beating of the clock grew louder, and the great weights became visible, floating and swaying above. The tower now narrowed, and we crawled rather than climbed among beams, through holes, and into the heart of the clock itself, like animalculae creeping amid the machinery of an old-fashioned chronometer, until we stood among the bells. Thence we watched in the gray dimness the life-springs of the huge timekeeper working and shuddering. The bells were rusty; their tongues were rough with red decay. Suddenly the chimes boomed out around us; an iron arm arose in the gloom and smote the great bell twice; it was half-past 4 o'clock.

We crawled up between the lips of the bells to another and again another wooden stair and stood one hundred and fifty feet above the pavement, in an octagonal chamber, lighted by eight louver windows. From one of these, on the eastern side, had been removed the huge wooden lattice which at once serves to keep out foul weather, and to throw down the sound of church bells into the bosom of the city. And from below struggled faintly to our ears the distant din of traffic, the rumble of wagons, the hoof-beats of horses and the buzz of the City Buildings. Spires and cornices seemed to rise almost under our feet; the river's silver flickered from the south, and the yellow canal crawled beneath its bridges away to the rolling purple of the hills in the north.

"Must we climb out through this window?" was our first nervous interrogation.

"Oh, yes," replied Watson, "it can't be done any other way."

Above projected a huge cornice, below was nothing but a sheer precipice of smooth stone. The writer saw and trembled, and inwardly wished himself at home; and when Peter Depretz got out of the window to execute a dance on the narrow cornice underneath for the purpose of inspiring us with courage, the fear only increased. Then a young man clambered up to a loophole within, Klein fastened the steel hooks of a grappling ladder to the cornice, which projected twenty-five feet above us, and the top rung of the vibrating stairway was made fast to a rope, which the young assistant tied firmly about a beam within. But the ladder swung backward and forward over the precipice, until we began to experience the familiar feeling of nightmare.

After having read that hideous but most artistically Gothic romance by Victor Hugo, *The Dwarf of Notre Dame,* one is apt to have a frightful nightmare about steeple-climbing, and we remember such unpleasant experience. The dreamer finds himself, perhaps, straddling a stone dragon at a vast altitude from the gabled city below; the clouds float far beneath him; the ravens shriek in his ears; above him springs into the very vault of heaven a vast peak of carven stone—a precipice roughened only with gargoyles, griffins, hippogriffs, dragons—all the hideous imaginations of the midiaeval sculptors. He flees from a pursing monster below, and climbs the dizzy eminence above with frantic despair. The diabolic pursuer pauses, to grin with satiated rage at his victim's agony of fear. Suddenly the gargoyles grin; the stony monsters open their giant mouths; the vast steeple trembles with awful animation; the gargoyle seizes the fugitive's heel with his teeth. The victim shrieks and falls into the abyss of peaked roof below, bounding from carven projections, wheeling, turning, circling, ricochetting in the ghastly fall. There is no more intense fear than this fear of falling in nightmare, and the spectacle of the swaying ladder without the Cathedral steeple yesterday produced a wide-awake realization of that horrible fancy.

"Take a good drink of whisky," observed Weston, proffering a well filled flask; "it will give you nerve without producing giddiness, since you seem frightened."

Then Weston produced a thick leathern strap, and buckled it tightly about the reporter's waist, also fastening a strong harness strap under and over his right thigh. To these straps the end of a new rope was made fast, and one other end passed up the ladder to the loophole window, twenty-five feet above, where it was taken in and tied to a beam. Klein then ran up the ladder, which shuddered under him as though trying to shake him off and down on the stone steps of the façade below, and Weston endeavored to induce the reporter to follow. The latter was by that time in a shivering fit and on the point of backing down, when Depretz seized him by the thigh and pulled him outward, with a gruff "Confound you, come out or I'll pull you out!" Then he came out and went up the quivering ladder, feeling all the while as though the steeple were reeling.

On arriving at the cornice above, a strong rope stretched through the loophole window afforded an excellent handrail, when the ladder was pulled up, made fast to another cornice above, and the climbing operation repeated for another twenty-five feet. We then found ourselves perched on the narrow cornice at the base of the tall, bare peak, whence the flag was flying fifty feet further up. It may be worth while to mention here that all the party had encased their feet in India-rubber, which clings well to roughened stone, and facilitates the work of climbing. The ladder was left hanging to the cornice by its iron teeth for the descent.

Weston then clambered up the slope of the spire with the agility of a monkey, planting his feet against the stone and ascending the lightning-rod hand over hand. Arrived at the summit, he bestrode the cross, lowered a third rope, with which he hauled up a block-and-tackle and a larger rope, and made preparations for our ascent. The block-and-tackle was firmly bound over the arms of the cross, the large rope riven through it and fastened below around the reporter's chest, while the lighter rope was tied to the leathern belt about his loins, to serve as a stay-rope in case of accident. Then seizing the lightning-rod the work of ascent was rendered comparatively easy. Just below the cross there is a little cornice which affords a temporary foothold, and thence it was not difficult, with the aid of the lightning-rod, to climb into the arms of the cross, when the novice was tied to the lightning-rod itself. The northern arm of the cross served admirably for a footstool and the summit for a seat. It is cut octagonally, with facets upon the summit, converging cut-diamond style to a little point. The summit of the cross has a surface equivalent to about two feet square.

Fear gradually passed off while thus seated, and it was possible to turn and look in any direction over the city. From the great height, two hundred and twenty-five feet, every portion of the city encircled by the hills was distinctly visible. The City Buildings and the surrounding edifices seemed dwarfed to toy-houses; the circular fountain-basin of the City Park seemed like a ring of muddy water at the foot of the Cathedral; the summits of the synagogue's minarets were visible below; in every direction the city lay out in regular squares like an elaborate map. For three or four blocks, north, south, east and west, the centers of thoroughfares were distinctly visible, with wagon-teams, buggies and carriages straggling along, apparently no larger than flies. The crowds below, with faces upturned to the cross, were liliputians; even with a small opera glass it was difficult to distinguish faces. All the Plum street canal bridges from the elbow eastward, were plainly visible; Mill Creek shimmered with a golden gleam in the west, and the Ohio curved in blue serpentine in the south. We seemed to stand above the city smoke and the evening mists; sounds from below came faintly to the ear, like echoes of another world; the tone of the giant clock below striking the chimes and the hour of five, were weird and thin; the least whisper was audible; the sky seemed nearer, and the ripple of fleecy clouds, coming up from the west, in white breaker lines against the sea of azure, seemed purer and clearer than ordinary. From our eminence it was impossible to obtain, by looking down, any accurate idea of the prodigious height—the foreshortening of the spire, to the last cornice we had left, gave it the appearance of being but ten or twelve feet high.

"Suppose," we horrifically observed, "that the cross should give way, and fall down!"

"See!" replied Weston, giving the summit a violent shake with both hands—"she rocks!"

It was true; the cross trembled and shuddered an instant, and then gave four distinct rocks—earthquake tremblings they seemed to us. Another shake caused it to rock still more violently, and shook us in our seats.

"For God's sake," we frantically yelled, "stop!"

"It's perfectly safe," observed Weston, apologetically. "I rocked it just to show you that it was safe. If it didn't rock it would be out of plumb. All properly built stone spires rock, and wooden spires rock horribly."

"Suppose," we again suggested," that the steeple should take fire below us!"

"Then I should run down the lightning rod and carry you on my back."

"Besides," observed Klein, "the steeple is as solid as the everlasting hills. The fire might burn out the wooden shell within, but the heat would escape through the windows, and we could get to the windward side of the cross, you know."

The flags and wreaths were carefully detached, and the copper-barbed top of the lightning rod, which had been removed for the decorations, was replaced in its socket. Then Weston took a small flag and threw it down. It was awful to watch its descent. It flew and flew in circles, described somersaults, trembled, collapsed, extended, and finally, after many seconds, flattened out on the roof.

"I want you to stand up on the top of the cross, right on the top," exclaimed Weston, commencing to detach the cords which held the reporter to the lightning-rod. His indifference to danger inspired the visitor with sufficient confidence to perform the feat, and extend his arms for an instant 225 feet above *terra firma*. Suddenly the reporter caught sight of something that caused him to clutch the lightning-rod convulsively and sit down. Weston's braces were adorned with great brazen buckles, which bore in ghastly bas-relief the outlines of a skull and crossbones.

"What on earth do you wear such ill-omened things for?" we asked.

"Oh," replied he, laughing and dancing on the northern arm of the cross, "I thought I'd get smashed up some day, and took a fancy to these suspenders, as they serve to remind me of my probable fate. You seem to believe in omens. Well, I tell you I never like to do climbing on Friday, although I know it's all foolishness."

After inspecting the initials of the climbers cut into the summit of the cross, we performed a descent which seemed far easier than the ascent. As we re-entered the belfry the clock boomed out six times, and the "Angelus" chimed in measured strokes of deeply vibrating music from the big bell. The mists climbed higher as the sun commenced to sink in a glory of mingled gold and purple, and a long streamer of ruby light flamed over the western hills. "That is a lovely view," exclaimed Weston, "but I think it is not so fine as the bird's eye view of the city by night, sparkling with ten thousand lights. You must come up on the cross some fine night with me."

The reporter shivered and departed.

Part II

"ENORMOUS AND LURID FACTS":
LANGUAGE, FOLKLIFE, AND CULTURE

12

CHEEK

There is a picturesque force of laconic expressiveness about certain American slang-terms which has brought them into familiar use even among persons who ordinarily eschew slang in common conversation. Such a term is "cheek." Cheek comprises in one syllable all that is usually expressed in such words as assurance, self confidence, impudence and insolence, the significance of cheek, largely depending on the context. For example, if we say that it is necessary to have some cheek in order to get along in the world, we mean self-confidence. But if we observe that a certain person has "more cheek than a brass monkey" or "a government mule," we mean that he is impertinent to an astonishing degree, and has little or no regard for the feelings of his fellow-men. What we propose to consider, however, is what part does cheek play in success. It would be folly to generalize cheek in the person of any one type of cheekiness; for they are multitudinous and varied. But cheek, as the opposite of timid delicacy, may be considered in a general way through its effects.

A timid man, however talented, has a poor chance in a race with a shrewd and cheeky man, of infinitely less ability. The former may catch up in time when the momentum which cheek has given his rival begins to die out; the timid man may be sometimes the winning tortoise. But his tendency to underestimate himself, his comparative ignorance of the world, and his dread of appearing rude or uncultivated—all these causes—in fact, which tend to produce his timidity, are very hurtful to his chances of success in life. The world usually regards timidity an indication of incapability; and there must be some general truth at the bottom of such a tendency. The cheeky man, even after he has been discovered to have too much self-confidence, usually manages to keep ahead. Moreover, he learns rapidly as he goes, and his faith in his own capacity aids him marvellously well. He forces a way for himself while others beg and plead for it. He considers himself as good a man as any other upon the face of the earth; and this democratic spirit enables him to bring himself directly in contact with men from whom the timid shrink with dismay in consequence of their comparative weakness. Moreover he can adapt himself to any society, and familiarize himself with people whom delicate persons dread to meet. He resents an insult quickly, relies much upon his physical vigor and, to use his own expression, "knows how to take care of himself." He compels persons to listen to him who hate to see him, and obliges people who inwardly despise him to respect him outwardly. And if he be really a sharp and shrewd type of this class, when you ask him how he gets along so well in the world, he will answer,—"My dear fellow, it is very simple. I have plenty of cheek; and I know the value of it, and how to use it to the best advantage." But suppose the enquirer goes further, and asks, "What is cheek? what causes it? how can it be acquired?"—then the answer would probably be,—"Cheek is confidence in one's self, courage, impudence, power to adopt one's self to all circumstances; you may not acquire it, although you may repress your rational timidity in time to a great extent; you must be born with cheek to be cheeky," or words to that effect.

Then, what does cheek in the best sense depend on? It depends upon physical vigor to a great extent. It is the self-confidence inspired by perfect health and natural energy which must be inherited to possess. Broad shoulders and strong muscles, a loud and dominating voice, a big beard, a fearless eye, a carriage that seems to suggest the belief, "I am as good as the next man, and fear no one,"—these will do more to help a man along in life than much learning and wisdom. The race to the strongest!—the survival of the fittest! This is why the world regards timid men with suspicion. There is nothing about them which imposes and forces itself upon the spectator,—no strong physical individuality,—no violent magnetism of voice and eye,—none of that bodily power which compels reluctant attention and imposes a respect like that we give to certain fierce animals we dare not refuse to caress lest they should become angry.

A little illustration from newspaper life. Some years ago a certain newspaper circle in one of the Eastern cities opened to admit a new reporter. He was a man of forty years of age, weighed about two hundred pounds, had a great brown beard, an aquiline face, and large grey eyes. He had had far less experience than any of his comrades, was partly deaf, spoke in a low voice, and was an inferior writer; but it was soon found that he had no equal as a newsgatherer. With the same chances as the rest he obtained news no one could procure, interviewed parties who had refused to see any other newspaper men,—even the cheekiest,—got full particulars of secret sessions of municipal bodies which nobody else could get,—fathomed mysteries which baffled the skill of the most experienced,—and universally secured more attention than his fellows. No one could understand his "good luck" as they called it at first, his "peculiar tact," as they styled it later on. He explained in this way; "You are all young men; I have the air of a middle-aged man; I have a ponderous aspect and a dignified look; I have big whiskers and a big beard. It has been my experience that people always pay more attention to what might be called "heavy-looking men" than to any others; and I rely largely upon that fact." This was not a case of cheek; but only a little illustration of what the physical advantages which self-confidence is generally based upon may accomplish in a calling which demands mental, not physical, superiority.

13

THE CREOLE PATOIS

——— ⊷⊰⊹⊱⊷ ———

I

Although the pure creole element is disappearing from the *Vié faubon,* as creole children called the antiquated part of New Orleans, it is there nevertheless that the patois survives as a current idiom; it is there one must dwell to hear it spoken in its purity, and to study its peculiarities of intonation and construction. The patois-speaking inhabitants—dwelling mostly in those portions of the quadrilateral farthest from the river and from the broad American boundary of Canal Street, which many of them never cross when they can help it— are not less *bizarre* than the architectural background of their picturesque existence. The visitor is surrounded by a life motley-colored as those fantastic populations described in the *Story of the Young King of the Black Isles;* the African ebon is least visible, but of bronze-browns, banana-yellows, orange-golds, there are endless varieties, paling off into faint lemon tints, and even dead-silver whites. The paler the shade, the more strongly do Latin characteristics show themselves; and the oval faces, with slender cheeks and low broad brows, prevail. Sometimes in the yellower types a curious Sphinx visage appears, dreamy as Egypt. Occasionally, also, one may encounter figures so lithe, so animal, as to recall the savage grace of Priou's *Satyress.* For the true colorist the contrast of a light saffron skin with dead-black hair and eyes of liquid jet has a novel charm, as of those descriptions in the Malay poem *Bidasari,* of "women like statues of gold." It is hard to persuade one's self that such types do not belong to one distinct race, the remnant of some ancient island tribe, and the sound of their richly vowelled creole speech might prolong the pleasant illusion.

It must not be supposed, however, that the creole dialect is the only one used by these people; there are few who do not converse fluently in the French and English languages, and to these acquirements many add a knowledge of the sibilant Mexican-Spanish. But creole is the maternal speech; it is the tongue in which the baby first learns to utter its thoughts; it is the language of family and of home. The white creole child learns it from the lips of his swarthy nurse; and creole adults still use it in speaking to servants or to their little ones. At a certain age the white boys or girls are trained to converse in French;

judicious petting, or even mild punishment, is given to enforce the use of the less facile but more polite medium of expression. But the young creole who remains in Louisiana seldom forgets the sweet patois, the foster-mother tongue, the household words which are lingual caresses.

Now the colored inhabitants of the *carré* regulate the use of the creole after the manners of their former masters, upon whose time-honored customs they base their little code of urbanity. Let us suppose you are dwelling in one of the curious and crumbling houses of the old quarter of the town, and that some evening while dreaming over a pipe as you rock your chair upon the gallery, the large-eyed children of the habitation gather about you, cooing one unto the other in creole like so many yellow doves. Invariably you will then hear the severe maternal admonition, "Allons, Marie! Eugène! faut pas parler créole devant monsieur; parlez Français, donc!" Creole must not be spoken in the presence of "monsieur"; he must be addressed in good French, the colonial French of Louisiana that has been so much softened by tropicalization.

The general purpose of these little sketches will not admit of any extended linguistic dissertation, otherwise it would be a pleasant task to follow the foot-prints of many philological harvesters, and glean something in fields where French, English, and American scholars have reaped so well. It would be interesting to trace back the origin of the creole to the earlier ages of Latin-American slave colonies, showing how the African serf softened and simplified the more difficult language of his masters, and made to himself the marvelous system of grammar in which philologists have found material for comparison with the tongue of Homer and the speech of Beowulf. But the writer's purpose is to reflect the spirit of existing things rather than to analyze the past, to sketch local peculiarities and reflect local color without treating broadly of causes. It will be sufficient, therefore, to state that the creole patois is the offspring of linguistic miscegenation, an offspring which exhibits but a very faint shade of African color, and nevertheless possesses a strangely supple comeliness by virtue of the very intercrossing which created it, like a beautiful octoroon.

That word reminds one of a celebrated and vanished type—never mirrored upon canvas, yet not less physically worthy of artistic preservation than those amber-tinted beauties glorified in the Oriental studies of Ingres, of Richter, of Gérôme! Uncommonly tall were those famous beauties—citrine-hued, elegant of stature as palmettos, lithe as serpents; never again will such types re-appear upon American soil. Daughters of luxury, artificial human growths, never organized to enter the iron struggle for life unassisted and unprotected, they vanish forever with the social system which made them a place apart as for splendid plants reared within a conservatory. With the fall of American feudalism the dainty glass house was dashed to pieces; the species it contained have perished utterly; and whatever morality may have gained, one cannot help thinking that art has lost something by their extinction. What figures for designs in bronze! what tints for canvas!

It is for similar reasons that the creole tongue must die in Louisiana; the great social change will eventually render it extinct. But there is yet time for the philologist to rescue some of its dying legends and curious lyrics, to collect and preserve them, like pressed blossoms, between the leaves of enduring books.

The creoles of the Antilles seem to have felt more pride in the linguistic curiosities of their native isles than the creoles of Louisiana have manifested regarding their own antiquities. In Trinidad fine collections of creole legends and proverbs have been made, and an excellent grammar of the dialect published; in Martinique, hymn books, *paroissiens,* and other works are printed in creole; the fables of La Fontaine and many popular French fairy tales have found creole translators in the West Indies, while several remarkable pamphlets upon the history and construction of the West Indian dialects are cited in Parisian catalogues of linguistic publications. But it was not until the French publishers of *Mélusine* showed themselves anxious to cull the flora of Louisiana creole that the creoles themselves made any attempt to collect them. Happily the romantic interest excited throughout the country by George Cable's works stimulated research to further exertion, and even provoked the creation of a Franco-Louisianian novel, written by a creole, and having a considerable portion of its text in patois. Nevertheless nothing has yet been attempted in Louisiana comparable with the labors of MM. Luzel and Sébillot in Bretagne; no systematic efforts have been made to collect and preserve the rich oral literature of the creole parishes.

The inedited creole literature comprises songs, satires in rhyme, proverbs, fairy tales—almost everything commonly included under the term *folklore.* The lyrical portion of it is opulent in oddities, in melancholy beauties; Alphonse Daudet has frequently borrowed therefrom, using creole refrains in his novels with admirable effect.

Some of the popular songs possess a unique and almost weird pathos; there is a strange naïve sorrow in their burdens, as of children sobbing for lonesomeness in the night. Others, on the contrary, are inimitably comical. There are many ditties or ballads devoted to episodes of old plantation life, to surreptitious frolic, to description of singular industries and callings, to commemoration of events which had strongly impressed the vivid imagination of negroes—a circus show, an unexpected holiday, the visit of a beautiful stranger to the planter's home, or even some one of those incidents indelibly marked with a crimson spatter upon the fierce history of Louisiana politics.

II

One finds among the creole literature many charming apocrypha—popular love songs far too perfect in arrangement and versification to have been created by the uneducated and simple race which invented the creole idiom. The true creole poetry—the slave poetry improvised according to African methods—manifests its origin by the quaint construction of its stanzas, by the simplicity of its images, above all by the systematized reiteration of sonorous phrases, by a recurrent motive like that of Gottschalk's *Bamboula:*

> "Foulard *rivé*
>   *Moin té toujours tini;*
> Madras *rivé,*
>   *Moin té toujours tini;*
> Des Indes *rivé,*
>   *Moin té toujours tini;*
> Capitaine second
>   Cé yon bon gaçon . . .

> *"Tout moune tini,*
>   *Tout moune* yo aimé;
> *Tout moune tini,*
>   *Tout moune* yo chéri,
> *Tout moune tini,*
>   Yo Doudou à yo;
> Tousse moin tout seule,
>   Pas tini cila moin."

This is Guadaloupe, not Louisiana, creole, and is cited only because the writer has not at hand any specimen of the Louisiana creole ditty which offers an equally forcible example of the reiteration of phrases. Whenever in Louisiana creole one finds a poem in which there is no recurrent motive or motives, it is tolerably certain that no colored man composed it. As a specimen of evidently apocryphal creole I may quote a stanza of the song *Dipé mo 'oir toi, Adèle,* which has been set to music:

> "Quan' mo pas 'oir toi, Adéle,
>   Mo senti m'apé mouri;
> Mo vini comme ein chandelle
>   Qui apé allé fini;

Mo pas 'oir rien su la terre
    Qui capab dans la rivière
Mo capab dans la rivière
    Tété moin pou' pas souffrir."

It will be observed that in each of the quatrains composing the above eight-line stanza the first line rhymes with the third, and the second with the fourth. In true creole poetry such versification is scarcely ever found, although a far simpler form of rhyme is occasionally used. The recurrent motive or theme may change its position with every stanza; it may begin one line and terminate the next; it may disappear and reappear at irregular intervals, like a serpent crawling through a cotton patch, yet it is never totally absent. Veritable creole ballads are usually constructed of very slender material; they contain comparatively few images; but these images are as oddly combined and alternated as the patchwork upon an old-fashioned country bed-quilt:

"Belle Amerikaine,
    Mo l'aimin toi!
Belle femme,
    Mo l'aimin toi!

"M'allé à l'Havane
Pou coupé canne—
Pou bail toi l'arzan,
    Belle Amerikaine!
M'allé à l'Havane, zamie,
Pou coupé canne, zamie,
Pou bail toi l'arzan,
    Belle Amerikaine!
        Cézaire,
    Mo, l'aimin toi!
        Belle femme
    Mo l'aimin toi!" etc.

A popular creole ditty this, with a beautiful melancholy air, yet there is little in it save a reiterated declaration of love for the beautiful "American" *Cézaire* (probably an English-speaking colored stranger), and a promise to cut sugarcane in Havana, so as to earn money for her. Among the older creole ballads a complete versified narrative may sometimes be found, but not often; the ditty usually presents a series of random fancies, connected only by the recurrent motive spun athwart them. Many of these melodious curiosities must have been lost, for we find numberless refrains wandering about like spirits disembodied, mournful witnesses to the existence of important ballads which have passed away forever. Analysis of these broken remnants often reveals some purely African elements. Old colored folk who remember how to dance the *Congo* and the *Calinda* still chant African choruses, but without knowing the meaning of the words. That such words should be remembered at all is probably due to the influence of fetich beliefs—to faith in the virtue of syllables muttered by Voudoo sorcerers in former times.

The animal fables are worthy of serious attention; they are full of grotesque humor, vivid fancy, and they offer the best material for study of the idiom. Furthermore, they are very rich in household sayings and original proverbs worthy of conservation. Another interesting portion of creole literature is purely satirical, intensely acute, but never positively violent. Among unpublished collections already made in New Orleans, I have seen compositions in which various high and mighty personages of the old *régime* were lampooned with singular audacity, as though creole Louisiana had its periodical Saturnalia, when, as during the Roman festival, slaves might mock their masters *ad libitum.*

The apocryphal creole lyrics—the imitations of the slave songs by native *literati*—are distinguishable from the negro compositions, and possess less chrestomathic value, just as all the Spanish imitations of the *seguiriyas jitanas* are not worth one true gypsy ballad. Still, this *white* creole literature is not without intrinsic beauty, and in several of its best compositions set to music we find odd bits of negro creole occasionally preserved, like rare black pearls beaded with white ones. It is also to be observed that educated masters of the slave idiom have made capital translations into it from other languages, or taken down from dictation by former servants many admirable recitals, legends, ballads. Writing in creole for amusement is less frequent now than it was some years ago, when *Le Carillon* came out weekly with three fourths of its columns in patois. The files of the dead periodical are philologic curiosities, and within them may be found many creole antiquities preserved, like ephemerides in amber. Even lately articles or letters in creole sometimes appear in those extraordinary parish papers printed in French without and in English within. The last creole satire published in *L'Abeille de la Nouvelle-Orléans* was a metrical contribution ridiculing an unpopular sanitarian during the epidemic of 1878.

Among the colored population of the old quarter the creole survives like some plant that has almost ceased to flower, though the green has not yet departed from its leaves. One can find many scattered petals of folklore, few entire blossoms. Education is slowly but surely stifling the idiom. The later colored generation is proud of its correct French and its public-school English, and one must now seek out the older inhabitants of the carré in order to hear the songs of other days, or the fables which delighted the children of the old *régime*. Happily all the "colored creoles" are not insensible to the charm of their maternal dialect, nor abashed when the invading *Amerikain* superciliously terms it "Gombo." There are mothers who still teach their children the old songs—heirlooms of melody resonant with fetich words—threads of tune strung with *grigris* from the Ivory Coast. So likewise, we need not doubt, are transmitted the secrets of that curious natural pharmacy in which the colored nurses of Louisiana have manifested astounding skill—the secret of fragrant herb medicines which quench the fires of swamp fever, the secret of miraculous cataplasms which relieve congestions, the secret odorous *tisanes* which restore vigor to torpid nerves—perhaps also the composition of those love philters hinted at in creole ballads, and the deadly *ouanga* art as bequeathed to modern Voudooism by the black Locustas of the eighteenth century.

14

THE CREOLE DOCTOR

Some Curiosities of Medicine in Louisiana

The Northerner who decides to settle in New Orleans will find after the experience of a few summers in the Louisiana climate that he has become more or less physiologically changed by the struggle of his system with those novel atmospheric conditions to which it was obliged to adapt itself. According to the constitutional peculiarities of the individual, the effects of acclimatization may vary—while some persons suffer considerably, others endure very little positive discomfort; but all are subjected to a certain physical transformation. A rosy complexion invariably fades out; the blood partly loses its plasticity, as the proportion of red corpuscles greatly diminishes; and susceptibility to changes of heat and cold becomes singularly intensified. For Southern Louisiana is an especially pyrogenic region; the conditions are febrile; the general aspect of the healthiest natives is that of convalescents as compared with the ruddy look of Northern people; and the well-known ivorine pallor of the Creole suggests to inexperienced eyes a recent attack of malaria. The changes in the blood accompanying acclimatization necessarily involve corresponding changes in regard to diet and habits of life; but while the appetite may be maintained by the use of acidulated drinks, or such gentle stimulants as claret-and-water, one's capacity for intense or prolonged exertion steadily diminishes, and finally passes away. Nothing resembling the electrical vim—the almost furious energy—of the Northwestern American will endure under this sun, and yet the physical languor which supervenes may be eventually compensated by increased capacity for rapid mental work.

During this process of enervation the stranger is peculiarly liable to fever, and of fevers (which in epidemic years, all seem to lose their special characteristics and to interblend with the dominant evil) there is a surprising variety. Some, like the *dengue,* seem to bray the muscles as with fingers of iron; in others, the victim may shiver with cold under the heat of a July sun—there are different kinds of remittent, intermittent and other malarial affections which are easy of treatment, and slow torpid fevers which scorn the power of quinine and so sap the nervous energy as to leave the victim prostrate for months. The acclimated citizen rarely suffers from these maladies; but woe to the incautious and energetic stranger who attempts to live in this sub-tropical and pyrogenic region, indifferent to the danger of excessive fatigue, or the perils of self-exposure to sudden changes of temperature!

Even in view of the fact that the city is but a few feet above the level of the sea, and to a large extent below that of the river, the humidity of the air is remarkable. Unless constructed with a precaution inspired by thorough knowledge of atmospheric conditions, brick houses are apt to prove damp and undesirable residences. Frame buildings are much more healthy, being little affected by those sudden changes of temperature which often represent more than thirty degrees in twenty-four hours, and will cause a cold sweat to start from every square inch of a hastily built brick dwelling. It is not easy to accustom one's self to these atmospheric variations; even the natives suffer from the irregularities of heat and cold; and if there be any specially Creole disease, it is consumption. Flannel underwear becomes a necessity of life in this region of border warfare between the winds of the North and the winds of the tropics. It is not, however, until the blood has been thinned and the recuperative vitality lessened by the first summer's sojourn that the settler in Louisiana finds the South also has its winter—snowless here, but severe on those particularly sensitive to dampness, for the humid chill seems to penetrate to the bones. Even the cool nights of fall and spring have breezes that seem to blow from a region of thawing snows.

That the thermometer in Southern Louisiana rarely mounts so high during the torrid months as it does in the Northwestern or Northeastern States is sometimes appealed to as an evidence that our summers are less oppressive. But this inference is erroneous. A heat of 85° or 90° here is more difficult to endure than much higher temperatures in dryer air; for the moist atmosphere sometimes has the weight of the vapor-laden air of a Russian bath. Any protracted elevation of the temperature to the figure 100° in the shade would prove fatal here to hundreds, and if sunstrokes are less common in New Orleans than elsewhere, it must be remembered that summer is a "dead season" here, that there is comparatively little work done in the sun, and that all who can comfortably afford it leave the city. Our summer nights are cooler than in the North, but not really more refreshing,—for the coolness is a humid one, the coolness of heavy dews and sometimes of miasmal emanations—signalled in spring and fall by visible white vapors. Much of the unhealthiness of the night air has been attributed to the ubiquitous Spanish moss (*tillandsia nenenoides*) which lends such phantasmal beauty to the Louisianian and Floridian woods—an aspect as of some vast and mysterious mourning for vanished gods—but which really absorbs ozone in quantities so enormous as to affect the atmosphere.

Other singular facts connected with the climatic conditions in Southern Louisiana might be cited; but enough has been already stated to show that the question of salubrity or insalubrity of the region for strangers can be fully answered by no one who has not passed through the experiences of thorough acclimatization, involving sundry constitutional changes. It was during my own struggles with such novel conditions of climate that I first became interested in the subject of Creole medicine—a natural art rapidly becoming obsolete—whose traditions have never been collected, much less published, and whose secrets are being buried every year with some one belonging to the old French-speaking generations of colored nurses and domestics.

Every people possesses its particular domestic medicines; and many of the best domestic remedies for trifling ailments are common to all civilized countries; but where the conditions of life and climate are more or less exceptional, home-medicines are proportionately peculiar. It is this fact which lends some real importance to the study of Creole medicine; and it is worthy of remark that in the old slave-days physicians were far less often summoned to prescribe for trifling ailments, inasmuch as every household was skilled in the use of remedies at once natural and simple. How the knowledge of these was first acquired I cannot pretend to explain; but it is not unreasonable to believe that in many cases the African slave was able to teach his master. Any one who attempts to study the evolution of Creole negro folklore, negro patois, negro melody, or those strange practices generally classed under the name Voudooism might certainly gather many valuable facts by personal observation alone; but the true significance of much that was singular in the old slave-life can only be fully understood by those who have studied Africa profoundly. It is to men like General Faidherbe or Berenger-Ferand or Boilat—it is especially to ethnological authorities upon the subject of West African races and their customs—that we must look for the proper explanation of many mysteries regarding the beliefs and the folklore of American slaves; nor can one hope without some knowledge of the anthropology of those regions that furnished black laborers to our cane and cotton-fields to attempt a thoroughly trustworthy history of what is called Creole medicine.

My own experiences have not enabled me to make any noteworthy observations of the more purely African features of this somewhat occult art; but they enabled me to know the real skill of colored nurses in dealing with local fevers and other ailments of a less serious character. Among several curious remedies for which I had to thank these mysterious people I will cite only two. The first was a cure for bilious fever—which cure was brought to me in a small earthenware jug, piping hot. It was a drink which had a reddish color, an agreeable odor, and an unpleasantly bitter taste. I was told to let the fluid cool before drinking, and not to be frightened at the results, which proved alarming, for dizziness and difficulty of breathing were among them. But the draught restored me to complete health; and I may say that I even felt unusually well for several months subsequently. I wanted to obtain the recipe from the negress who prepared the medicine; but this, to my surprise, she refused to given even in exchange for what I believed to be a rather handsome remuneration. Furthermore she declared the medicine was *bien dangereuse,* that I could not use it without instructions, and that I could not find "the plant." I knew there were at least four ingredients in the preparation; but the color and odor, at least, were not due to any very unfamiliar simples.

The second remedy was a very simple one for inflammation or congestion of the eyes; and was told me by an old colored woman who had the reputation of being a Voudoo, but whom I never suspected of belonging to that confraternity. She was able to comprehend the interest I felt in Creole folklore, and collected for me a number of little songs and proverbs in the patois. Her recipe was this: "Take a fresh Creole egg [egg laid in Louisiana]; separate the yolk carefully from the white, and then beat up the white into a light, fine foam. Then take a strip of cotton or linen about six or eight inches wide; fold up the egg-foam in it so as to form a cataplasm wide enough to cover both eyes, and go to bed with the cataplasm well attached by knotting the ends of the linen or cotton folds about the head." This simple egg poultice, thus left to dry upon the eyes, proved in my case remarkably efficacious, although I cannot imagine that there is any special virtue in albumen. I must also state that I recommended the cataplasm with good results in instances where hot or cold compresses had failed, for some reason or other, to reduce inflammation.

The reluctance of the negress who prepared me the potion above referred to, either to sell or give away the secret, I found to be shared by most of the colored people from whom I attempted to procure the same kind of information. It is really only the Creole gentleman or lady, accustomed to command this class, and habituated to their habits and beliefs, who can obtain their absolute confidence in such matters. The greater number of the recipes cited in this article I could not have obtained but for the aid of Creole friends; and I am especially indebted to a scholarly Spanish physician, Dr. Rodolfo Matas, now president of the New Orleans Medical Association, for many valuable facts and suggestions. He called my attention to the fact that a patient scientific inquirer might discover under the fantastic surface of Creole empiricism material of larger medical importance than that which formed the pharmacopeia of those old Arabian pharmacists and practitioners whose treatises have only been carefully studied by Europeans within the last few years. Of course such investigations would demand an uncommon knowledge of sub-tropical flora, and years of practical study in Louisiana and the Antilles. Many prescriptions given to me I find it impossible to utilize for this article, simply because the names of the herbs are given in Creole or in African terms only, for which I can find no English or scientific equivalent.

As my Spanish friend pointed out to me, the whole of this empirical home-medicine may be classed under three heads: 1. Simples, or vegetable remedies; 2. Remedies into whose preparation animal substances enter; 3. Imaginative medicine, consisting less in actual curative methods than in prac-tices, semi-religious and semi-superstitious—the Magic of the Blacks, African in its origin, yet queerly blended with ideas borrowed from Catholicism and distorted grotesquely in the borrowing. This last division deserves attention in a special article; and I cannot attempt to treat it in the present essay. Of the other divisions, the first is far larger and more hygienically interesting; it is much more extensive than the samples I am able to cite can give any idea of, and to do it justice would require an exhaustive knowledge of Louisiana botany, especially a knowledge of our swamp plants.

Tisanes, or those preparations classified by our Creoles under the gen-eral name of teas (*thés*),—being infusions of medicinal herbs obtained by boiling the leaves,—occupy a larger place in Creole medicine than do the tisanes recognized by English or American pharmaceutical science as worthy of clas-sification in dispensatories. There are hundreds of them. Some are too famil-iar to need more than an allusion,—such as the orange leaf, lemon leaf and sassafras teas. *"Mo pas boi dithe pou fieve li"* ("I'm not going to drink tea for his fever"), is a Creole proverb referring, not to tea proper, which is not a favorite beverage with our native French-speaking population, but to those warm herb infusions administered in fever. The following recipes are among the most interesting in the little collection I have been able to make of Creole medicine belonging to the first and second divisions of the subject.

Chills and Fever—For this familiar disorder several queer tisanes are recommended: 1. Tea prepared with the leaves of the pimento (pepper plant); 2. thick black coffee mingled with fresh lemon-juice to be taken three times a day; 3. snake-root (*serpen-taria*) in whiskey—I do not know how strong the infusion is made; 4. tea made from the leaves of the *"cirier-batard"* (*Myrica gale*), a small cupful to be swallowed three times a day. In addition to these hot drinks, alternated sometimes with draughts of claret or spiced beer, well heated, the patient may be ordered to put cay-enne pepper in his shoes every day for nine days. In the absence of quinine or other recognized febrifuges, some of the above remedies are not to be scoffed at. The plant called by our Creoles the *cirier batard* has, moreover, been utilized in various ways by regular medical science, owning to its astringent qualities. Its aromatic properties are said to have a purifying effect upon the air of the swamps which it loves. In North America its geographical range extends from Louisiana to Greenland. The roots of the *Myrica* contain so much tannin that they can be utilized with great success in the manufacture of ink.

But the most interesting fact contained in the above samples of empiricism is the mention of lemon-juice. Lemon-juice as a remedy for certain forms of fever was known to the Creoles long before Tomasso Crudelli discovered the reason of its value, and advocated its use in the marasmal regions of Italy. Only at the last meeting of the International Medical Congress held in Copenhagen, the discoverer of the *bacillus malarii* strongly recommended the planting of malarial regions with lemon trees, and addressed the learned body with much success on the merits of lemon-juice as a febrifuge.

Coffee, considered a febrifuge in the domestic medicine of most hot countries, is administered largely in typhoid fever; but the infusion is made with the green berries in whiskey, a dose three times a day. To alleviate the cerebral symptoms, a live pigeon is cut open and the warm, bleeding surfaces applied to the head.

Leaves of the lettuce (*lactucarium*) are boiled to form a tea, said to be very efficient in cases of sleeplessness. This lettuce-leaf tea is administered in large quantities before going to bed.

Geranium-leaf tea, a delightfully fragrant beverage, is frequently given as a remedy for nausea. The interior of a fowl's gizzard, boiled with tea, is also recommended.

A cold in the head is treated in many ways, and also has its own special tisane,—a sort of celery-leaf tea. The tea is sweetened with honey, and a few drops of paregoric are usually added. Among other remedies I may mention doses of castor oil warmed with molasses; also roasted onions, with molasses and butter, to be swallowed before retiring; and finally, a gargle made with olive oil, honey, vinegar and a little paregoric.

Boiled leaves of the honeysuckle are said to make an excellent gargle for sore throat. Parsley-leaves in vinegar are also used exteriorly. Another exterior application consists of a white onion roasted in the embers, then cut in half, and each half applied to the neck until cold. This operation is repeated three times each night.

The honeysuckle (*Lonicera caprifolium*) is known to medical practice. The expressed juice of the plant has long been recommended as a remedy for the stings of bees or wasps,—to be rubbed into the puncture. The fruits of all the varieties are said to be emetic and cathartic; and some varieties have been used by physicians in practice. The variety called *periclymenum* has been used in France as a gargle. Is this bit of Creole medicine a colonial inheritance from the mother country?

There are other local remedies for sore throat, of a character altogether too mediaeval to allow of their being mentioned in print. I doubt, however, if these are Creole; for I have heard of similar medicine among the peasantry of Europe.

Indigestion introduces us to another tea, very fragrant and soothing, made from bay leaves and leaves of the mint-plant. A little whiskey is usually added. Sugar water is also recommended.

Melonseed tea is given in jaundice, and also in several other forms of disease. But the great remedy is carrot-juice; the carrots are first scraped, then squeezed through muslin. A cup of this juice is believed to be efficacious in the extreme.

For tetanus cockroach tea is given. I do not know how many cockroaches go to make up the cup; but I find that faith in this remedy is strong among many of the American population of New Orleans. A poultice of boiled cockroaches is placed over the wound. In Louisiana this insect (*Blatta Orientalis*) grows to a positively amazing size; and a very few would make quite a large plaster. Oil of copaiba is also recommended to rub the body with in case of tetanus; but there is nothing especially Creole in the use of the latter remedy. Powdered sulphur, salt, and tallow are likewise used as a mixture to rub the person with; and cockroaches fried in oil with garlic for indigestion.

An immense variety of remedies for diarrhoea are known in Creole medicine; I will name only a few. Tea made with an infusion of pecan husks, pecan bark and the leaves of the pecan tree steeped in whiskey are very popular. This is doubtless due to the astringent quality of the pecan, rich in tannin. Another remedy consists in a hot drink made by roasting rice, and subsequently pouring boiling water on the grains. Hot water in which toast has been steeped is also given. Flaxseed tea, administered in so many ailments, is recommended likewise. Hot tea made with dandelions is said to be another efficacious cure. Milk and starch intermingled are often taken; also eggshells ground or powdered, and drunk in water. Finally the banana fruit (used otherwise in a hundred ways by our motley population) is advocated as possessing excellent curative properties. The fruit should be plucked or selected green, cut into thin slices, placed in a vessel, softened to a pap by having boiling tea poured upon it, and then absorbed.

As remedies for palpitation of the heart there are other extraordinary "teas." One, to be drunk morning and evening, is made by boiling parsley-root. Another is made with asparagus. A third is prepared with wild sage, "golden rod" (*solidago odorata*), and a plant called *l'herve à chevreuil* by Creoles, which I cannot at present obtain the botanical name of. This must be taken three times a day.

There is also a tea for rheumatism made from the leaves of the plant called by the Creoles *chou-gras*. An infusion of the berries of the same herb in whiskey is used to rub the afflicted part with. This herb is neither more nor less than the common pokeberry (*phytolacca decandra*).

Chillblains are not altogether uncommon in Louisiana, where the frosts are light and cold "spells" have rarely a duration of more than three days. Lemon-juice is used to rub the place with. There are several decidedly original remedies for other ailments of the feet. For cold feet it is recommended that the members be wrapped in newspapers and the socks or stockings pulled on over the paper. This is also said to prevent cramps. For sore feet foot-baths of salt (rock salt) and water, or lye and water, or hot water poured over fresh mint-leaves or elder-leaves, are administered.

There are Creole remedies for headache, which by reason of their savage simplicity seem worthy of an African origin. These chiefly consist in applications to the forehead, temples or head of fresh leaves, which are changed as soon as the leaf begins to dry or wrinkle up. Leaves of the wild plantain are very popular for this method of cure; fig-leaves, elder-leaves and orange-leaves are also used. But the orange-leaf is usually smeared with lard before being applied. Another remedy is to pour a little hot water, mixed with laudanum, into the ear. Wild plantain-leaves, dipped in cold water, are very often used to allay inflammation of the eyes, when the fresh skin of a certain fish, or the excellent egg poultice, is not immediately procurable.

In swelling of the glands of the throat the swollen gland should be well rubbed with tallow; and the tallow smeared on thoroughly melted by holding close to the skin, without actually touching it, the blade of a knife heated in the flame of a lamp or candle. Some say the point of the heated blade only should approach the skin, and that the point should be moved so as to describe a cross immediately over the gland. This seems to be a purely superstitious idea.

In erysipelas a poultice of almond-leaves and rice flour is generally applied to the sore. Almond-leaves, it may be observed, are also considered to possess special virtue and healing qualities in relation to affections of the eyes.

For overheating of the blood,—an imaginary disorder,—tea made with the leaves of wild chicory is recommended, but tea made with the leaves of the *patate de Guinée* (potato vine) or leaves of a plant called *hooli* may be substituted. Somebody told me that *hooli*, or, as he termed it, *ahouli*, took its name from the Spanish *alheli* or alete, a corruption of the Arabic *al-khaili*, "the gilly-flower." But I am inclined to suspect an African origin for the word; moreover, the *hooli* shown me strongly resembles the plantain, having a large fleshy leaf, which when steeped in water makes the liquid ropy by reason of some viscid secretion. I must leave botanists to decide the scientific appellation of this, as well as of several other queer plants, one of which, bearing a little blue flower, is used to make a tea said to allay nervousness.

A favorite medicament for teething is furnished by the *chien dent*,—dog's grass, quitch grass or couch grass (*triticum repens*),— which grows wild on many of our New Orleans sidewalks or *banquettes*. An infusion of the leaves is used to rub the infant's gums with.

There is a very funny remedy for earache which is popular among the most ignorant classes of French-speaking colored people, and perhaps among many equally ignorant whites. Of course the familiar plug of wool or cotton steeped in laudanum is in vogue here as well as everywhere else; but a much more efficacious remedy is alleged to be a plug of *laine-de-negre* poked into the ear. And the oddest idea connected with the practice is that the wool in question must not be asked for, but must be snipped off the owner's head surreptitiously, in order to render it efficacious. When duly stolen, and moistened with laudanum, the wool never fails to cure!

These recipes may serve to convey some idea of the nature and variety of Creole medicine, a subject much larger, however, than this essay can justly indicate, and including much that must be left to the ethnologist and the folklorist to properly utilize. Probably Angelo de Gubernatis might find in Creole medicine-lore some new material for his *Mythologie des Plantes;* but this material belongs to a class of the theme which I cannot at present attempt to touch. It has a special interest only to folklorists and those who have the leisure and the opportunity to study the question of African survivals in the West Indies and America. On the other hand, the herb medicine of the Creoles deserves some scientific attention. So far as my limited observation enables me to judge, the most valuable part of Creole medicine has been developed by climatic necessities. Febrifuges, indeed, form the most important portion of this domestic medicine; and the art of preparing these, as well as various sudorifics and diet-drinks, seems to have been evolved by an experience not without serious value.

Finally, let me request the reader to observe that I have used the word "Creole" only in its popular sense,—just as we used to say in slave days, a "Creole negro," or as we say to-day, a "Creole egg." Many of these prescriptions and ideas are of negro origin; and but few of them are now ever used by the educated French-speaking people of Louisiana, with the exception of certain tisanes the medical value of which has been latterly recognized by physicians.

15

THE LAST OF THE VOUDOOS

In the death of Jean Montanet, at the age of nearly a hundred years, New Orleans lost, at the end of August, the most extraordinary African character that ever gained celebrity within her limits. Jean Montanet, or Jean La Ficelle, or Jean Latanié, or Jean Racine, or Jean Grisgris, or Jean Macaque, or Jean Bayou, or "Voudoo John," or "Bayou John," or "Doctor John" might well have been termed "The Last of the Voudoos"; not that the strange association with which he was affiliated has ceased to exist with his death, but that he was the last really important figure of a long line of wizards or witches whose African titles were recognized, and who exercised an influence over the colored population. Swarthy occultists will doubtless continue to elect their "queens" and high-priests through years to come, but the influence of the public school is gradually dissipating all faith in witchcraft, and no black hierophant now remains capable of manifesting such mystic knowledge or of inspiring such respect as Voudoo John exhibited and compelled. There will never be another "Rose," another "Marie," much less another Jean Bayou.

It may reasonably be doubted whether any other negro of African birth who lived in the South had a more extraordinary career than that of Jean Montanet. He was a native of Senegal, and claimed to have been a prince's son, in proof of which he was wont to call attention to a number of parallel scars on his cheek, extending in curves from the edge of either temple to the corner of the lips. This fact seems to me partly confirmatory of his statement, as Berenger-Feraud dwells at some length on the fact that the Bambaras, who are probably the finest negro race in Senegal, all wear such disfigurations. The scars are made by gashing the cheeks during infancy, and are considered a sign of race. Three parallel scars mark the freemen of the tribe; four distinguish their captives or slaves. Now Jean's face had, I am told, three scars, which would prove him a free-born Bambara, or at least a member of some free tribe allied to the Bambaras, and living upon their territory. At all events, Jean possessed physical characteristic answering to those by which the French ethnologist in Senegal distinguish the Bambaras. He was of middle height, very strongly built, with broad shoulders, well-developed muscles, an inky black skin, retreating forehead, small bright eyes, a very flat nose, and a woolly beard, gray only during the last few years of his long life. He had a resonant voice and a very authoritative manner.

At an early age he was kidnapped by Spanish slavers, who sold him at some Spanish port, whence he was ultimately shipped to Cuba. His West-Indian master taught him to be an excellent cook, ultimately became attached to him, and made him a present of his freedom. Jean soon afterward engaged on some Spanish vessel as ship's cook, and in the exercise of this calling voyaged considerably in both hemispheres. Finally tiring of the sea, he left his ship at New Orleans, and began life on shore as a cotton-roller. His physical strength gave him considerable advantage above his fellow-blacks; and his employers also discovered that he wielded some peculiar occult influence over the negroes, which made him valuable as an overseer or gang leader. Jean, in short, possessed the mysterious obi power, the existence of which has been recognized in most slave-holding communities, and with which many a West-Indian planter has been compelled by force of circumstances to effect a compromise. Accordingly, Jean was permitted many liberties which other blacks, although free, would never have presumed to take. Soon it became rumored that he was a seer of no small powers, and that he could tell the future by the marks upon bales of cotton. I have never been able to learn the details of this queer method of telling fortunes; but Jean became so successful in the exercise of it that thousands of colored people flocked to him for predictions and counsel, and even white people, moved by curiosity or by doubt, paid him to prophesy for them. Finally he became wealthy enough to abandon the levee and purchase a large tract of property on the Bayou Road, where he built a house. His land extended from Prieur Street on the Bayou Road as far as Roman, covering the greater portion of an extensive square, now well built up. In those days it was a marshy green plain, with a few scattered habitations.

At his new home Jean continued the practice of fortune-telling, but combined it with the profession of creole medicine, and of arts still more mysterious. By-and-by his reputation became so great that he was able to demand and obtain immense fees. People of both races and both sexes thronged to see him—many coming even from far-away creole towns in the parishes, and well-dressed women, closely veiled, often knocked at his door. Parties paid from ten to twenty dollars for advice, for herb medicines, for recipes to make the hair grow, for cataplasms supposed to possess mysterious virtues, but really made with scraps of shoe-leather triturated into paste, for advice what ticket to buy in the Havana Lottery, for aid to recover stolen goods, for love powers, for counsel in family troubles, for charms by which to obtain revenge upon an enemy. Once Jean received a fee of fifty dollars for a potion. "It was water," he said to a creole confidant, "with some common herbs boiled in it. I hurt nobody; but if folks want to give me fifty dollars, I take the fifty dollars every time!" His office furniture consisted of a table, a chair, a picture of the Virgin Mary, an elephant's tusk, some shells which he said were African shells and enabled him to read the future, and a pack of cards in each of which a small hole had been burned. About his person he always carried two small bones wrapped around with a black string, which bones he really appeared to revere as fetiches. Wax candles were burned during his performances; and as he bought a whole box of them every few days during "flush times," one can imagine how large the number of his clients must have been. They poured money into his hands so generously that he became worth at least $50,000!

Then, indeed, did this possible son of a Bambara prince begin to live more grandly than any black potentate of Senegal. He had his carriage and pair, worthy of a planter, and his blooded saddle-horse, which he rode well, attired in a gaudy Spanish costume, and seated upon an elaborately decorated Mexican saddle. At home, where he ate and drank only the best—scorning claret worth less than a dollar the *litre*—he continued to find his simple furniture good enough for him; but he had at least fifteen wives—a harem worthy of Boubakar-Segou. White folks might have called them by a less honorific name, but Jean declared them his legitimate spouses according to African ritual. One of the curious features in modern slavery was the ownership of blacks by freedmen of their own color, and these negro slave-holders were usually savage and merciless masters. Jean was not; but it was by right of slave purchase that he obtained most of his wives, who bore him children in great multitude. Finally he managed to woo and win a white woman of the lowest class, who might have been, after a fashion, the Sultana-Validé of this Seraglio. On grand occasions Jean used to distribute largess among the colored population of his neighborhood in the shape of food—bowls of *gombo* or dishes of *jimbalaya*. He did it for popularity's sake in those days, perhaps; but in after-years, during the great epidemics, he did it for charity, even when so much reduced in circumstances that he was himself obliged to cook the food to be given away.

But Jean's greatness did not fail to entail certain cares. He did not know what to do with his money. He had no faith in banks, and had seen too much of the darker side of life to have much faith in human nature. For many years he kept his money under-ground, burying or taking it up at night only, occasionally concealing large sums so well that he could never find them again himself; and now, after many years, people still believe there are treasures entombed somewhere in the neighborhood of Prieur Street and Bayou Road. All business negotiations of a serious character caused him much worry, and as he found many willing to take advantage of his ignorance, he probably felt small remorse for certain questionable actions of his own. He was notoriously bad pay, and part of his property was seized at last to cover a debt. Then, in an evil hour, he asked a man without scruples to teach him how to write, believing that financial misfortunes were mostly due to ignorance of the alphabet. After he had learned to write his name, he was innocent enough one day to place his signature by request at the bottom of a blank sheet of paper, and, lo! his real estate passed from his possession in some horribly mysterious way. Still he had some money left, and made heroic efforts to retrieve his fortunes. He bought other property, and he invested desperately in lottery tickets. The lottery craze finally came upon him, and had far more to do with his ultimate ruin than his losses in the grocery, the shoemaker's shop, and other establishments into which he had put several thousand dollars as the silent partner of people who cheated him. He might certainly have continued to make a good living, since people still sent for him to cure them with his herbs, or went to see him to have their fortunes told; but all his earnings were wasted in tempting fortune. After a score of seizures and a long succession of evictions, he was at last obliged to seek hospitality from some of his numerous children; and of all he had once owned nothing remained to him but his African shells, his elephant's tusk, and the sewing-machine table that had served him to tell fortunes and to burn wax candles upon. Even these, I think, were attached a day or two before his death, which occurred at the house of his daughter by the white wife, an intelligent mulatto with many children of her own.

Jean's ideas of religion were primitive in the extreme. The conversion of the chief tribes of Senegal to Islam occurred in recent years, and it is probable that at the time he was captured by slavers his people were still in a condition little above gross fetichism. If during his years of servitude in a Catholic colony he had imbibed some notions of Romish Christianity, it is certain at least that the Christian ideas were always subordinated to the African—just as the image of the Virgin Mary was used by him merely as an auxiliary fetich in his witchcraft, and was considered as possessing much less power than the "elephant's toof." He was in many respects a humbug; but he may have sincerely believed in the efficacy of certain superstitious rites of his own. He stated that he had a Master whom he was bound to obey; that he could read the will of this Master in the twinkling of the stars; and often of clear nights the neighbors used to watch him standing alone at some street corner staring at the welkin, pulling his woolly beard, and talking in an unknown language to some imaginary being. Whenever Jean indulged in this freak, people knew that he needed money badly, and would probably try to borrow a dollar or two from some one in the vicinity next day.

Testimony to his remarkable skill in the use of herbs could be gathered from nearly every one now living who became well acquainted with him. During the epidemic of 1878, which uprooted the old belief in the total immunity of negroes and colored people from yellow fever, two of Jean's children were "taken down." "I have no money," he said, "but I can cure my children," which he proceeded to do with the aid of some weeds plucked from the edge of the Prieur Street gutters. One of the herbs, I am told, was what our creoles call the "parasol." "The children were playing on the *banquette* next day," said my informant.

Montanet, even in the most unlucky part of his career, retained the superstitious reverence of colored people in all parts of the city. When he made his appearance even on the American side of Canal Street to doctor some sick person, there was always much subdued excitement among the colored folks, who whispered and stared a great deal, but were careful not to raise their voices when they said, "Dar's Hoodoo John!" That an unlettered African slave should have been able to achieve what Jean Bayou achieved in a civilized city, and to earn the wealth and the reputation that he enjoyed during many years of his life, might be cited as a singular evidence of modern popular credulity, but it is also proof that Jean was not an ordinary man in point of natural intelligence.

16

New Orleans Superstitions

—⊷ ⧫ ⊶—

I

The question "What is Voudooism?" could scarcely be answered to-day by any resident of New Orleans unfamiliar with the life of the African west coast, or the superstitions of Hayti [Haiti], either through study or personal observation. The old generation of planters in whose day Voudooism had a recognized existence—so dangerous as a motive power for black insurrection that severe measures were adopted against it—has passed away; and the only person I ever met who had, as a child in his colored nurse's care, the rare experience of witnessing a Voudoo ceremonial, died some three years ago, at the advanced age of seventy-six. As a religion—an imported faith—Voudooism in Louisiana is really dead; the rites of its serpent worship are forgotten; the meaning of its strange and frenzied chants, whereof some fragments linger as refrains in negro song, is not now known even to those who remember the words; and the story of its former existence is only revealed to the folklorists by the multitudinous débris of African superstition which it has left behind it. These only I propose to consider now; for what is to-day called Voudooism in New Orleans means, not an African cultus, but a curious class of negro practices, some possibly derived from it, and others which bear resemblance to the magic of the Middle Ages. What could be more midiaeval, for instance, than molding a waxen heart, and sticking pins in it, or melting it slowly before a fire, while charms are being repeated with the hope that as the waxen heart melts or breaks, the life of some enemy will depart? What, again, could remind us more of thirteenth-century superstition than the burning of a certain number of tapers to compel some absent person's return, with the idea that before the last taper is consumed a mysterious mesmerism will force the wanderer to cross rivers and mountains if necessary on his or her way back?

The fear of what are styled "Voudoo charms" is much more widely spread in Louisiana than any one who had conversed only with educated residents might suppose; and the most familiar superstition of this class is the belief in what I might call *pillow magic,* which is the supposed art of causing wasting sicknesses or even death by putting certain objects into the pillow of the bed in which the hated person sleeps. Feather pillows are supposed to be particularly well adapted to this kind of witchcraft. It is believed that by secret spells a "Voudoo" can cause some monstrous kind of bird or nondescript animal to shape itself into being out of the pillow feathers—like the *tupilek* of the Esquimau *iliseenek* (witchcraft.) It grows very slowly, and by night only; but when completely formed, the person who has been using the pillow dies. Another practice of pillow witchcraft consists in tearing a living bird asunder—usually a cock—and putting portions of the wings into the pillow. A third form of the black-art is confined to putting certain charms or fetiches—consisting of bones, hair, feathers, rags, strings, or some fantastic combination of these and other trifling objects—into any sort of a pillow used by the party whom it is desired to injure. The pure Africanism of this practice needs no comment. Any exact idea concerning the use of each particular kind of charm I have not been able to discover; and I doubt whether those who practice such fetichism know the original African beliefs connected with it. Some say that putting grains of corn into a child's pillow "prevents it from growing any more"; others declare that a bit of cloth in a grown person's pillow will cause wasting sickness; but different parties questioned by me gave each a different signification to the use of similar charms. Putting an open pair of scissors under the pillow before going to bed is supposed to insure a pleasant sleep in spite of fetiches; but the surest way to provide against being "hoodooed," as American residents call it, is to open one's pillow from time to time. If any charms are found, they must be first sprinkled with salt, then burned. A Spanish resident told me that her eldest daughter had been unable to sleep for weeks, owing to a fetich that had been put into her pillow by a spiteful colored domestic. After the object had been duly exorcised and burned, all the young lady's restlessness departed. A friend of mine living in one of the country parishes once found a tow string in his pillow, into the fibers of which a great number of feather stems had either been introduced or had introduced themselves. He wished to retain it as a curiosity, but no sooner did he exhibit it to some acquaintance than it was denounced as a Voudoo "trick," and my friend was actually compelled to burn it in the presence of witnesses. Everybody knows or ought to know that feathers in pillows have a natural tendency to cling and form clots or lumps of more or less curious form, but the discovery of these in some New Orleans households is enough to create a panic. They are viewed as incipient Voudoo *tupileks*. The sign of the cross is made over them by Catholics, and they are promptly committed to the flames.

Pillow magic alone, however, is far from being the only recognized form of maleficent negro witchcraft. Placing charms before the entrance of a house or room, or throwing them over a wall into a yard, is believed to be a deadly practice. When a charm is laid before a room door or hall door, oil is often poured on the floor or pavement in front of the threshold. It is supposed that whoever *crosses an oil line* falls into the power of the Voudoos. To break the oil charm, sand or salt should be strewn upon it. Only a few days before writing this article a very intelligent Spaniard told me that shortly after having discharged a dishonest colored servant he found before his bedroom door one evening a pool of oil with a charm lying in the middle of it, and a candle burning near it. The charm contained some bones, feathers, hairs, and rags—all wrapped together with a string—and a dime. No superstitious person would have dared to use that dime; but my friend, not being superstitious, forthwith put it into his pocket.

The presence of that coin I can only attempt to explain by calling attention to another very interesting superstition connected with New Orleans fetichism. The negroes believe that in order to make an evil charm operate it is necessary *to sacrifice something*. Wine and cake are left occasionally in dark rooms, or candies are scattered over the sidewalk, by those who want to make their fetich hurt somebody. If food or sweetmeats are thus thrown away, they must be abandoned without a parting glance; the witch or wizard must not look back while engaged in the sacrifice.

Scattering dirt before a door, or making certain figures on the wall of a house with chalk, or crumbling dry leaves with the fingers and scattering the fragments before a residence, are also forms of a maleficent conjuring which sometimes cause serious annoyance. Happily the conjurers are almost as afraid of the counter-charms as the most superstitious persons are of the conjuring. An incident which occurred recently in one of the streets of the old quarter known as "Spanish town" afforded me ocular proof of the fact. Through malice or thoughtlessness, or possibly in obedience to secret orders, a young negro girl had been tearing up some leaves and scattering them on the sidewalk in front of a cottage occupied by a French family. Just as she had dropped the last leaf the irate French woman rushed out with a broom and a handful of salt, and began to sweep away the leaves, after having flung salt both upon them and upon the little negress. The latter actually screamed with fright, and cried out, "Oh, pas jeté plis disel après moin, madame! pas bisoin jeté disel après moin; mo pas pé vini icite encore" (Oh, madam, don't throw any more salt after me; you needn't throw any more salt after me; I won't come here any more.)

Another strange belief connected with these practices was well illustrated by a gift made to my friend Professor William Henry by a negro servant for whom he had done some trifling favor. The gift consisted of a "frizzly hen"—one of those funny little fowls whose feathers all seem to curl. "Mars'r Henry, you keep dat frizzly hen, an' ef eny niggers frow eny *conjure* in your yard, *dat frizzly hen will eat de conjure."* Some say, however, that one is not safe unless he keeps two frizzly hens.

The naughty little negress at whom the salt was thrown seemed to fear the salt more than the broom pointed at her. But she was not yet fully educated, I suspect, in regard to superstitions. The negro's terror of a broom is of very ancient date—it may have an African origin. It was commented upon by Moreau de Saint-Méry in his work on San Domingo, published in 1796. "What especially irritates the negro," he wrote, "is to have a broom passed over any part of his body. He asks at once whether the person imagined that he was dead, and remains convinced that the act shortens his life." Very similar ideas concerning the broom linger in New Orleans. To point either end of a broom at a person is deemed bad luck; and many an ignorant man would instantly knock down or violently abuse the party who should point a broom at him. Moreover, the broom is supposed to have mysterious power as a means of getting rid of people. "If you are pestered by visitors whom you would wish never to see again, sprinkle salt on the floor after they go, and sweep it out by the same door through which they have gone, and they will never come back." To use a broom in the evening is bad luck: *balayer le soir, on balaye sa fortune* (to sweep in the evening is to sweep your good luck away), remains a well-quoted proverb.

I do not know of a more mysterious disease than muscular atrophy in certain forms, yet it is by no means uncommon either in New Orleans or in the other leading cities of the United States. But in New Orleans, among the colored people, and among many of the uneducated of other races, the victim of muscular atrophy is believed to be the victim of Voudooism. A notion is prevalent that negro witches possess knowledge of a secret poison which may terminate life instantly or cause a slow "withering away," according as the dose is administered. A Frenchman under treatment for paralysis informed me that his misfortune was certainly the work of Voudoos, and that his wife and child had died through the secret agency of negro wizards. Mental aberration is also said to be caused by the administration of poisons whereof some few negroes are alleged to possess the secret. In short, some very superstitious persons of both races live in perpetual dread of imaginary Voudoos, and fancy that the least ailment from which they suffer is the work of sorcery. It is very doubtful whether any knowledge of those animal or vegetable poisons which leave no trace of their presence in the blood, and which may have been known to some slaves of African birth, still lingers in Louisiana, wide-spread as is the belief to the contrary. During the last decade there have been a few convictions of blacks for the crime of poisoning, but there was nothing at all mysterious or peculiar about these cases, and the toxic agent was invariably the most vulgar of all—arsenic, or some arsenious preparation in the shape of rat poison.

II

The story of the frizzly hen brings me to the subject of superstitions regarding animals. Something of the African, or at least of the San Domingan, worship of the cock seems to have been transplanted hither by the blacks, and to linger in New Orleans under various metamorphoses. A negro charm to retain the affections of a lover consists in tying up the legs of the bird to the head, and plunging the creature alive into a vessel of gin or other spirits. Tearing the live bird asunder is another cruel charm, by which some negroes believe that a sweetheart may become magically fettered to the man who performs the quartering. Here, as in other parts of the world, the crowing hen is killed, the hooting of the owl presages death or bad luck, and the crowing of the cock by day presages the arrival of company. The wren (*roitelet*) must not be killed: *c'est zozeau bon Dié* (it is the good God's bird)—a belief, I think, of European origin.

It is dangerous to throw hair-combings away instead of burning them, because birds may weave them into their nests, and while the nest remains the person to whom the hair belonged will have a continual headache. It is bad luck to move a cat from one house to another; seven years' bad luck to kill a cat; and the girl who steps, accidentally or otherwise, on a cat's tail need not expect to be married the same year. The apparition of a white butterfly means good news. The neighing of a horse before one's door is bad luck. When a fly bothers one very persistently, one may expect to meet an acquaintance who has been absent many years.

There are many superstitions about marriage, which seem to have a European origin, but are not less interesting on that account. "Twice a bridesmaid, never a bride," is a proverb which needs no comment. The bride must not keep the pins which fastened her wedding dress. The husband must never take off his wedding ring: to take it off will insure him bad luck of some kind. If a girl who is engaged accidentally lets a knife fall, it is a sign that her lover is coming. Fair or foul weather upon her marriage day augurs a happy or unhappy married life.

The superstitions connected with death may be all imported, but I have never been able to find a foreign origin for some of them. It is bad luck to whistle or hum the air that a band plays at a funeral. If a funeral stops before your house, it means that the dead wants company. It is bad luck to cross a funeral procession, or to count the number of carriages in it; if you do count them, you may expect to die after the expiration of as many weeks as there were carriages at the funeral. If at the cemetery there be any unusual delay in burying the dead, caused by any unlooked-for-circumstances, such as the tomb proving too small to admit the coffin, it is a sign that the deceased is selecting a companion from among those present, and one of the mourners must soon die. It is bad luck to carry a spade through a house. A bed should never be placed with its foot pointing toward the street door, for corpses leave the house feet foremost. It is bad luck to travel with a priest; this idea seems to me of Spanish importation; and I am inclined to attribute a similar origin to the strange tropical superstition about the banana, which I obtained, nevertheless, from an Italian. You must not *cut* a banana, but simply break it with the fingers, because in cutting it you *cut the cross*. It does not require a very powerful imagination to discern in a severed section of the fruit the ghostly suggestion of a crucifixion.

Some other creole superstitions are equally characterized by naïve beauty. Never put out with your finger the little red spark that tries to linger on the wick of a blown-out candle: just so long as it burns, some soul in purgatory enjoys rest from torment. Shooting-stars are souls escaping from purgatory: if you can make a good wish three times before the star disappears, the wish will be granted. When there is sunshine and rain together, a colored nurse will tell the children, "*Gadé! djabe apé batte so femme.*" (Look! the devil's beating his wife!)

I will conclude this little paper with selections from a list of superstitions which I find widely spread, not citing them as of indubitable creole origin, but simply calling attention to their prevalence in New Orleans, and leaving the comparative study of them to folklorists.

Turning the foot suddenly in walking means bad or good luck. If the right foot turns, it is bad luck; if the left, good. This superstition seems African, according to a statement made by Moreau de Saint-Méry. Some reverse the conditions, making the turning of the left foot bad luck. It is also bad luck to walk about the house with one shoe on and one shoe off, or, as a creole acquaintance explained it to me, "*c'est appeler sa mère ou son père dans le tombeau*" (It is calling one's mother or one's father into the grave). An itching in the right palm means coming gain; in the left, coming loss.

Never leave a house by a different door from that by which you entered it; it is "carrying away the good luck of the place." Never live in a house you build before it has been rented for at least a year. When an aged person repairs his or her house, he or she is soon to die. Never pass a child through a window; it stops his growth. Stepping over a child does the same; therefore, whoever takes such a step inadvertently must step back again to break the evil spell. Never tilt a rocking-chair when it is empty. Never tell a bad dream before breakfast, unless you want it "to come true"; and never pare the nails on Monday morning before taking a cup of coffee. A funny superstition about windows is given me in this note by a friend: "*Il ne faut pas faire passer un enfant par la fenêtre, car avant un an il y en aura un autre*" (A child must not be passed through a window, for if so passed you will have another child before the lapse of a year.) This proverb, of course, interests only those who desire small families, and as a general rule creoles are proud of large families, and show extraordinary affection toward their children.

If two marriages are celebrated simultaneously, one of the husbands will die. Marry at the time of the moon's waning and your good luck will wane also. If two persons think and express the same thought at the same time, one of them will die before the year passes. To chop up food in a pot with a knife means a dispute in the house. If you have a ringing in your ears, some person is speaking badly of you; call out the names of all whom you suspect, and when the ringing stops at the utterance of a certain name, you know who the party is. If two young girls are combing the hair of a third at the same time, it may be taken for granted that the youngest of the three will soon die. If you want to make it stop raining, plant a cross in the middle of the yard and sprinkle it with salt. The red-fish has the print of St. Peter's fingers on its tail. If water won't boil in the kettle, there may be a toad or a toad's egg in it. Never kill a spider in the afternoon or evening, but always kill the spider unlucky enough to show himself early in the morning, for the old French proverb says:

> "Araignée du matin—chagrin;
> Araignée du midi—plaisir;
> Araignée du soir—espoir"

(A spider seen in the morning is a sign of grief; a spider seen at noon, of joy; a spider seen in the evening, of hope).

Even from this very brief sketch of New Orleans superstitions the reader may perceive that the subject is peculiar enough to merit the attention of experienced folklorists. It might be divided by a competent classifier under three heads: I. Negro superstitions confined to the black and colored population; II. Negro superstitions which have proved contagious, and have spread among the uneducated classes of whites; III. Superstitions of Latin origin imported from France, Spain, and Italy. I have not touched much upon superstitions inherited from English, Irish, or Scotch sources, inasmuch as they have nothing especially local in their character here. It must be remembered that the refined classes have no share in these beliefs, and that, with a few really rational exceptions, the practices of creole medicine are ignored by educated persons. The study of creole superstitions has only an ethnological value, and that of creole medicine only a botanical one, in so far as it is related to empiricism.

All this represents an under side of New Orleans life; and if anything of it manages to push up to the surface, the curious growth makes itself visible only by some really pretty blossoms of feminine superstition in regard to weddings or betrothal rings, or by some dainty sprigs of child-lore, cultivated by those colored nurses who tell us that the little chickens throw up their heads while they drink to thank the good God for giving them water.

17

THE MUSIC OF THE MASSES

Airs from the Streets and Variety Halls—Tunes That the Barrel Organs and Whistlers Execute

There is plenty of newspaper and book space and a wealth of critical ability devoted to the treatment of the music of the elect and select, but it is small notice in that region and from that quarter that the music of the people gets. The few with souls attuned to harmony, and with trained and culti-

vated musical taste, gather to enjoy the noble harmonies of Wagner, the superb symphonies of Beethoven, but the music of the spheres is not more distinct from or inaudible to the great masses of the people. The oratorio is for the few, the ballad for the many. The lofty strains of the music of Mendelssohn, of Mozart, of Handel, of Haydn swell through the vaulted and frescoed halls, and awaken the enthusiasm of the coldly critical, but the simple song-makers's melodies are ground from the barrel organs, whistled from all the street corners, hummed over the forge and in the harvest field; they float out upon the air, kept time to by the hammer, the scythe, the whetstone, the sewing machine. The music of the masters dies away among the peaks and cliffs in the pure upper air; the music of the ballad-makers lives forever in the green valleys, echoing from heart to heart, from soul to soul among the lowly.

> "Oh, Love, they die in yon rich sky.
>   They faint on field, or hill or river,
> Our echoes roll from soul to soul,
>   And live forever and forever."

Calm criticism and professional enthusiasm for the one; tears and laughter for the other. Through all time the song singers have been a power for good or evil. A song has cut off a King's head; a ballad has made a revolution. Kingly decrees and iron bars were useless to curb the power and lessen the dangerous influence of Beranger; and the exile and persecution of Roget de

Lisle could not destroy the deathless Marseillaise, or make it less a terror to tyranny. Here is a field for the investigator, rich and fascinating beyond comparison: to trace the history of the song, the ballad, the vaudeville, the chanson, how through all history they have softened or hardened hearts, won the loves of tender maids or made iron the muscles of fighting men, brought low the oppressor, uplifted the oppressed, comforted souls sore stricken, and brought tears to evil eyes and laughter to lips unused to it. In every field of human experience the ballad is a mighty power. What more sinister and threatening than—

> "And shall Trelawny die?
>   And shall Trelawny die?
> Thou twenty thousand Cornish men
> Shall know the reason why."

What more suggestive in bold and fearless threat than—

> "To the Lords of convention 'twas Claverhouse spoke
> Ere the King's crown go down there are heads to be broke.
> Then let each cavalier who loves honor and me,
> Come follow the bonnets of Bonnie Dundee."

What has done more to reconcile bitter enemies than—

> "Under the sod and the dew,
> Waiting the judgment day,
> Under the roses the blue,
> Under the lilies the gray."

But it is our purpose to speak of the popular song music of America only, and especially of that of to-day.

In the early days of the country, the only songs of the people were the ballads brought over from the old country, and the children were taught to sing "Killarney," "The Meeting of the Waters," "Sweet Afton," "Jamie's on the Dark Blue Sea," "Lancashire Lass," "Lass o' Lowrie," "Annie Lawrie," "The Watcher," "Roll on, Silver Moon,", "Sally in Our Alley," "Auld Robin Gray," "Bonnie Doon," "Bonnie Dundee," "Rocky Road to Dublin," "Fine Old English Gentleman," "Sweet Jessie, the Flower of Dumblane," etc., with all the old English religious and political airs. These were the songs taught our grandfathers and grandmothers in their childhood, and this is why the "Old Folks at Home" still delight to listen to the Old Irish, English, and Scottish melodies, renewing, as they do, the associations of "Long, long ago," and filled as they are for them with haunting memories of happy times gone long ago and forever.

Afterward, when the young Republic attained a government and nationality of its own, it demanded a popular music of its own, and a race of sentimental and patriotic song-writers sprung up to answer the demand. These gave us such songs as "Hail Columbia," "Yankee Privateer," "Woodman, Spare that Tree," "Red, White and Blue," "Independence Day," "Star Spangled Banner," "Home, Sweet Home," "Forty Years Ago," "Old Oaken Bucket," etc. But the American songwriters drew largely upon the music of the old countries, and many of our popular airs are taken bodily from that source.

Afterwards came the school of Negro Melodists, and it gave us some of the purely American ballads, the sweetest, best and most truly characteristic. Such songs as "Jim Crow," "Rosa Lee," "Walk Jaw Bone," "Who's Dat Knocking?" "When I Gits in a Weaving Way," "Way Down upon the Suwanee River," "Old Kentucky Home," "Massa's in de Cold, Cold Ground," "Kemo Kimo," "Down in Tennessee," "Oh Susanna," "Carry Me Back to Ole Virginny," "Ole Virginny Never Tire," "Dandy Jim of Caroline," "Picayune Butler," "Nelly Bly," "Essence of Old Virginny," "Lily Dale," "Darling Nelly Gray," "Nelly was a Lady," and the hundreds of other songs of this class. In this the master, and perhaps the only purely original song-writer of America, was Stephen Foster, and there is nothing sweeter and truer in ballad music than "Old Folks at Home," "Massa in de Cold, Cold Ground," and "Jenny with the Light Brown Hair."

Contemporary with this school was a set of sentimental songs of a coarser grain, set to airs drawn mostly from the Cremorne Garden, Argyle Rooms and the variety halls of London, though others seem to be original with our own song writers, such as "Old Dog Tray," "Jordan is a Hard Road to Travel" and other songs of a like character that achieved temporary popularity.

Later came the great civil war, with its notable additions to the popular music of the land, and its revival of patriotic airs. It gave us "Rally Round the Flag," "Tramp, Tramp," "Babylon is Fallen," "Marching Through Georgia," "Tenting Tonight," "Just Before the Battle, Mother," "Mother, I've Come Home to Die," "When this Cruel War is Over," "Maryland, my Maryland," "Dixie," "Bonny Blue Flag," "John Brown's Body," "Battle Hymn of the Republic," "Tell my Mother I died Happy," "Mother, is the Battle Over?" "Year of Jubilo," "Away Goes Cuffy," "What's a Hungry Darkey Gwine to Do?" "Death of Ellsworth," "When Sherman Marched Down to the Sea," "Drummer Boy of Shiloh," "When Johnny Comes Marching Home," "On Shiloh's Bloody Hill, "The Rebel Riders," "Bound to Run the Blockade," "Up with our Banner Bright," "The Wilson Zouave," "Brave Boys Are They," "Marching Along," and so on.

The colleges have occupied a song field peculiar to themselves, and have given us among hundreds of others, "Benny Havens," "Fair Harvard," "Peter Gray," "Upidee," "Litoria," "One Fish Ball," "The Jolly Young Sophomore," "The Mountains," "The Wooden Spoon," etc., with the scores of secret society songs.

Since the war there has been a run of such popular songs as the "Captain with his Whiskers," "Captain Jinks," "Up in a Balloon," "Goodbye, Liza Jane," "Pretty Little Polly Perkins," "Sarah's Young Man," "Bell goes a Ringing for Sara," "Shabby Genteel," "Pulling Hard Against the Stream," "Just as Good as Gold," "Flying Trapeze," "Down in a Coal Mine," "Ever of Thee," "Rosalee the Prairie Flower," "Hard Times Come Again No More," "Pat. Malloy," "Lannigan's Ball," "Finnigan's Wake," "Shoo Fly," "Castles in the Air,", "Put Me in my Little Bed," "Whipporwill," "Too Genteel," "Eileen Aroon," "The Mill in the Valley," "Tassels on Her Boots," "Mabel Waltz," "Good Bye, John," "Five O'clock in the Morning," "Nobody's Child," with all the list of "Claribel's" exquisite songs, and all the list of Will. Hays' sloppy melodies.

To-day nearly all the popular airs originate in the variety theater, or from the opera bouffes, and they are turned out by the hundred. Most of them are the merest nonsense and silliness, and are never heard more than once or twice. Some live through this very silliness. A jingle of meaningless words is set to some little snatch of melody that catches the popular ear and, presto, the jingle and the tune is in everybody's mouth, and the air is whistled by everybody capable of a pucker of the lips. One performer bases his claims to popular recognition and to a weekly salary on a song called "Flewy Flewy," a pretty air with such words as:

"The snail he dragged a rail,
  Flewy, Flewy, Flewy, Flewy,
Snail he dragged a rail,
  Flewy an'a John'
Snail he dragged a rail,
Dragged it with his tail—
Wasn't that a pretty drag?
  Flewy an'a John.
"Camel climbed a tree,

Flewy, Flewy, Flewy, Flewy,
Camel climbed a tree,
    Flewy an'a John.
Camel climbed a tree
To catch the bumblebee.
Wasn't that a pretty climb?
    Flewy an'a John."

And so on for half a dozen stanzas. Others of these variety airs have real merit, in words or music, or, rarely, in both. Often a rude ballad strikes a chord in the popular heart, and without musical or literary merit wins its way to great popularity among a certain class, or perhaps among all classes. An instance of this is the absurd song about Jim Fisk, and how "he never went back on the poor." It has made him the hero of the canaille.

It is false in sentiment, false in fact, outrageous in rhyme, rhythm and melody, and yet it makes the galleries roar and yell. Two years ago it was first sung in this city, at the National Theater, by a wretched balladist, who called herself Maude de Lisle, and whose recommendations were a plain face, an awkward form and a weak, cracked voice. Every night the song was *encored* with yells and howls that threatened to raise the roof. It created a *furore* among the class of attendants at that theater. It crowded the galleries nightly, and the singer was often recalled six or seven times, and her engagement was continued two weeks in consequence.

A sure sign that a song has made a success or a hit in a new field is the fact that such a new song will immediately be followed by any quantity of parodies, imitations and paraphrases. There is not one of the popular songs that is not parodied a hundred times over. Some of the songs strike so decidedly upon a new vein of originality as to create a new school in the variety music. Such, for instance, as "Lannagan's Ball," "Champagne Charlie," "Hildebrand Montrose," "Pretty as a Picture," "Walking Down Broadway," "On the Beach at Long Branch," "Sailing on the Lake," "Mulligan Guards," and the negro camp-meetings airs of the Hampton Students, Jubilee Singers, and "Old Black Joe" of Milt. Barlow. As soon as a song makes a success in English, it is immediately parodied in Low Dutch or Irish dialect. "Hildebrand McGuffin," and half a dozen others. "Mulligan Guards," first produced by Harrigan and Hart, was a great success, and at once it gave rise to a regular school of such songs—"Skidmore Guards," "Doherty Fusileers," "Brannagan's Band," "Gallant Sixty-ninth," "The Dutch Galoots," "Black Shootileers," "Fogarty Musketeers," "Hoolahan Musketeers," "The Tra-la-la-loo," "Ashantee Recruits," "Since Terry Joined the Gang," "Shoot the Hat," "The Ginger Blues," etc.

The "Drum Major," "Captain Jinks of the Horse Marines," "Captain with his Whiskers," "Captain Cuffs of the Glorious Buffs," etc., belong to another "school." Billy Morris' Minstrels used to parody every new sensation in the drama, and after "Under the Gaslight," they gave "Under the Kerosene Lamp;" after "Enoch Arden" they gave "In a Garden;" after "Colleen Bawn" they gave "Boilin' Cawn;" after "Ticket of Leave Man" they gave "Take It and Leave Man," and so on. So some ridiculous parody regularly follows the successful ballad. "Little Maud" is followed by "Little Fraud," "Up in a Balloon" by "Down in a Coal Mine," "Walking Down Broadway" by "Spooning on the Sands," "Gliding Down the Stream," by "Sailing on the Lake," "Darling, I am Growing Old," by "Darling, I am Growing Bald," "Wait till the Moonlight falls on the Water" by "Wait till the Gas-light falls on the Gutter," "Molly Darling" by "Dolly Varden," "You'll Never Miss the Water till the Well Runs Dry" by "You'll Never Miss the Lager till the Keg Runs Dry," and "You'll Never Miss de Coat till de Man's Gone Out," "Old Folks at Home" by "Young Folks at Home," "Tommy, Make Room for Your Uncle" by "Tommy, Make Room for your Aunty," "Pull down the Blind" by "Pull Down Your Vest" and "Make Doun dem Blinds," "Flewy Flewy" by "Sphew Flu," "Eileen Alana," by "A Lean Banana." "What is Home Without Mother," by "What is Home without a Mother-in-Law." Sometimes the parody supersedes the original entirely as in the case of "Little Fraud" and "Death of Ellsworth."

Not one out of a hundred of the so-called popular songs of the day contain any merit of any kind. Usually the words are silliness itself. When sentiment is attempted it is mawkish and sickening. When wit is attempted, the result is melancholy. It is usual to select some foolish verses appearing in the "ladies' magazines" or sentimental weeklies and set them to music, and such a song as "Put Me in My Little Bed," or "Put Away His Little Shoes," "Mother, I've Come Home to Die," is manufactured.

The song-makers make up in energy and fruitfulness what they lack in ability. There are songs about everything under the heavens—and in the heavens, too, for that matter. Every new slang phrase is the nucleus for a new song, every new style of garment, every new thing in the dramatic, social, political, religious and financial worlds.

Anything will do for a subject. A stick, a stone, a great scoundrel, a great warrior, a great thief, a street corner, a buggy ride, a little dog, that little dog's tail, a holiday, a show, an accident, a dog fight, a scandal, a wedding, a divorce. Even one song is made the subject for another; or a song is made of the titles of others. Everything is fish for the ballad-writer. Here is a list of song subjects given at random to illustrate this point: "The Bashful Lover,"

"Bloated Young Aristocrat," "Donkey Race," "Croquet," "Clown in the Pantomime," "Chap Wot Plays the Cornet," "Dog and Cat," "Dashing West End Swell," "The Elderly Beau," "Enoch," "Footsteps on the Stairs," "Hanki Panki," "I Wish I'd Been Born a Girl," "I'm a Twin," "Come and Kiss Me," "Little Church Around the Corner," "Moet and Chandon," "Marriage Fee," "Old Oaken Bucket," "The Periwinkle Man," "The Village Green," "Roguish Cora," "Sorrows of a Spinster," "Strike While the Iron Is Hot," "Up in the Air," "Charley Ross," "Oh Dat Watermelon," "There's a Letter in the Candle," "The Old Kitchen Floor, "The Charcoal Man," "The Clam Man's Gal," "Courting in the Rain," "It's Funny When You Feel That Way," "The Lazy Club," "The Pretty Waiter Girl," "Tra la-la Lazy Club," "Tra La-La George," "The Things a Young Lady Wears," "When Charlie Plays the Drum," "Circus Show," "Twenty-seven Cents," "Riding in the Street Car," "There is no Harm in Kissing," "Say Yes, Pussy," "If Ever I Cease to Love," "Dutchman's Little Dog," "The Country Cousin," "The Chinese Giant", "The Goat," "Go Way Bumblebee," "Soup, Starch and Candle," "Single Gentlemen, how do You Do?" "There's Where You Make Your Mistake," "Ten Thousand Miles Away," "The Cymbal Man," "The Conductor," "Charley's Sunday Out," "The Girl at the Sewing machine," "Her heart was True to Poll," " It's Funny how They do it, but They do," "Something," "My Nose," "Nothing," "Sunlight of My Soul," "Bunch of Radishes," "Turkey in the Straw," "The Higgenbottom Sisters," "Blue Grass," "Don't Give Yourself Away," "Shine Your Boots?" "The Beer Jerker," "The Boston Fire," "Don't Wake the Baby," "Gal That Danced in Baba," "The Hypochondriac," "Wat d'ya say?" "Keep off the Grass," "Let de Guilty Man Escape," "The Matinee Brigade," "Patent Rubber Bustle," "Pull Back Dress," "Schooner of Lager," "Smoke House Graduates," "Tom Collins," "Telephone," "Violets Dipped in Dew," and so on, a larger sheet than this paper could be filled with titles in diamond type.

Some clever things are done in the way of meaningless jingles. This one is well known:

"I saw Essau kissing Kate,
    And the truth is we all three saw,
For I saw Essau, she saw me,
    And she saw I saw Essau."

Here is the noble chorus of Kemo Kimo:

"Kemo kimo, dar or whar, in come Sally singing my hi,
my ho, my rump stump, flumididdle sometimes penniwinkle,

linktum nip cut, hit 'em with a brick bat. Patrick Murphy, Donahue Flannigan, rot gut purgatory, sing song Kitty can't you Kime oh."

Here is another from "Heathen Chinee:"
Chic-ee-ri-chi-chi-chic-chow-la,
Chic-ee-ri-chi-ee-nic-pee-nau
Ee-gat-wee-dust-ee-cant-ee-kee
Ee-can nobee-ought-bee Chinee-coo.

The following is supposed to be an immitation of a barrel organ"

"Quar, quar, quar, quar, quar, quar, quar,
Quar, quar, quar, quar, quar-rr, quar,
Quar, quar, quar, quar, quar, quar, quar,
Quar-r-r-r-, quar, quar, quar, quar."

It is supposed to be playing the air of "Pop Goes the Weasel." Run it over in your head, and see how it goes. It isn't bad if you do it artistically. This is the chorus from one of Tony Pastor's songs:

"One-ery, two-ery, tickery seven,
Alaba, clackaba, ten or eleven,
Ping, Pang, Whiskey Dan,
Tiddletum, toddletu, twenty-one."

Here's another:

"For his bom, bom, bom, and tingle, tingle, tingle,
Bom, bom, bom, and jingle, jingle, jingle,
Won the heart of pretty Polly Pringle:
Pretty Polly Pringle liked his bom, bom, bom."

The bom, bom, bom is supposed to be the base drum, and the jingle, jingle, jingle the cymbals. An old and well-known jingle is:

"School, shool, shool, aroon,
Shool a shag a rack, shool a bub a coo;
First time I saw silly bally a-a-a,
Discum bibble all a boo, slow reel,"

Another is:

> "Hokey pokey winkey wum,
> Polly ma goo kum a lung kung,
> Hangery wangery ching a ling chung.
> The King of the Cannibal Islands."

"Upidee," "B-a-ba," "Chocachelunk," "Upidee," "Bingo" and others are in the college *repertoire*, along with "Caesar of Ostrich" and "Felis Sedet by a Hole."

All the old nursery jingles are used, the object being to carry forward the melody in some sort of vocal utterance, however absurd. So, often we hear to a sprightly air the old familiar:

> "Intry mintry cutry corn.
> Apple seed and apple thorn;
> Wire bier limber lock,
> Six geese in a flock;
> Sit and sing by the spring,
> Y-o-u-t-out,"

AND:—

> "Onery twoery tickery tee,
> Holibo crackibo danderee,
> Pinpon musket John,
> Twiddledum twoddledum twenty-one."

And:—

> "I-ry u-ry ickery Ann
> Philasy pholasy Nicholas John:
> Queevy quavy Irish navy
> Strinklum stranuklum buck."

But the most extraordinary of these jingles we ever heard set to music is:

> "That or this or him or whender,
> Dum pole greasy de tie

Swuad o' bededdler baker,
Old Tweezer bededdler rat dang."

Akin to these are the nonsense songs like the "Flewy Flewy" quoted and others, ranging through all degrees from the jingle absolute, where the greater the distance from any glimmer of sense or consecutiveness or coherency the better, up to the verse when there begins to appear some evidence of sanity on the part of the writer. Such a song is the old timer marriage of the monkey:

"Monkey married the baboon's sister,
Smacked his lips and then he kissed her;
Kissed so hard he raised a blister—
　　She sot up a yell.

"The bridegroom put on some court-plaster,
Stuck so fast it couldn't stick faster,
Sure it was a sad disaster,
　　But it soon got well.

"What do you think the bride was dressed in?
White gauze veil and green glass breast-pin,
Red kid shoes. She was quite interesting.
　　Oh, she was a belle.

"The bridegroom put on a clean shirt collar,
And red cravat that cost a dollar,
Ruffled shirt, the style to foller.
　　He cut a stunning swell."

Of a piece with this is Van Amburg's show:

　　"First comes the African polar bear,
　　　Oft called the iceberg's daughter,
　　She's been known to drink three kegs of beer,
　　　Then call for soda water.

　　"She wades in the water up to her knees
　　　Not fearing any harm,
　　And you may grumble all you please,
　　　And she don't care a darn.

Chorus—"The elephant now goes round,
    the band begins to play,
    The boys around the monkeys cage
    Had better keep away.

   "Next comes the Anaconda boa constrictor,
    Oft called Anaconda for brevity;
He's noted the world throughout
    For his age and his great longevity.
He can swallow himself, crawl through himself;
    And come out again with facility.
He can tie himself up in a double beau knot,
    And wink his tail with the greatest agility.
Chorus—"The elephant now goes round, etc.

But little better than this is the famous "Hildebrand Montrose," of which the following specimens will do:

   "My name is Hildebrand Montrose,
Some folks they call me Charley,
In my buttonhole I wear a rose;
I can Francais vooley parley.
My hair is auburn ringlets, My eyes are azure dark,
The girls they call me birdie,
Like the swallows in the park.
Chorus—Ta-ta, ta-ta, my baby dear,
      I'll meet you in the park
    If the weather it is clear,
      It'll strike you with a feather:
    Every daisy knows
      The darling of the ladies
    Is Hilderbrand Montrose.

His necktie is golden scarlet,
   This most exquisite fellow;
He looks like a Christmas present
   Under his silk umbrella;
His boots are patent-leather,
   He never pays his bills;
He always drinks plain soda,

And eats up tooth-pick quills.
   Ta-ta, ta-ta, etc.
Au revoir, au revoir,
   You should hear him say;
I must go and buy some gum-drops
   For Clanville across the way.
All the girls together
   Are dying for a beau.
Of course the individual
   Is Hildebrand Montrose.

   Chorus.

He parts his hair in the center,
Chalks his paper collars;
His papa is very wealthy—
   Worth a million dollars
In Big Bonanza mining stocks.
   His voice is quite soprano,
You ought to hear him sing Love's Chidings
   On a Fogarty piano.

   Chorus.

Bye-Bey! Bye-Bey!
   I must tear myself away
Before the bright aurora
   Gilds the summer clouds so gay.
The ladies, heaven bless 'em,
   Positively knows (sic)
Their choicest little treasure
   In Hildebrand Montrose.

The Dutch parody runs thus:

Olive oil, olive oil,
   My baby pet.
I'll meet you in dot park
   Ven de vedder it vos vet.
I strike you mit a pretzel,

I vill you up mit vine,
Der darlings of der ladies
   Vos Jakey Bumblestein.

The Irish parody on the chorus is:

Tra-la-la! Tra-la-lu! My darling pet:
I'll meet you in the park when the weather it is wet,
I'll strike you with a turkey leg, I'll smoother you with the stuffin'
For the darling of the ladies is Hildebrand McGuffin.

Some of the airs of the variety halls are so pretty and taking that they are promoted to higher and more select circles. They find their way into the orchestras and to the private parlors of the rich and cultivated and critical. "Beautiful Bells," arranged as a waltz, was played by the Cincinnati Orchestra at the Cincinnati assemblies two winters ago, and the lovely belles of our best society swept and swayed to the strains that had their origin in the variety room, and were first sung by painted women in scant skirts and soiled tights. Nilsson created a furore with "Way Down Upon the Suwanee River." Aimee made a sensation with "Pretty as a Picture," and the tender melancholy of "Massa's in the Cold, Cold Ground," the exquisite beauty and infinite mournfulness of "Old Kentucky Home," the sprightly playfulness of "Seeing Nellie Home," and "Jenny with the Light Brown Hair," and "Touch the Harp Lightly, My Pretty Louise," the pleading tenderness of "Don't be Sorriful, Darling," and the honest sentiment and pure pathos of "Pulling Hard Against the stream," have won their way to a higher and better life among people who never invade the bounds of the concert halls. Other songs that deserve to be made exceptions where there is such an overwhelming preponderance of trash, are "Be Merry on Christmas Day," "Castles in the Air," "Shabby Genteel," "Norah O'Neil," "Take This Letter to My Mother," "Letter in the Candle," "The Old Cabin Home," "Love Among the Roses," "The Dreamy Waltz," "Old Log Cabin in the Lane," "Memory Bells," "My Old Wife and I," "You'll Miss Me When I'm Gone," "Slavery Days," "The Vagabond," "No One to Love," "Eileen Alana," "Under the Willow," and others. Of course there is a long list of popular and pretty melodies and sentimental songs that do not properly come under the head of variety airs, though they were sung from the stage everywhere, for everything is fair game in that quarter. If the church song writer puts out a song which has the ring to catch the people it is quickly taken up by the vaudeville singers, and we have negro song and dance men howling "Hold the Fort," or bedizened women in flesh-colored tights singing "Sweet By and By," sandwiched between "Big, Fat Nance" and "Hildebrand Montrose."

In another article on this subject we will endeavor to draw out other points of interest concerning the ballad music of the day, and give other interesting specimens of the kind of stuff that is accepted as the music of the masses.

18

BLACK VARIETIES

The Minstrels of the Row

Picturesque Scenes Without Scenery

The attractive novelty of theatricals at old Pickett's tavern, on the levee, by real negro minstrels, with amateur dancing performances by roustabouts and their "girls," has already created considerable interest in quarters where one would perhaps least expect to find it; and the patrolmen of the Row nightly escort fashionably dressed white strangers to No. 91 Front street. The theater has two entrances, one through the neat, spotlessly clean bar-room on the Front street side, the other from the sidewalk on the river side. The theater is also the ball-room; and when the ancient clock behind the black bar in the corner announces in senile, metallically-husky tones the hour of 12, the foot-lights are extinguished, the seats cleared away, and the audience quickly form into picturesque sets for wild dances.

It is a long, low room, with a staircase at the southwest corner, ascending to the saloon above; an unplastered ceiling of clean white pine plank, resembling an inverted section of steamboat deck, a black wooden bar at the south-east corner, and rude wooden benches of unpainted plank arranged along the walls and across the room from the bar to the stage. This stage consists of a wooden platform, elevated about a yard from the floor; and the little room under the staircase at the left side serves as the green-room. Tallow dips, placed about a foot apart, serve for footlights. Strips of white muslin sewed together form the curtains, which are attached by rings to a metal rod in the ceiling, and open and close much after the manner of the curtains of an old-fashioned, four-posted bedstead. These curtains were made by a mild-mannered brown girl called Annie, remarkable for deep, dark eyes, light, wavy hair, and wonderful curves of mouth, chin and neck; but poor Annie is no better than she ought to be, and loves to smoke a great, black, brier-root pipe.

Ere the curtain rose we found it extremely interesting to glance over the motley audience, largely made up of women less fair, but not less frail than Annie.

A sharp-faced Irish girl, with long fawn-colored hair and hard gray eyes; a pretty and ruddy-faced young white woman, very neatly built and fashionably dressed, the wife of a colored bar-keeper; a white brunette, with unpleasantly deep-set black eyes and long curly hair, who feigns to have colored blood in her veins; a newly arrived white blonde, who last week followed a roustabout hither from Ironton through some strange and vain infatuation; the notorious Adams sisters; a young Cincinnati woman of evil repute, whose parents live but a few squares up town, and have not for years exchanged word or look with their daughter, though she almost daily passes by the old home; and one Gretchen-faced woman, with rather regular features and fair hair, who has lately deserted a good home at Portsmouth to become the mistress of a stevedore—these comprised the white women present. Excepting the bar-keeper's little white wife, they evidently preferred to sit together. But the picturesqueness of the spectacle was rendered all the more striking by the contrast.

Every conceivable hue possible to the human skin might be studied in the dense and motley throng that filled the hall. There were full-blooded black women, solidly built, who were smoking stogies, and wore handkerchiefs of divers colors twined about their curly pates, after the old Southern fashion. Some of these were evidently too poor to own a whole dress, and appeared in petticoat and calico waist alone; but the waists had been carefully patched and washed, and the white petticoats were spotlessly clean and crisp with starch. Others were remarkably well dressed—excepting their ornaments, which were frequently of a character calculated to provoke a smile. One little negro woman had a flat locket with a brilliantly-colored picture painted on it, and at least six inches in diameter, suspended from her ebon neck by a golden chain. Gold or imitation, yellow and glittering, flashed everywhere in ear pendants against dusky cheeks, in massive rings upon strong black hands, in fair chains coiling about brown necks or clasping bare brown arms.

It is a mystery how many of these women, who can not afford to buy two dresses, or who have to borrow decent attire to go out of doors, can refuse to part with their jewelry in almost any extremity, but we have been reliably assured that such is the case. As a rule, these levee girls do not invest in bogus jewelry. It was curious to observe the contrast of physical characteristics among the lighter-hued women; girls with almost fair skins frequently possessing wooly hair; dark mulattoes on the contrary often having light, floating, wavy locks. One mulatto girl present wore her own hair—frizzly and thick as the mane of a Shetland pony—flowing down to her waist in gipsy style. Where turbans were not worn among the fairer skinned, the hair was generally confined with a colored ribbon. At least three-fourths of the audience were women, and of these one-third, perhaps, were smoking—several of the white girls were chewing. Of the men present, the great number were roustabouts, in patched attire, often of the most fantastic description. Four musicians played lively old-time tunes before the stage, and through the half-open door at the other end of the theater glimpses were visible of an expanse of purple, star-studded sky, a more deeply purple expanse of rippling river, the dark rolling outline of the Kentucky hills, and a long line of yellow points of light, scattered along the curving shore as far as the eye could reach. From without, the cool, sweet river air occasionally crept in by gentle breaths, and from within, the dim light of trembling candle-flame, the blue wreaths of heavy tobacco smoke, the sound of vociferous laughter and the notes of wild music, all floated out together into the white moonlight.

The little stage curtain rose, or, rather, parted, upon a scene originally ludicrous in itself, which evoked a shout of mingled glee and amusement from the expectant audience. The six performers were, with one exception, very dark men, with pronounced negro features; but they had exaggerated their natural physiognomical characteristics by a lavish expenditure of burnt cork and paint. The mouths of the end-men grinned from ear to ear; their eyes appeared monstrous, and their attire could not have been done justice to by any ordinary play-bill artist. It was a capital get up in its line, such as white minstrels could hardly hope to equal. The three principal performers were professionals from Louisville. The right end man had a tambourine with a silver rim, which he unfortunately smashed during the evening by knocking it against his pate, and as a tambourine performer he can not have many white rivals, tapping the instrument against his hand, elbow, knee, head, foot, with a rapidity which almost defied the eye to follow it.

After the first musical performance minstrel jokes were in order, including odd conundrums, "hits" at the patrolmen, and miscellaneous jokes of a humorous, but always innocent description. Here is a specimen:

"How dy'e feel to-night, Mr. Royal?"

"I feel's as if I was in de clouds; an' angels pouring 'lasses all over me."

"Well, Mr. Royal, I want to prepose a kolumdrum to you. Kin you spell 'blind pig' with two letters?"

"Cou'se I kin. Blind pig?—let's see!—pig? P-g, pig."

"Wrong, sir; wrong. B-l-i-n-d, blind, p-i-g, pig—blind pig. Thar's an 'i' in pig, an' you left out the eye."

"But if he's got an eye, he can't be a blind pig."

[Roars of laughter.]

"Hev' you got a wife, Mr. Moore?"

"Yes."

"Isn't it sweet to hev' a nice little wife?"

"Yes."

"When you git up in de morning she kin give you a s-t-r-o-n-g cup of coffee."

"Yes."

"An' give you nice, strong butter?"

"No; not strong butter."

"An' give you a nice, strong hug?"

"Yes."

"An' kiss you at the door, and say, 'By-by, baby; dream of me?'"

"Yes."

"An' when y'ar just gone out the front way, open de back door an' let a great big black niggar in de back way?"

Then they sung a song, with a roaring chorus, called "Cahve de Possum," after which came more jokes, and then a most comical scene—really the best performance of the evening—between two men, one attired as a woman, with an enormously exaggerated "pull-back," and the other costumed as a journeyman whitewasher. The effects of this scene upon the audience was extremely interesting. The women not only laughed but screamed and leaped in their seats, to fall back and laugh till the tears ran down their cheeks. A well built young black woman named Lucy Mason, whose face still bore the scars of a recent razor-slash, then came upon the stage, attired in a short petticoat with scalloped edges; striped stockings, which displayed a pair of solid, well-turned legs; and boy's brogans. She danced a break-down very fairly, and was several times called out. Then a little roustabout, from New Orleans, danced a jig; and the performance closed with a lengthy but very comical extravaganza entitled "Damon and Pythias." To the curious visitor, however, the merits of the performance, although an excellent one, were far less entertaining than the spectacle of the enjoyment which it occasioned—the screams of laughter and futile stuffing of handkerchiefs in laughing mouths, the tears of merriment, the innocent appreciation of the most trivial joke, the stamping of feet and leaping, and clapping of hands—a very extravaganza of cachination.

Midnight twanged out from the ancient clock, laughter was heard only in occasional chuckles, a roustabout extinguished the footlights with his weatherbeaten hat, the bar became thronged with dusky drinkers, and the musicians put their instruments by. Then the room suddenly vibrated in every fiber of its pine-planking to a long, deeply swelling sound, which suddenly hushed the chatter like a charm. Half of the hearts in the room beat a little faster—hearts well trained to recognize the Voices of the River; and the sound grew stronger and sweeter, like an unbroken roll of soft, rich, deep thunder. "The Wildwood," shouted a score of voices at once, and the throng rushed out on the levee to watch the great white boat steaming up in the white moonlight, with a weird train of wreathing smoke behind her, and dark lovers of swarthy levee girls on board.

19
AMONG THE SPIRITS

An *Enquirer* Reporter Communicates with His Father

⊷ ⧻◆⧻ ⊶

"Be thou a spirit of health, or goblin damned,
Bring with thee airs from heaven or blasts from hell,
Be thy intents wicked or charitable,
Thou com'st in such questionable shape
That I will speak to thee"

*   *   *

"I am thy father's spirit,
Doom'd for a certain term to walk the night."

—*Hamlet: Scene IV.*

After his last visit to No. 16 Barr street, the reporter resolved to go through a course of purification before again presuming to enter that ghostly temple; for his spiritualistic friend had maliciously suggested that the spirits objected to him as being physically and psychically filthy. He began by taking a bath, and washed himself seven times in a mystic manner. Moreover, he promised to abstain from tobacco, to live on mush and milk, to wear a clean shirt, to black his boots every morning, and to forswear swearing. Alas for the fragility of such promises, so aptly compared to pie-crusts! He longed after the flesh-pots of Egypt, and devoured beefsteak rare the very next morning; he neglected his linen; and he found it hard to confine himself to five cigars a day. However, he actually succeeded in sticking to his last resolution for six long and weary days; but happening to look at the office clock last Friday afternoon, and finding himself twenty minutes behind time for the seance, he unfortunately said something at the very last moment that the recording angel must have put down in black and white. It was therefore with horrible qualms of conscience that he entered Mrs. Smith's parlor.

The reporter was kindly received by the medium, who looked younger and prettier than ever. "Your last report was a very fair one," she said, smiling; "but you made some dreadful mistakes in describing that room up-stairs. The windows are *not* at the north side, and the closet is *not* in the west wall, and there *is* a carpet upon the floor."

The reporter apologized for the inaccuracy, and promised to correct it, excusing himself at the same time for his unpunctuality.

"My husband has not yet come home from the gallery," said the me-dium [Mr. Smith is a photographer]; but this lady, Mrs. ———, will take his place in the circle.

The lady to whom the reporter was now introduced looks much more like a medium than Mrs. Smith. She is not tall, but of a physique as robust as that of Mrs. Hollis, with dark hair and steady, piercing black eyes, a rather high forehead, and lips indicative of great power of will. She is evi-dently a person of much force of character, yet withal of a frank and kindly manner. The reporter regrets being unable to give her name—especially as her husband happens to be a prominent citizen of Cincinnati. After some brief conversation the three proceeded upstairs and commenced prepara-tions for the seance.

"You don't like to tie Mrs. Smith yourself, I believe?" said the black-eyed lady, with a peculiar smile.

"Indeed I had rather not," pleaded the reporter; "I don't know how."

"Well, you must at least fasten the rope behind the chair; and you must examine the room. You can tack down her dress to the floor if you like, and tie her feet to the chair."

The reporter declined to act upon the last two somewhat malicious suggestions; but he examined the room, and tied the rope as desired. The preparations made were similar to those described in his last report; the medium's dress being nailed to the floor; the doors locked and fastened with pen-knives, etc. Then the tin trumpet was placed in the middle of the floor, but out of the reach of any one in the circle; the gas was put out, and the sitting commenced. It may be as well to mention here that the reporter took good care to satisfy himself that the medium was securely fastened, at the same time remarking, that so far as he was personally concerned his possible convictions would not be weakened or strengthened by the fact of Mrs. Smith being fettered or unfettered; but that having to lay a statement before the public it were just as well that the usual course was adopted. Mrs. ——— observed that the spirits preferred that the medium should be tied.

For nearly an hour the circle waited for news from the Spirit-world, at first beguiling the time with conversation, and a little singing in which all joined. The musical hymn with the well-known refrain—

"On the other side of Jordan,
In the green fields of Eden,
There is rest for the weary,
There is rest for you—"

was sung several times, and also several other pieces; but the spirits appeared to be unwilling. The conversation gradually slackened, until the circle sat in a dreary silence, interrupted only by the occasional cries of children in the street at play, or the rumble of a passing vehicle.

"I really hope we are not going to be disappointed this time," said the medium, finally breaking the silence. "It would be too bad."

"I wish Mr. Mitchel would come and speak to the gentleman," said Mrs. ———.

"Who is Mr. Mitchel?" asked the reporter.

"Why," answered the medium, "a spirit, of course."

"Yes; but I meant to ask what he was before he became a spirit."

"Well, he says he is the brother of Professor Mitchel—the astronomer, that used to live here, you know. He first began to communicate with us nearly six years ago, when he told us some very strange things about a little private affair of our own—things we didn't know anything about beforehand—and he also told us the name of a man who he said could give us further information. Father was a strict church-member at that time, and did not, of course, believe in Spiritualism; but he went after this man just for curiosity, and found him at last after a good deal of trouble. The man was a kind of artist—used to touch up pictures. He told my father everything that the spirit had referred to. Mitchel nearly always attends our sittings now; and sometimes you would be surprised at the manifestations he gives. He will talk in a loud, deep voice—just like a person in the flesh, and sing, and stamp on the floor.

"I think, said Mrs. ———, "that we are talking too much. When you talk, Mary, it makes you too positive. We had better sing something. Don't you know some song?"—to the reporter.

The reporter sang some songs in a very dismal voice, until the bells announced that it was six o'clock. An hour and a quarter had passed away.

"The spirits are going to do something, I know," suddenly exclaimed Mrs. ———, in tones of quiet satisfaction. "I feel an unusually strong influence. They will certainly lift that trumpet. Do you feel the influence strongly, Mary?"

"Not as strong as I generally do," answered the medium.

"Do you feel the influence?"—to the reporter.

"I have no idea what the 'influence' is like—except from reading Bulwer Lytton's fantastic tales. He speaks of such an influence in one of his horrid stories, as a 'ghastly exhalation' rising through the floor—a vague, but awful description, isn't it? How does the influence affect you?"

"Why, a strange kind of numbness creeps all over me, as if my whole body was 'going to sleep' in the sense that one's foot is said to go to sleep. This feeling is accompanied by a curious sense of *expansion,* as it were: my hands, for instance, seem to increase in size. But I can not describe the feeling properly. Ah! I felt a hand laid on my arm this moment. We had better continue singing; the spirits like it."

Suddenly the reporter distinctly felt the fingers of a hand touching, first the lower part of his right thigh, and then his knee in a rapid succession of taps. The taps seemed to be given by the first finger and thumb of a right hand—a heavy, strong hand—which closed as they touched the reporter's thigh, as though in the attempt to pinch slightly without hurting. The sensation, at the same time, was extremely peculiar, each tap being followed by a very faint shock as of electricity. The reporter naturally started.

"Did you touch me, Mrs. ———?"

"No, sir. You had better take hold of my hands."

The reporter did so, but the ghostly touches were continued, and the strange shocks accompanying them became stronger. Mrs. Smith still sat at the opposite side of the room, occasionally talking while the spectral hands were tapping the reporter's knee. He endeavored to catch hold of them, holding both of Mrs. ———'s hands with his right, and seeking the ghostly hands with his left. But he could not touch them. Then another hand, a very small one, was laid upon the upper part of his right arm, and closed its fingers upon the limb for an instant, sending a peculiar, but not disagreeable, thrill through the reporter's frame.

The trumpet then began to move along the floor, making a strange tinkling sound as it passed over the carpet. Then came a succession of faint taps, which sounded as though made by the index-finger of a hand.

"The spirit wants to say something, evidently," said Mrs. ———. "Do you want anything?"—to the spirit.

"Yes."—[three taps.]

"What is it?"

[No answer.]

"Are we sitting right?"

"No!"—[a single emphatic tap.]

"What is the matter?"

[No answer.]

At that moment the trumpet was raised from the floor, and struck the reporter heavily on the right thigh three times. Then it repeated the operation on his knee.

"Perhaps somebody has their legs crossed," said Mrs. ———. "Have you, sir?"

"Yes." The reporter had his right leg crossed over his left for some time. He uncrossed them at once.

"You must not sit that way according to the rules of the seance. The spirits don't like it. Is it all right now?"—to the spirit.

Three emphatic taps; and three blows with the trumpet on both of the reporter's knees. The touch of the trumpet did not produce the peculiar shock caused by the touch of the fingers. A moment after, the spirit laid the trumpet down in its first position and departed.

"I wonder if that could have been Mitchel?" said Mrs. ———.

The state of affairs had now become really interesting. After a minute or two the trumpet was moved again, but this time with apparent difficulty, as though the ghostly fingers were too unsubstantial for the task.

"I guess that's Maudie," said the medium.

"No; I should rather think it is one of this gentleman's relatives—the spirit is so weak. It is always weak the first time it tries to speak."

The tinkling noise seemed to move in the direction of the medium. Then there came a distinct sound of *kisses*—kisses in quick succession, as though coming from the small, chubby lips of a child; and the word "Mamma" was repeated in a distinct, soft whisper.

"Ah! that's Maudie," said the medium. "What is it, darling?"

"Why isn't papa here."

"If we knew you wished to speak to him, darling, we would not have formed the circle without him."

"Won't you bring some flowers next time?"

"Yes, dear."

The spirit then seemed to go to Mrs. ———, and kissed her. The child-voice asked once more for flowers; and the trumpet was returned to its place.

Again the reporter felt a hand laid upon his knee—a strong, heavy hand, like the hand of a man, and the touch was accompanied by the same strange electric thrill as before. The trumpet was again raised. It was first laid on the visitor's knees, and then brought over to where the medium was sitting. A voice spoke through it in a deep, hoarse whisper.

"Some spirit wishes to speak with the gentleman," said the medium.

The trumpet then appeared to be brought to within about four inches of the reporter's face, and the voice addressed him by a name by which he is unknown to his friends in this country, but which he at once recognized. The reporter did not mention this fact to the medium for private reasons; and no one but himself caught the name. The greater part of the sentence following was indistinguishable; but the word "father" was distinctly uttered.

"Do I understand you to say that you are my father?'

"Yes"—[feebly].

"Please give your name."

[Two indistinguishable whispers.]

"Your full name, please."

Three indistinct whispers. The whispers sounded much like the full name, but the reporter wished to hear it distinctly given. The middle name is a curious one, and the reporter's father never was in America, or known to any person in this country, so far as can be ascertained.

"Please try again?"

"Charles"—the rest indistinguishable.

Several more unsuccessful efforts were made. Then a whisper came— "I shall try to grow stronger," and the trumpet was laid down.

In about a minute it came again, and the voice clearly and distinctly uttered the full name:

"Charles Bush H——."*

"That is the name."

"I am your father, P——."†

"Have you any word for me?"

"Yes."

"What is it?"

"Forgive me"—in a long whisper.

"I have nothing to forgive."

"You have, indeed"—very faintly.

"What is it?"

"You know well"—distinctly.

"Will you write it?"

"I don't know how."

"There is a pencil and paper upon the table."

"I will try. I will try to grow stronger."

The trumpet was replaced for several minutes, after which the spirit returned.

"I wronged you: forgive me"—a loud, distinct whisper.

"I do not consider that you have."

---

*I.e. Hearn.

†I.e. Patricio (or Patrick as he was called as a child), Lafcadio's original first name.

"It would be better not to contradict the spirit," interrupted the medium, "until it has explained matters."

"I do not wish to contradict the spirit in the sense you imply," answered the reporter. "*I thoroughly understand the circumstance alluded to;* but I wish to explain that I have long ceased to consider it as a wrong done me." *To the spirit*—"Please state explicitly the circumstance you refer to."

"You know."

"Am I to understand that you prefer not to speak of it in the circle?"

"Yes."

"Will you write it?"

"I will try."

The trumpet was once more replaced. After waiting a few minutes the reporter, inadvertently, and, he believes, noiselessly *crossed his feet in the dark;* and to his surprise immediately received a heavy blow from the trumpet on the *left* foot, which happened to be uppermost. The trumpet rang again with the stroke, and was violently tapped, as with strong fingers. It is needless to say that the reporter uncrossed his feet without delay.

"That must be Mr. Mitchel," said Mrs. ———.

"Is that you, Mitchel?" inquired the medium.

"Yes; the father wishes to speak with his son. He would write to him, but he has not yet learned the law by which that can be done." This was spoken in the loud, deep, clear voice of a vigorous man.

"Will he be able to write?"

"Not yet. But it *can* be done"—with a remarkably strong emphasis upon the word in italics. The voice seemed to come from the floor, immediately at the reporter's feet.

In a short time the former voice again spoke; but only to testify pleasure "at meeting my son," and promising to endeavor to gain strength for a more satisfactory communication. Then followed a sound as of footsteps, moving around the reporter's chair, and seeming to die away in the direction of the wall—heavy footfalls, as of a man; yet the slight floor did not respond to the heavy tread by the faintest vibration.

"You had better ask Mr. Mitchel to assist your father," said Mrs. ———. "He will answer any questions you may wish to put."

"You are better acquainted with Mr. Mitchel than I am," answered the reporter. "Be kind enough to ask him for me."

"Mr. Mitchel," said the lady, "will you please let this gentleman know what his father wishes to say?"

No answer.

"This is a reporter, Mr. Mitchel. He intends to publish his experience at this seance."

"Humph!" said the spirit, in a slightly sarcastic manner.

"Don't you think it would help our cause, Mr. Mitchel?"

A long, weary sigh, and a succession of taps upon the trumpet.

Just at that moment a loud knock sounded upon the door; the trumpet fell upon the carpet with a loud crash, as if dropped from the ceiling. The spell was broken.

"Ah! that spoils our sitting for the remainder of the evening," said Mrs. ———, turning up the gas, and opening the door to admit Mr. Smith.

"Why, it is after seven o'clock," said that gentleman. "I am sorry to have broken up the sitting, but I did not suppose you were having any manifestations."

The seance had lasted more than two hours.

Mrs. Smith was still sitting, exactly as she had been tied previous to the performance; her dress strongly nailed down to the floor; and the ropes fastened exactly as they had been before the *seance commenced.* The reporter examined the knots he had made, and found them intact.

In conclusion the author of this statement wishes to inform the readers that he has endeavored to lay before them a plain, unvarnished report of facts. He can offer no explanation of them, but leaves the reader to his own conclusions. It may be well to mention, however, that the words uttered by the Voice regarding something it refused to explain more fully appeared to allude to a rather curious bit of private family history. The reporter can not conceive of any possible means by which the secret of the name given by the Voice could have come to the knowledge of either of the lady mediums present—especially as even the steps necessary to produce mesmeric clairvoyance had not been taken. The person supposed to speak to the visitor had spent the greater part of his life in Hindostan,* and had been buried at sea in the Mediterranean in 1866. Neither of the parties concerned have, or ever did have, any relatives or connections, however distant, in the United States.

---

*The Persian name of India, often applied to the whole Indian peninsula.

20

SOME STRANGE EXPERIENCE

The Reminiscences of a Ghost-Seer

———— ✠ ————

"They do say the dead never come back again," she observed half dreamingly; "but then I have seen such queer things!"

She was a healthy, well built country girl, whom the most critical must have called good looking, robust and ruddy, despite the toil of life in a boarding-house kitchen, but with a strangely thoughtful expression in her large dark eyes, as though she were ever watching the motions of Somebody who cast no shadow, and was invisible to all others. Spiritualists were wont to regard her as a strong "medium," although she had a peculiar dislike of being so regarded. She had never learned to read or write, but possessed naturally a wonderful wealth of verbal description, a more than ordinarily vivid memory, and a gift of conversation which would have charmed an Italian *improvisatore*. These things we learned during an idle half hour passed one summer's evening in her company on the kitchen stairs; while the boarders lounged on the porch in the moonlight, and the hall lamp created flickering shadows along the varnished corridors, and the hungry rats held squeaking carnival in the dark dining-room. To the weird earnestness of the story-teller, the melody of her low, soft voice, and the enthralling charm of her conversation, we cannot attempt to do justice; nor shall we even undertake to report her own mysterious narrative word for word, but only to convey to the reader those impressions of it which linger in the writer's memory.

"The first thing I can remember about ghost-people," she said, "happened to me when I was quite a little child. It was in Bracken County, Kentucky, on a farm, between Dover and Augusta—about half way between the towns—for I remember a great big stone that was set up on the road just above the farm, which they called the 'Half-way Stone,' and it had a big letter H cut on it. The farm-house was away back from the river, in a lonely place, among woods of beech and sugar-trees; and was one of the weirdest old buildings you ever saw. It was built before there were any nails used out West; so you can imagine how old it was; and I heard that the family who first built it had many a terrible fight with the Indians. Before the house ran a rocky lane full of gutters and mud holes; and behind it was a great apple orchard, where very few apples grew, because no one took care of the trees. Great slimy, creeping plants had grown up about them, and strangled them; and the pathways were almost grown over with high weeds, and strong rank grass; and owls lived in some of the trees, but the family seemed to be afraid to shoot them. At the end of the orchard yawned a great, deep well, unused for many years; cats and dogs and rabbits had found graves in the fetid black water; the stones were green with moss and slime; the bucket was covered with moss; and great black snakes which lived in holes in the sides of the well used to wriggle out on sunny days and blink their wicked, slimy eyes at the house. This well was at the mouth of a deep hollow, choked up with elder-brush and those creeping plants that can never be killed, and there were black-snakes, garter-snakes and dry-land moccasins living there. Near the hollow on the other side flowed a clear "branch" of water, over a bed of soft blue clay, which we used to roll into "slate pencils" and make mud pies of. One time we wanted to make a little mill-dam there, to drown some geese in, and while digging into the blue clay with a grubbing-hoe we found four great big Mexican dollars buried there. We did not know what they were then, and we brought them to the farmhouse, where they took them from us. Some time afterwards two men came and bought the piece of ground where we had found the money, and they set to digging; but nothing more was ever found there.

"The farmhouse looked as if it had been built a hundred years ago, but those who built it built well and strong, for it was sound from roof to foundation. Many of the big trees in the orchard, planted by them, had rotted and died, and the bark was peeling off over nests of the gray wood-lice that burrowed under it; but the old house was still strong. It was a very queer, antiquated structure, with ghostly looking gables, and great limestone chimneys towered up at each end of it. There were four big rooms, two up stairs and two down stairs, and a little kitchen built against the house, making a fifth room; there were five old-fashioned doors of heavy planking, and there were eight or ten narrow windows, with ever so many tiny panes of glass in them. The house was built of heavy sarsaparilla logs, with floors of black walnut, and walls ceiled with blue ash; and there were no shelves, but only recesses in the walls—small, square recesses, where books and little things were kept. The clapboards were fastened down on the roof with wooden pegs, and the flooring was pegged down to the sleepers. Between the planking and the logs of the south room on the first floor there was an old Revolutionary musket built into the wall. The north room, next to this, was never occupied.

"I remember that room well; for the door was often open, although no one of the family ever entered it since an old lady named Frankie Boyd had died there, years before, of consumption. She had lingered a long time, and coughed a great deal, and used to spit on the wall beside the bed. The bed was an old-time piece of furniture, with posters; and all the furniture was old-fashioned. There was an old-fashioned clothes-chest with legs; an old-fashioned rocking-chair, with great heavy rockers; and an old-fashioned spinning-wheel. One of the old lady's dresses, a black dress, still hung on the wall where she had placed it the last time she had taken it off; but it had become so old and moth-eaten that a touch would have crumbled it like so much burnt paper. The dust was thick on the floor, so thick that the foot would leave an impression in it; and the windows were yellow like parchment for want of cleaning.

"They said that the old lady used to walk about that room, and that no one could sleep there. Doors used to open and shut without the touch of human hands; and all night long the sound of that rocking-chair rocking, and of the spinning-wheel humming, could be heard through the house. That was why nobody ever went into that room. But the ghost of Frankie Boyd was not the only ghost there. The house had once been owned by the Paddy family, and Lee Paddy, the "old man," and all his children, had died in the room used when I was there for a kitchen, and had been buried in the family graveyard, on the north side of the house, under the shadow of a great locust tree. After Frankie Boyd died the house fell into the hands of her nephew, a man named Bean, who had a rich father, a scientific old gentleman, in Lewis County. Both father and son were queer people, and the old man's eccentricity at one time nearly lost him his life. Some one killed an immense blacksnake on his farm, and the scientific Mr. Bean had it cooked for dinner after the manner of cooking salmon. Then he invited a friendly neighbor to dine with him. They say that the neighbor was delighted with the repast, and declared that he had never eaten finer salmon. But when Old Bean told him that he had eaten a black snake which John killed yesterday morning, the shock nearly killed him, and he staggered home to get his shot-gun. Bean did not dare to leave his home for weeks afterwards.

"After the death of Frankie Boyd, the old farmhouse in Bracken County of course became a weirder and ghostlier place than ever—a scary place, as the slaves around there used to call it. It was a dreadfully creaky place, and no one could pass out or down the old staircase without making a prodigious creaking and crackling. Now at all hours of the day or night those stairs creaked and creaked, and doors opened and banged, and steps echoed overhead in the rooms upstairs. I was a very little girl then and had a little boy-playmate, who used to run about with me all over the farm, digging in the blue clay, running after the fowls, watching the great snakes that glided about the noisome well, climbing the strangled apple trees in search of withered and shrunken apples, and throwing pebbles at the great, ugly horned owls that used to sit there among the creepers, blinking with their great yellow eyes. We did not know why the house was haunted by such odd noises; and the old negro servants were strictly forbidden to tell us anything about the queer things that walked about there. But, nevertheless, we had a perfect horror of the house; we dreaded to be left in it alone; we never entered it on sunny days, except at meal time, and when foul weather forced us to stay in-doors the folks often found us sitting down and crying in a corner. We could not at first tell why we cried, further than that we were afraid of something undefinable—a vague fear always weighed upon us like a nightmare. They told us to go upstairs, one evening after dark, and we had to go without a light. Something came after us, and stepped up the stairs behind us, and touched our heads, and followed us into the room, and seemed to sob and moan. We screamed with fear, and the folks ran up with a lantern and took us down stairs again. Some one used also to play with the rusty old musket that had been built into the wall, and would get under the black walnut floor, knocking loudly and long; and all the time the rocking-chair creaked and thumped in the north room. Bean had got used to it all; but he seldom went up stairs, and the books in the old recesses became black with layers of clammy dust, and the spiders spun thick, glutinous webs across the windows.

"It came to pass about six months after the dead had followed us into the dark room upstairs, that a great storm came down through the woods, wrestling with the ancient trees, tearing away the serpent-creepers in the garden, swelling the springs to torrents, and the old farmhouse rattled through all its dry bones. The great limestone chimneys and the main building stood the test bravely: but the little kitchen building where all the Paddy family had died, was shattered from clapboards to doorstep. It had been built in a very curious fashion, a fashion passed away and forgotten; and the cunning of modern house builders could not rebuild it. So they pulled it down, log by log, and brought destruction upon many spider colonies, and mice nests, and serpent holes; building a new pinewood structure in its place, with modern doors and windows. And from that time the strange noises ceased and the dead seemed to rest, except in the room where the yellow spittle had dried upon the walls and the old-fashioned furniture had become hoary with years of dust. The steps on the staircase died away forever, and the knocking beneath the floor ceased.

"But I must not forget to tell you one more curious thing about the place. There was a hen-house near the grave of the Paddy family; and the hens were great in multitude, and laid eggs by hundreds. Somehow or other we could scarcely ever get any eggs for all that. The hens were thin, spectral birds, which looked as if they had been worn out by anxiety and disappointment. Something or other used to steal their eggs the moment they were laid; and what it was no one ever pretended to know. The old negro cook hinted that the ghosts of the Paddy family sucked the eggs; but as we could never find even an egg-shell, this supposition did not hold good. Traps were laid for polecats, weasels, coons, and every variety of wild egg-thieves; but none were ever seen there or caught; and the poultry ceased to propagate their species, so that fresh relays of poultry had to be purchased ever and anon. I don't know whether the old farmhouse still stands, or whether Bachelor Bean has been gathered to his fathers, for it is many years since I left there to live with friends at Dover.

"I had another experience, of a much more unpleasant kind, I think, during the time I remained at Dover. All the country round there is hilly; and there are two broad turnpike roads winding out of the city—one called the Maysville pike, the other the Dover pike, running from Dover beyond Minerva. Now, both of these pikes have been the scene of violent death; and both are said to be haunted. Of the latter fact I have the testimony of my own eyes—which, I make bold to remark, are very sharp eyes.

"About four miles from Dover, on the Maysville pike, the road, following the winding of the hills, crosses a rude bridge of rocks and timber over a swift stream, and curves into the shape of a gigantic horse-shoe. This place is called 'Horse-shoe Bend,' is situated between two hills, and is wild and 'scary' in the extreme. Since the occurrence which gave a specter to Horse-shoe Bend, few have the courage to pass the spot after nightfall; and those who must, put spurs to their horses and gallop by as though the Devil were riding behind them; for the specter of a suicide haunts the bend.

"I can't well remember when it happened, but I do not think it was more than half a dozen years ago; and I even forget the man's name. I only know that he was a married man, pretty well-to-do, and lived at Rock Springs, below Augusta. One day he left his home on business, and was detained in town beyond his usual hour for returning. It was a bright, frosty winter's night; the pike was white and hard as iron, and his horse's hoofs made merry music on the long trot home, until he saw his farmhouse and its shadow lying black and sharp on the fields, and the blood-red glow of the wood fire in the great limestone fireplace. Then it occurred to him, strangely enough, to dismount, tie his horse to a tree, and creep softly up to the window. His wife sat by the fire, but not alone; the arm of a stranger was about her waist, and the fingers of a stranger were playing with her hair. Then he turned, sick at heart, from the window, and crept along in the shadows to where his horse stood, and mounted and rode away, recklessly, madly, furiously. People who looked out of their windows as he passed say they never saw man ride so before. The hard pike flashed into fire under the iron hoofs of the flying horse, the rider cursed like a fiend, and the great watchdogs in the farmhouses, howled as though a specter were sweeping by. Neither horse nor horseman ever returned. Some little school children next morning passing by Horseshoe Bend, in the golden light of the early sun, saw the farmer hanging from a tree by his bridle rein; and the horse laying by the side of the road, dead, and frozen like his rider. Preacher Holton and Sam Berry cut down the body; but the specter of the suicide has never left the spot. They say the only way to make the spirit of a suicide rest is to bury the body with a stake driven through it. I don't know whether that is true; but I know that every time I passed Horse-shoe Bend I could see the farmer leaning against a tree, dressed in his gray winter suit, and the horse lying down by the side of the road. You could see the very woof of the cloth, the very hair of the black horse: yet the moment you got near enough to touch the specter with the hand, it passed away like the flame of a candle blown out. I have often seen it.

"I don't know very much about the history of the apparition which haunts the other pike; I have forgotten the name, but I have seen the thing which walks there. About three miles from Dover, on the way to Minerva, is a toll gate, and about a mile and a half above the toll gate is a place called Firman's Woods, a hilly place, with trees. In a hollow by the side of the road at this point, a farmer was murdered for his money, and his body flung into the brush. He had ridden over that road a hundred times, and paid many a toll at the toll-gate; everybody knew his grizzled beard and broad-brimmed hat when he passed by. On the night of the murder he had disposed of some stock and was returning home with a well filled pocketbook, when he met another horse-man traveling toward Minerva. Perhaps he was incautious with his new ac-quaintance; perhaps he foolishly displayed the greasy pocket-book, fat with rolls of green bills, for on reaching Firman's Woods the stranger stabbed him to the heart with a bowie-knife, hid the corpse in the hollow, and galloped off with the dead man's money. The victim of the murder has never found the sleepy rest of death. A spectral rider gallops nightly along the pike, sometimes flying past the toll-gate invisible, his horse's hoofs echoing loud and sharply of cold nights, and splashing through the mud with a soggy sound on rainy evenings. But he is only seen at Firman's Woods—a shadowy figure, headless and horrible. I have seen it, and beheld it dissolve like the flame of a candle in a strong current of wind.

"The most frightful experience I ever had—at least the one which fright-ened me most—was in the town of Minerva. I was working for a family there as cook, and my room was a dark and shadowy apartment, in the back of the building. It had a window, but the window gave scarcely any light, because it faced a higher building across the alley, and had not been cleaned for years. I thought there was something queer about the room, because the first day I came to the house Joe ———— took me upstairs with a candle in his hand, and said, 'You won't be afraid to sleep here, will you?' Well, I said, 'No.'"

[Here we ventured to ask the narrator what Joe's other name was, but she objected, for private reasons, to mention it, and we had to content ourselves with the fact that Joe was the proprietor of the house and a man of family.]

"I worked there only one day. When supper was over, and the dishes had been washed up, and everything put in order, I went upstairs to bed. I remember that I felt afraid—I could not tell why—to blow the candle out; but I thought the folks would scold me for wasting candles, so I blew it out at last, and crept into bed, and tried to pull the covers up over me. I found I could not move them at first; they seemed to be nailed to the foot of the bed. Then I gave a very strong pull, and succeeded in getting the clothes up, although it seemed as if a heavy weight had been lying on them. Suddenly I felt a distinct pull back—something was pulling the clothes off of the bed. I pulled them back again, and they were again pulled off. Of course I felt frightened; but I had seen and heard strange things before, and concluded to lie down quietly and let the clothes be, because I thought that if I would let the Thing alone, it would let me alone. And at last I fell asleep.

"I don't know how long I slept; but I had a hideous nightmare, and awoke panting in the dark, feeling that something was in the room with me. About a minute afterward it put its fingers on my mouth, and then stroked my nose. I thought of getting up, but I was too frightened to move; when I felt an immense hand placed on my chest, pressing me down to the bed—a hand so vast that it covered me from shoulder to shoulder, and felt heavier than iron. I was too frightened to faint, too spell-bound to scream, too powerless to move under that giant pressure. And with the pressure came horror, a horror of hell, unspeakably awful, worse than the ghastly enchantment of a thousand nightmares. I remember that I would have wished to die but for the hideous fancy that my ghost would go out in the dark to that awful Thing. The hand was suddenly removed, and I shrieked like a maniac in the dungeon of a lunatic asylum. Every one heard that shriek; and they came running up with lights and white faces. They showed me the doors and the windows securely fastened, and showed me that no human being had been in the room besides myself; but I did not need to be told that. I left the house next day.

"There was something of the same kind in a house in Lexington, where I used to live. It had once been owned by a lady named Jane ————, a slaveholder in the days before the war; but she had passed to the place of Shadows, and her house had fallen into other hands. Still her sins haunted it—haunted it horribly. They say that one winter's night, many years ago, she had whipped a negro slave to death with her own hands for some trifling act of disobedience. He was a powerful man, but they had stripped and securely tied him so that resistance was impossible, and the woman beat him with a leather strap, dipped in water, for eight consecutive hours. And the body died and was buried under the floor, and became green with rottenness; but the ghost of the man walked about and groaned, and tormented all who lived in the building. The woman used to sit on her doorstep all night crying in the moonshine, while the ghost groaned within. At last she moved away, and died in another neighborhood; but even when I was there the specter used to pull the bedclothing off the beds down stairs, if any one dared to sleep there.

"I have seen and heard many odd things of this kind; and once I saw what they call a wraith or a double, but I don't think you would find them so interesting as my last experience in a Cincinnati house. It was on West Fifth street, and I was working there both as cook and chambermaid. There was a story connected with the house, which I never knew correctly, and will therefore not attempt to relate, beyond that a certain young girl died there and came back afterwards. But I was not told about this circumstance until I had worked there for some time. It happened one evening, about dusk, that I went upstairs to one of the bed-rooms on an errand; and I saw a young lady, all in white, standing before the mirror, tall and silent. The sun had set the color of blood that evening, and a faint rosy-glow still mingled with the gloomy gray, so that objects were plainly discernible and sharply outlined. Now, as I had left all the boarders at supper, I thought on first entering the room that the figure before the mirror must be that of some lady visitor, whose coming I had not known. I stood for a moment and looked at her, but did not see any face, for her back was turned to me, and, as she seemed unusually tall, I thought that the blackness of her hair was lost in the blackness of the shadows above the mirror. But it suddenly occurred to me to glance at the mirror. I did so. There was the figure, tall, silent and white, but there was no face or head visible. I approached to touch the white shadow; it vanished like the flame of a candle vanishes, or as the breath vanishes from the mirror that has been breathed upon.

"People call me a medium, sometimes, and ask me to sit in dark circles and help to call up spirits. I have always refused—do you wonder at it? I tell you the truth, sir, when I say that far from refusing to leave the dead alone, I would be only too happy if they would leave me alone."

21

HACELDAMA

Humanity and Inhumanity in the Shambles
Hebrew Slaughters, Gentile Butchers, and Consumptive Blood-Drinkers

— ⇌ —

It is true that from a merely commercial standpoint, the daily sacrifice of beeves in the slaughter-houses of the Tallow District possesses little interest compared with the porcine holocausts of Bank street; and the fact that a Hebrew butcher cuts the throat of a bullock with a peculiarly-shaped knife is of less moment to the practical minded than the fact that the hog may be killed, scalded, cleaned and cut-up in the wonderfully brief period of three minutes. But there is always an interest attaching to the violent taking of life, which has no connection with results of profit and loss; there is always food for curiosity in the haceldama: the sight of slaughter will never cease to exercise a certain fascination upon those unfamiliar with its horrors. And the higher the organization of the victim, the greater must be the interest in its sufferings. This truth was fully recognized by the bloodthirsty rulers of imperial Rome. When Commodus gave those famous exhibitions of his extraordinary skill in slaughter, which were witnessed, it is said, by a million spectators, he delighted the rabble by the butchery of the most rare and curious animals, brought at an enormous expense from all parts of the known world to Rome. The skill of the "imperial sagittary, beautiful as an Antinous and majestic as a Jupiter, whose hand was so steady and whose aim so true that he was never known to miss," must have afforded of itself a most entertaining spectacle. But the principal pleasure of the exhibition lay, after all, in the sight of the death-throes of the beautiful animals turned loose in the arena,—in the satisfaction of a monstrous bloodthirstiness, in beholding animal agonies of a totally novel description. The sight of a headless ostrich running at full speed after having been decapitated by a crescent-headed arrow was vastly more entertaining than the movements of a chicken after having been beheaded; and the dying agonies of an elephant or a hippopotamus much more interesting than the sufferings of a bull or a boar,—for the simple reason that they were more horrible. The animals most susceptible to suffering were, consequently, most sought after; and the human animal was, of course, in high requisition. And, for somewhat analogous reasons, we consider the sights of a slaughter-house more interesting than the sights of a pork factory—the slaughter of a bullock of more moment than the violent death of a hog. Indeed, of all domesticated animals the hog shares our sympathies the least; its proverbial stupidity and omnivorous gluttony are not in its favor; modern hygiene extols the wisdom of the Hebrew Lawgiver in pronouncing the hog an unclean animal; and the Moslem portrays the ghoul of his superstition with the snout and ears of a monstrous hog. The rotting bodies of the dead, the foulest ordure, the most offensive carcasses, are not less palatable to the hog than the most savory vegetable; a nice fat baby, a fowl, and even its own newly-born young, are greatly relished by this cannibal creature. It was discovered some years since in London that a certain unconscionable stock-raiser had actually contracted with several of the city hospitals for old poultices and plasters which had done service; that he had been fattening his hogs upon this hideous diet. The exact amount of suffering endured by a hog in the slaughter-house is even to the most humane a matter of less interest than the suffering of a more finely organized animal; and to evoke pity for the former would be a task of more than ordinary difficulty. But there are scenes daily to be witnessed in the slaughter-houses of the Tallow District which deserve the observation of the curious, and the attention of the humane. The Society for the Prevention of Cruelty to Animals might find much good work to do in that neighborhood.

On a boiling summer day it is not, indeed, a pleasant neighborhood to visit; its very gutters seem foul with the foetor of slaughter, and its atmosphere heavy with the odors of death,—impregnated with globules of blood. Its unpleasantness has rendered it an unfamiliar neighborhood to a large portion of the community, who have no interests in those businesses for which it is famous, and who have no desire to linger longer amid its stenches than they can possibly help. There is very little attention given by a carnivorous community—our Hebrew brethren excepted—as to how the beeves and fatlings which furnish flesh meat for general consumption come by their death, but many a beefeater would feel more concern regarding his daily diet did he but witness the death agonies of the last bullock slaughtered by his favorite butcher. The flavor, delicacy, and nutritive properties of mutton and beef depend more upon the method of slaughter than is generally supposed, and of this fact a few visits to the Quarter of Shambles would suffice to convince any intelligent observer.

To describe one Gentile slaughter-house is to describe the majority of those in the district—huge frames mostly, often painted black or red (appropriate hues of death), oftener whitewashed, with long, low pens in the rear, offal-gutters traversing the main floor from wall to wall, and great doorways yawning upon the streets in front, and exhaling heavy and deathly aromas. The impression left by a visit to the first is confirmed rather than varied by visits to half a dozen more—an impression of gloom and bad smells; daylight peering through loose planking; the head of a frightened bullock peering over the pen door; blood, thick and black, clotting on the floor, or oozing from the nostrils and throats of dying cattle; entrails, bluey-white and pale yellow; fresh quarters and sides hanging up; butchers, bare-legged and bare-armed, paddling about in the blood; naked feet encrusted with gore, and ill-shaped toes dyed crimson with the red fluid oozing up and clotting between them. Children stare in half terror, half curiosity through the open doorways, and greedy hogs are fattening on the blood and entrails which pass down to them through the offal gutter. Half the slaughter-houses keep hogs for scavengers, and it is to be observed that such hogs are seldom heard to squeal—they only grunt out their deep satisfaction, their sense of repletion and their regret that their cavernous bellies are not larger. The dull thud of the slaughterer's axe, the bellowing and stamping of terrified cattle, the slash of entrails flung into the gutter, the click-clack of steel, sharpened upon steel, an occasional curse flung at an unruly cow, and the grunting of the hogs aforesaid are the pleasant sounds which accompany the vision.

All this, however, is the brighter side of the picture—the mere background to darker and fouler things—the general impression unrelieved from its vagueness by certain sharply defined features of horror which linger in the memory of the observer long after their attendant circumstances have faded out. The inexperience of the half-grown boys, too often employed as butchers, the torture of maddened steers, the agony of a bullock under a rain of ill-placed blows, are much more unpleasant matters than entrails and odors. It is well, perhaps, that the poor brutes are not gifted with facial expression, and that one of slaughter's greatest horrors is not thus visible in the slaughter-house. But it is certain that they are often aware of the fate in store for them, especially when permitted to peer through the pen-door into the slaughter-house, and see what is going on there. We noticed in one instance a strong proof of this fact. There were two cows in a pen; and there was a large square opening in the partition between the pen and the slaughter-house. It was the first slaughter of the day when one of the animals was dragged into the shambles and dispatched in a very bungling manner. The remaining cow watched the proceedings as though fascinated with terror—she saw her companion stricken down with the axe, saw the knife enter the throat, saw the blood pouring out, saw the butcher treading on the carcass, and the red fluid flushing out in spurts from the wound with each tramp of the men's naked feet. This part of the tragedy the poor vaccine mind was perhaps unable to fully comprehend, as she had probably never seen blood before, and could not exactly understand what was being done to her sister. Neither is it likely that she understood what those great masses of red and yellow hanging from the ceiling were; for there was no semblance to the living cow in them. But when she beheld the flaying, and the decapitation, and the ghastly, headless trunk, with severed windpipe protruding, and the entrails rolling out of the carcass, and the carcass itself divided and converted into great white and yellow masses of flesh and fat like those others hanging up further away,—then the poor cow must have had a dim understanding of what had happened to her companion, for she bellowed, and kicked, and turned her eyes away from the sickening sight, and perchance puzzled her poor brains in attempts to devise means of escape. Then at last came her turn; and the butchers approached with the fatal noose. But, while the cow had sense enough to be fully aware of the design of the men who approached her, with blood-encrusted arms and crimson feet, she had not sense enough to know that resistance was worse than useless. She was conscious only of danger,—danger of having her head cut off and her inside torn out, and of being turned into great masses of yellow fat and red meat;—and so she made violent demonstrations of brave despair. Wheedling and coaxing were in vain; and the butchers loudly cursed the poor cow. But at last the noose was flung about her neck, and they laid on the rope while she braced herself to resist. Then a great, yellow-haired brute of a man, with very large calves and very ugly feet, seized a pritch, and put out the poor cow's left eye. Still she would not enter the shambles; and the cruel ruffian thrust the iron spike into the other eye, and worked the point about in the socket. Frantic with agony, and trembling in every limb, the blinded and helpless animal leaped forward and butted the door in her pain. It was no trouble now to drag her into the place of slaughter, shivering with torture, and streams of mingled blood and tears rolling down from either eye.

"Got yer eyes sore, didn't ye?—ye d——d infernal beast. Thought I'd bring ye to."

And the brawny butcher brought down the axe, not on the right spot, but on the bleeding eye; and the wretched cow, who had never before, perhaps, known rougher hands than those of the milkmaid, gave such a hideous cry! It was not bellowing or lowing, but a cry between a shriek and a moan,—a cry half human, as of one in the agony of a nightmare,—a cry of prolonged and exquisite torture. The human heart would have heaved in horror at a cry of such anguish—anguish aggravated by the terror of helpless blindness. But the butcher only laughed, and swung the axe again and again in the most unscientific, bungling and brutal way. It took nine heavy blows to fell the miserable cow, all because the butcher knew nothing about his business. At last the poor carcass rolled over, and the knife opened a passage for the blood, and the butchers danced right joyously upon the belly of the cow. With every jump the blood-stream leaped, too, but the blood looked inky, as through turned black with agony, and thus reproaching the black cruelty of the slaughterers. So we found it elsewhere. In half a dozen slaughter-houses we did not find a single butcher who seemed to know his business, or who could fell a bullock with one well directed blow between the eyes. It may have been that we had an unfortunate knack of visiting a slaughter-house at an unpropitious time, but it would rather seem that too little attention is paid to the demands of humanity by employing inhuman and inexperienced men to kill. Such cruelty as we witnessed in the instance of the poor cow which uttered so unnatural a cry, is, we were subsequently informed, not uncommon. In the killing of sheep, too, we have seen men cruel through pure laziness—slowly plunging the knife into the poor creature's throat, and carelessly working it backward and forward, and making three or four efforts to break the vertebrae apart when one energetic effort would have sufficed. If the mutton-eaters and beef-eaters, contemplating their savory steaks and chops, could but know how the animals died that furnished that food—could but guess how every fiber of the tender meat vibrated in exquisite torture but a few hours before, it is doubtful whether they would have much stomach left for breakfast. Many a cruel butcher is earning good wages for bungling work, who would be more fitly employed in those horrible cannibal markets spoken of by recent African travelers, where human flesh is sold by weight, and human legs and arms dangle in the booths. The fiend who can laugh at the tortures of a blind cow, would certainly find rare amusement in severing a human throat, in watching human eyes roll in blood, and in listening to moans of human pain. And how amusing it would be to pry out a human eye with a pritchet.

Leaving such scenes as these for the interior of a Jewish slaughter-house is actually a pleasant relief. The one we visited was a neat and roomy edifice of brick, airy, well lighted, well ventilated, purified by running water, and it seemed to us less haunted by unsavory odors. The cattle saw nothing of the place of death until brought there for slaughter. Probably the neat and cleanly appearance of the place was partly due to its construction; but one almost felt on entering that the precepts of humanity were obeyed there. Near the office door sat a dark, swarthy man, with curly black beard, handsome aquiline features, and eyes shadowed by peculiarly long lashes—a face peculiarly Hebrew, grave almost to severity, and sternly calm. This was the Shochet, the Jewish butcher.

To be a Shochet a man must be thoroughly versed in the Hebrew doc-
trine, must be a member of a Hebrew congregation, must be humane, and
must be extremely dexterous in the use of the instruments of slaughter. Consequently the Hebrew butchers are without exception an educated and respectable class of people; and, as their profession calls for a dexterity and
knowledge not commonly possessed, it is a very profitable profession. Some
slaughterers can make two hundred dollars a month. The Shochet above referred to kills (or "cuts," as they generally term it) for nine different establishments, the Jewish houses paying him a regular monthly salary, and the Gentile
houses so much a head for every animal slaughtered. The Shochet can command good prices, and is more or less an autocrat in his profession; for, being
a scrupulous and religious man, he will permit no interference in his duties.
Many of the Gentile houses employ him for the sake of Hebrew custom; but
the meat stamped with his mystical seal will find ready purchasers not only
among the followers of either faith, but among all who seek for the best with
views hygienic or epicurean. Some of our leading hotels will purchase no other
beef but that bearing the Shochet's mark.

He is allowed to use but one weapon—the knife; and to kill in but one
manner—by severing the throat with one rapid, dexterous stroke. The knives
shown to us were peculiar in shape and temper. That for slaughtering bullocks
and calves had a blade over two feet in length, of a uniform breadth and
thickness throughout, pointless and square at the end; it was a thin blade, thin
as that of a small table-knife at the middle part, or a piece of printers' brass
rule; it was about three inches in breadth, bright as silver, keen as a razor and
tempered so that it would ring like a bell if tapped with the finger-nail. The
edge was a peculiar one—not a sloping edge like that of a razor, although
quite as keen, but an edge that seemed to roll in from the blade, smooth as
French note paper and that one might pass the tip of the finger over gently
without being cut. To sharpen such a knife is not an easy matter and requires
a peculiar skill. The knife for slaughtering sheep is not larger than a small
table-knife; but is shaped, tempered, and edged precisely like the other.

Now, every Shochet must have a certificate from his rabbi before he may
practice his calling; and in order to obtain such a certificate he must pass such
an examination as will convince his examiner of his fitness and dexterity. He
must even sharpen his knife in the rabbi's presence, so as to leave no percep-
tible roughness on its edge. Pass your finger over the blade of a new pen-knife
sharpened in the ordinary manner, and you will receive a painful cut. But the
Shochet's blade is even keener, although it will not cut you by a gentle touch;
and a wound inflicted by it on a healthy person will heal up without even the
ordinary soreness consequent upon other cuts. When the Shochet has an-

swered all questions satisfactorily and demonstrated his fitness for the office, he receives his certificate, and may obtain employment wherever he can.

Before killing an animal he must pass his thumbnail over the edge of the knife, and thus assure himself that the edge is both smooth and sharp, without the least flaw or roughness that might cause unnecessary pain.

He must take heed to inflict the least possible amount of suffering.

He must examine the edge of his knife after killing each animal, and if the edge is not perfectly true, he must either resharpen the knife or use another.

He must never inflict more than one cut, if possible.

He must examine the lungs of beeves and sheep killed by him, and under no condition is he allowed to place his mark upon the meat of an animal not found perfectly healthy in these organs.

And having discharged this duty conscientiously and found the animal healthy, the Shochet stamps the meat with the mystic characters בשר, or in English letters, "kosher," signifying sound; adding also, in Hebrew characters, the day and date of slaughter. Cruelty is never practiced in Hebrew slaughter-houses; at least never in the presence of the Shochet. His religion, his humanity, and the hygiene of his profession alike prohibit any unnecessary violence to the poor dumb brutes, and his keen eyes are always watchful.

Fifteen sheep are placed in a row, with their heads on the edge of the offal gutter, the fore legs and one hind leg of each sheep tied together. The Shochet approaches with his knife between his teeth. With one hand he lifts the head of the first sheep, and with the other gently parts the wool on the throat; then for an instant he presses the head well back with the left hand, and with the right touches the throat with the knife. The sheep jerks its head away with a hissing inhalation, much like the sound involuntarily uttered by a human on the receipt of a slight burn. There was no apparent effort in that slight, rapid movement of the knife, but the blood pours from a clean wound that has severed the neck half-way through. The animal has suffered no more actual pain than that inflicted by a slight burn on the skin. It kicks a little on finding its breath coming so short, snorts a little, and passes quietly away, while the Shochet feels the edge of his blade and seizes another victim. In no instance did we observe more than one rapid cut inflicted, and none of the victims exhibited signs of much pain.

But in the slaughter of bullocks the skill of the Shochet showed best to advantage. Most of the animals were in remarkably good condition, and very tractable; for they had been well used. An attendant entered the pen and slipped a noose about one of the animal's hind legs, while another within pulled at the hoisting apparatus. Resistance to the mechanical power thus employed was soon felt by the animal to be useless, and it found itself in the slaughter-house in an astonished condition. A few more pulls at the rope, and the animal was hoisted up by the leg until it was lying on its back, very much bewildered, but not in the least hurt. Then, while the head was held back by an attendant, the Shochet advanced, and the great, bright knife passed once across the vast neck like a gleam of lightning, while the blood leaped high into the air from a yawning cut six inches deep. It was a bright crimson, a healthy red, and leaped in jets from the neck at each beat of the dying heart, finally growing thicker, and slower, until its ripple on the floor ceased and it coagulated in bright red patches, in color and form miniatures of fleecy clouds reddened by a rosy sunset. The bullock kicked feebly a few times, and died as easily as the sheep had died. To do such execution at one stroke of that light, long, thin blade requires no little art. The Shochet never makes an apparent effort, never changes a muscle of his grave face, never missed the mark. And kosher meat is the tenderest, freshest, healthiest of all. Calves are killed in the same manner, except that they are hoisted up by both hind legs, and allowed to bleed more thoroughly. Even chickens are slain by the Shochet with a knife, and according to laws observed even in the remote antiquity when the smoke of sacrifice ascended in the wilderness, "and the Lord smelled a sweet savor."

It may not be generally known that, like New York, Cincinnati has its blood-drinkers—consumptives and others who daily visit the slaughter-houses to obtain the invigorating draught of ruddy life-elixir, fresh from the veins of beeves. Lawrence's slaughter-house, opposite the Oliver Street Police Station, has its daily visitants who drink blood; and the slaughter-houses of the Loewensteins, on John street, a few squares away, has perhaps half a dozen visitants of the same class. The latter places, indeed, have the principal custom of this kind (if custom it can be termed where the recipient is charged nothing); for the reason that all beeves are slaughtered there by a Shochet. Many who can drink the blood of animals slaughtered according to the Hebrew fashion, can not stomach that of bullocks felled with the axe. The blood of the latter is black and thick and lifeless; that of the former brightly ruddy and clear as new wine.

"We have two ladies and one young man coming here every day to drink blood," observed a slaughter-house proprietor yesterday. "We used to have a great many more, but they got well and strong and stopped coming. One woman came here for a year, and got wonderfully healthy and fat; she used to be a skeleton, a consumptive skeleton. We always slaughter in the Hebrew way; and the blood of cattle so killed is more healthy. It tastes like new milk from the cow."

"Why, did you ever drink it?"

"No, no!—what should I drink it for? I am too fat as it is. And you know"—with a pleasant laugh—"Moses forbid the Hebrews to use blood for a diet."

The Shochet passed by with his long knife. "I am going to cut a bullock now," he observed, "if you want a glass of blood."

It at once occurred to the writer to try the experiment for curiosity's sake, and give the public the benefit of his experience. A large tumbler was rinsed and brought forward, the throat of the bullock severed, and the glass held to the severed veins. It was filled in an instant and handed to us, brimming over with the clear, ruddy life stream which warmed the vessel through and through. There was no odor, no thickening, no consequent feeling of nausea; and the first mouthful swallowed, the glass was easily drained.

And how did it taste? Fancy the richest cream, warm, with a tart sweetness, and the healthy strength of the pure wine "that gladdeneth the heart of man!" It was a draught simply delicious, sweeter than any concoction of the chemist, the confectioner, the winemaker—it was the very elixir of life itself. The popular idea that blood is difficult to drink is an utter fallacy; and the most timid with the warm glass in his hand must be reassured by one glance at its clear contents. He will forget all the familiar feelings of sickness conjured up by that terrible word "blood"; it is not "blood" any longer in his eyes, but rosy life, warm and palpitating with the impulse of the warm heart's last palpitation; it is ruddy, vigorous, healthful life—not the essence, but the protoplasmic fluid itself—turned in an instant from its natural channel. No other earthly draught can rival such crimson cream, and its strength spreads through the veins with the very rapidity of wine. Perhaps the knowledge of its invigorating properties originated that terrible expression, "drunk with blood." That the first draught will create a desire for a second; that a second may create an actual blood-thirstiness in the literal sense of the word; that such a thirst might lead to the worst consequence in a coarse and brutal nature, we are rather inclined to believe is not only possible, but probable. The healthy and vigorous should respect the law of Moses in this regard. Perhaps it was through occasional indulgence in a draught of human blood, (before men's veins were poisoned with tobacco and bad liquor), that provoked the monstrous cruelties of certain Augustine Emperors. Perhaps it was such a passion that, as De Quincey has it, left Caligula, while toying with the polished throat of his wife, Caesonia, half distracted between the pleasure of caressing it, which he might do frequently, and of cutting it, which could be enjoyed but once.

22

THE MANUFACTURE OF YELLOW AND ROCKINGHAM WARE IN CINCINNATI

"I wouldn't like to have much of anything said about our goods in the newspapers," said the proprietor of the largest yellow and Rockingham ware pottery in the city.

"Why, pray?"

"Because it might bring me some more customers, and a few more customers would break me up, I think," said this singular man. "You see," he explained presently, "I'd rather keep my goods just stored up in the warehouses than to sell them at the present low price, and then run the risk of not getting even that."

There are many facts of great interest not generally known with respect to the manufacture and sale of potter's ware in the United States. For twenty years and more the fight has been going on between the manufacturers in this country and in Europe, to see which should have supremacy in America. The American potters strained every nerve, first to make wares which should be equal in every respect to those of the old country, and next, which was far more difficult, to sell goods as low as the imported goods could be sold. It was the aim, on the other hand, of the English potters and importers to put the foreign wares on the American market at so low a price that home manufacturers could not hope to compete with them. The importers had public opinion wholly in their favor at the start, for no American housekeeper would touch a piece of white granite ware unless she knew, or thought she knew, it to be the "real" imported English iron-stone china. A stone china soup tureen made in this country would be dropped like a hot potato.

The American potters seem at length to have gained the day. They could not destroy the stupid prejudice against home-made dishes, so they took advantage of it. They stamped their best white ware with

"The lion and the unicorn
A Fighting for the crown,"

And sold it as imported English ware—a pious fraud, which was excusable under the circumstances. The little *ruse de guerre* was so successful that, as a matter of fact, more white ware dishes made in Cincinnati and Trenton, New Jersey, are sold as imported English ware than are sold under the name of imported ware.

Our best potter's wares, both the white and yellow, are at length quite equal to the English goods, too. At a board of arbitration in England, to settle difficulties between employers and workmen in the potteries, specimens of American white ware were exhibited which were conceded by leading English manufacturers themselves to be equal in every respect to the English ware, and to be unsurpassed in strength, whiteness and durability. A statement to that effect was made very positively by Mr. Maddux, who is supposed to make the best English white ware that comes to this country.

Specimens of the best English yellow and Rockingham ware, too, when brought to this country and placed alongside the American ware, certainly gain nothing by the comparison. Indeed, for firm, glossy and brilliant enameling, it almost seems as if the palm must be given to the American manufacturer. So much, then, have the American potters accomplished. At the English arbitration meeting above mentioned, it was found on examination that the fine American white ware exhibited could be made in the United States quite as cheaply as it could be made in England and imported to this country—that is to say, with the present import duties. Should that democratic millennium ever arrive when there will be no tariff, then the American potters will go directly to the people with their wares, without the intervention of the great jobbing houses. The people will not suffer by the change, neither will the manufacturers. If anybody suffers it will be the importers.

"One thing remember," said the proprietor of the great Front street pottery, "the American manufacturers are not going to be beaten off. I regard it as only a matter of time when the large importing jobbing houses will cease to exist."

The pretty yellow and Rockingham ware is hardly appreciated as it ought to be, because it is so cheap. An eminent artist lately took up one of the common brown "tulip" pitchers which everybody has for milk and beer pitchers in Cincinnati, and said,

"Where in the world is that beautiful enameling done? It is as fine as anything I ever saw."

He was much surprised to find that the shining brown Rockingham pitcher was made out and out in Cincinnati, and that pretty pitchers and teapots of this ware were almost as common as brickbats in every household. The glazing on this ware is indeed unsurpassed. The perfect, brilliant gloss of a brown pitcher or teapot seems only to become brighter with time and usage.

The brown ware is the same as the yellow ware, except that it is stained or spattered with manganese before the glazing is burned in, and that gives it its brown and mottled appearance. The brown and mottled ware is called Rockingham ware. The mottling operation is called "spattling" in the pottery.

Cincinnati may be said to control the market in the West and South for this yellow and Rockingham ware. Goods are shipped from here as far as Dakota Territory and Texas. The Front street pottery alone can manufacture $100,000 worth of goods in one year. It is the largest yellow and Rockingham ware pottery in the United States, and the oldest pottery now in Cincinnati. Hard times affect the trade in this ware less than many other interests.

"Our kind of ware is such that the poorer people get, the more of it they buy," said the manufacturer.

The Front street pottery has existed exactly where it now stands for more than twenty-seven years. The clay for making the ware is brought from the Amanda Furnace, in Kentucky, a little above Ironton. It is a kind of fire clay.

All common clay contains iron, and the more iron there is in a clay the redder that clay will be when burnt. It is the iron that makes our common brick red after it is burnt. It is the iron in our common clay which makes it yellow before it is burnt. Burning brings out the iron rust color and shows it plainer. When the yellow ware is first molded it looks as white as the white ware. After it is baked the first time it becomes a beautiful cream color, then when it is glazed and burnt the second time the bright yellow iron color shines through the glaze, and leaves the ware the familiar tint known to everybody.

A housekeeper has no idea what a quantity and variety of work it took to make the big yellow bowl she mixes her cake in. It had to go through thirteen different processes in the pottery before it attained the dignity of a big yellow bowl. First, the clay which made it had to be brought one hundred and fifty miles down the river in a boat. Next, this clay had to be dumped into tanks or tubs, and washed and cut with great knives by machinery, and ground all up into a liquid with water, so as to be freed from the pebbles and hard lumps, which would ruin the bowl.

After being thoroughly washed and mixed with water, the clay, which was a dark, ash color at first, is a fluid which looks much like milk. But it is not done with yet—not yet clean and fine enough to make a yellow bowl. The milky fluid must be filtered through a silk bolting cloth, which is finer than a lady's finest silk dress. This bolting-cloth is made in Germany and imported. After the filtering, the liquid is pumped up and run into hydraulic presses, where the water is squeezed out and the clay left in a dough like state. In this state it is cut into great blocks, and then these blocks are ready to be made up into big yellow bowls for housekeepers to mix their husband's favorite tea cake in. The difference between a white bowl and a yellow bowl is in the clay—the clay of the white bowl containing no iron, and, therefore, not turning yellow when burnt.

The operation of molding a yellow bowl is very much like the operation of making mud pies; at least it looks so. After the mud of which our yellow bowl is made is all shaped up and molded, then it must have the pretty blue and white stripes put around it. The soft clay of the bowl is fixed upon a mold on a turning lathe, and so shaped and smoothed. The coloring matter—white and blue—is in two iron vessels which look something like teapots with long spouts. In one of these spouts the white coloring matter comes out through three little holes, so as to make the three white stripes. As the bowl flies around on the lathe the potter puts the iron teapot to his mouth and gives the liquid coloring a little puff out through the three tiny holes in the spout. The coloring matter goes out upon the soft clay bowl in three splotches, and the bowl flies around so fast that it distributes the color, and makes three stripes of the three splotches. A little space is left and three more white stripes are blown on. Then the potter takes up the other iron teapot and puffs a blue stripe on in the space between the two bundles of white stripes, and behold the yellow bowl is striped, six white stripes and a blue one in the middle.

The bowl must be set away and dried awhile, then it, with many hundreds, maybe thousands of other bowls, must be packed away in baked clay band-boxes, called "saggers," ready to be taken to the kiln and burnt. The kiln is a huge, dome-shaped structure of brick, and the piles of clay band-boxes are ranged all around its walls inside. The kilns at the Front street pottery are double, or two-story kilns, and this yellow and Rockingham ware pottery here in Cincinnati is believed to be the only pottery in the United States where the two-story kilns are in successful operation. The baking of the ware, so as to get it even all around the kiln, to have all the dozen or so fires just of the same hotness all the time, to bake the ware just long enough, so that it shall be ruined neither by being underdone nor overdone, is the profoundest secret of the whole pottery business. This part of it, the firing and baking, the proprietor of the pottery, except during two brief visits to England, has done with his own hands for more than twenty-seven years. His sons have learned the skill now, and the master himself is "not really obliged to do it for the sake of bread and cheese," as he expressed it, but still he does it all the same, hot or cold, rain or shine, probably from the force of habit now.

Is a yellow bowl done when it is baked? By no means. It is now called "biscuit ware," and when cool must be dipped into glazing and baked again. After the first baking, in the condition of "biscuit ware," this yellow ware is an admirable subject for the pupils of the Cincinnati School of Design to try their skill in painting on. The rough ware, before the glazing is put on, takes mineral colors beautifully, and nothing could be prettier to have in a house than pitchers, vases or jars which had been decorated with flowers and vines by the fair hand of the daughter of the house, or the lady of the mansion herself. It is pretty work, far more artistic than diagonal tucking and ruffling.

One would never know, to look at a shining yellow bowl or brown pitcher, how elaborate an affair is that glazing which gives the bowl or pitcher its perfect luster. The glazing is a composition which, when put under an intense heat, fuses, and makes a glassy coat all over the yellow bowl. This coat is glass, really. The solid materials for it are ground fine, mixed with water, and filtered, till a liquid is left which looks much like white-wash. The biscuit ware is dipped in this liquid, suffered to dry and then packed away into the kiln again, where it is baked at an intense heat, and the glazing fuses, hardens again and forms the brilliant glass coat of the yellow bowl.

The painting which has been, or at least might be put on under this glazing, comes out and shows brilliantly through the glassy coat. The yellow and red ware potteries are making now numbers of pots and vases of quite graceful and artistic shapes, and the School of Design people might ornament them beautifully. Even a handsomely painted yellow ware teapot wouldn't be a bad thing in a house.

One would never imagine again how many different places in the world must be called on to contribute materials for glazing the common yellow bowl. To make the glazing the potter brings borax from California, flint from Missouri and New Jersey, feldspar from Maine, and China clay from England. All these things and more go to make up the glass coat of the yellow bowl.

It requires five different molds to make a brown pitcher, and seven different molds to make a teapot. Some of the things made require even more molds than that.

A pleasant illustration of what a woman can do when she makes up her mind to it, is offered in the history of the Front street pottery. The successful manufacture of yellow and Rockingham ware in Cincinnati is due no less to a woman than to a man. More than twenty-seven years ago a brave young English married couple established the Front street pottery in their dwelling-house. They were very poor, but very determined. At first they employed but four or five persons besides themselves. Now this same pottery, when running its full complement, employs 120 persons.

The brave young English woman actually did all parts of the potter's work with her own hands.

"She knew more, in fact, about the business than I did, then," says her husband.

Girls are more largely employed in the potteries in England than in this country, and this woman had been "raised in a pottery," as she says. When but six-and-a-half years old she began to work there. She cut papers at first for the printing patterns. Then she went to carrying molds, and trimming and sponging the clay dishes. When only seven or eight years old she worked twelve hours a day in the pottery, and got $1.25 a week for it.

"Then they tried to put me at prentice painting," said she, "but I couldn't do it. I wouldn't sit still."

But everything else in the pottery the girl learned to do, from the ground up. When she and her husband started their little pottery, she entered the shop and worked like a man, doing everything that came to her hand, instructing and overseeing the work-men, molding the dishes, glazing them, packing them for burning, and anything and everything. All this time, too, she did her housework herself, and took care of her children, so that she might be said to have twice the work the men had to do.

In 1856 her husband went to England, and then this brave woman managed the pottery all by herself, preparing the clay, "bossing" the kilns, and making the sales, and everything else, and doing it all as well as any man, and better, far better than most men, till her husband came home.

She could do everything about the pottery, as was said, but she seemed to excel particularly in making sales. That was where she went beyond all the rest in the house, and so very successful was she that, although this remarkable woman has long since retired on her laurels, there were old customers still who refuse to buy unless they can deal with her. She visited England with her husband in 1873, and on their return the pottery was wholly remodeled and enlarged, the English improvements were introduced, until now the little pottery she and her husband started in their dwelling-house nearly thirty years ago is the largest and best arranged yellow and Rockingham ware factory in the United States. Naturally it is a matter of great pride and satisfaction to this brave and energetic lady. They have recently made some attempts at making majolica in the pottery.

In appearance Mrs. ——— is a tall, slender woman, with soft, brown eyes and a musical voice, nothing whatever "mannish"-looking about her. She has had ten children. Excellent as they are, it is possible that both she and her husband might be hopeful subjects for the city Missionary and the Ladies' Tract Society. Both were Methodists in the old country, but this is what the lady says now:

"I believe I've not been in church twenty times since I came to this country. I used to go at first; but whenever I did, I would always see some people there who had tried their best to cheat me in trade. These very people always took the most prominent part in the meetings, and when at last they went up and took sacrament right before my eyes, I couldn't stand it any longer, and I've never been to church from that day to this."

"I've often remarked that I wouldn't care if I had twenty such wives," said her husband admiringly.

Part III

OPINIONS OF AMERICA

23

Growth of Population in America

A very significant fact in the history of the United States was the announcement last year of an unexpected check in the growth of population. Such a
check would signify, among other things, an enormous increase in the difficulty of living. It is undeniable that the difficulty of living in America has
rapidly augmented within the last fifteen years. Twenty-five years ago there
were chances in America for the industrious poor such as had never been
offered in any other country,—except, perhaps, during a brief period in Aus-
tralia. Any steady and vigorous mechanic, really master of his trade, could
obtain wages enough to render it possible for him to start in business for
himself after a few years of wise economy; and thousands did so gain something better than independence. For the agricultural emigrant there were glorious chances of buying rich land in the West, and of eventually growing rich.
The illimitable Western plains were still a sea of green meeting the unbroken
circle of the clearest of skies; the now prodigious network of railroads had not
yet been spun over them, and buffaloes were grazing where street-cars are
running to-day. As the great lines began to spread there were new and wonderful opportunities for shrewd settlers to buy and build; and acres bought
then for a mere nominal price could now be scarcely purchased by covering
them with gold eagles. At no time and nowhere was the artizan or the farmer
more respected than in those days. Blacksmiths could attend balls in evening-
dress of the best cut; printers were walking about with diamond pins in their
shirt-fronts; and the ploughman of the hour might feel his labour lightened
by the prospect of becoming within a few years the lord of estates larger than
most European noblemen could boast of. Policemen in growing Western towns
were then receiving high salaries; and in summer patrolled their beats in dandy
uniform. It was a queer period—too queer to last; and there were strange
sights to be seen. Gambling, now pretty well suppressed, was then as fashionable as in the novels of Bret Harte. Kansas City; to-day an imposing town, was
then a fresh growth; and its streets of a morning are said to have often been
strewn white with playing cards thrown out of doors the evening before,—
because the gamblers would never run the risk of playing with the same pack
twice.

Within a quarter of a century America has been totally changed. The plains, the prairies of romance, can no longer be said to exist; they are covered with farms, villages, towns, cities. The railroads have not only "built up" the West; they have forced the expansion of industrialism to its utmost limit. Everywhere, instead of the old mushroom wooden town, structures of stone and iron, of brick and cement, are going up; and cities solid enough to endure for centuries stand on the site of mining camps. Everywhere the latest inventions are being utilized to the best advantage;—the steam-elevator, the electric lamp, the telephone, the district-telegraph. But everywhere, also, social conditions have hardened and stratified. There are no more chances to make a fortune in a day. Becoming more and more ordered, the West has also become more and more in all things like "the effete monarchies of Europe." Wealth throughout the whole vast Republic, indeed, is steadily setting into the hands of the few; and the capitalists have closed their ranks so well that only a genius can break his way into them. There are no more good lands to be purchased for mere song. There are no more high wages; and the prices of labour are being steadily cut down. Immense combinations or accumulations of invested capital crush competition, and render hopeless the most desperate efforts of common industry to achieve practical independence. Altogether the condition of the working-classes in America has become almost as hard as in any part of Europe, and is going, in all probability, to become harder. Unlimited capital and unlimited power to use it, in the hands of a small class, will certainly produce conditions impossible in England or in Germany.

The check upon the growth of population, may be due to other causes as well as to the increased difficulty of life, however; and it is probably because of such a conviction that the United States are now inclined to check emigration from Europe, rather than to encourage it. Estimates as to the future growth of population work out wonderfully on paper; but the real facts at last almost invariably belie the calculation. The truth seems to be that the increase of population is limited by other causes than the extent of territory, the character of resources, or even the conditions of existence. Perhaps it is limited by something in the race-character or race-nature itself. The American must have room—plenty of room; he will not submit willingly to cramping and squeezing. All the Anglo-Saxon race has the same feeling strongly marked; and this love of large space to work in, large space to live in, constantly develops instead of diminishing with the progress of our civilization. The population of America will probably never reach the gigantic figure once predicted for it. The space sufficient for a million Chinamen would scarcely satisfy the absolute wants of a thousand capable Yankees.

24

THE LABOUR PROBLEM IN AMERICA

⊷ ⫯⊱⊰⫯ ⊶

Henry J. Fletcher, a noted authority on the social history of railroad troubles in the United States, has contributed to the October *Atlantic Monthly* a remarkable paper on the problems involved by the colossal railroad strikes of recent years. The war between capital and labour in the United States offers peculiar features for study, and offers them upon an enormous scale. They are of the utmost importance to the sociologist; since they indicate the general lines of vast movements toward social transformation which are going on in Europe as well as in America,—though perhaps less clearly defined and less formidable in the older civilized societies, and though the last English coal-strike must not be forgotten. We may venture also to predict that their ultimate consequences will be reached first in the United States,—where social development having been unprecedentedly rapid, social transformation is likely to be also accomplished within a period of unexampled brevity.

In the early seventies, the writer of these lines can recollect that the contests between labour and capital in America usually ended in victories for capital. Various powerful trades-unions were broken up; and as the direct cause of these defeats seemed to be incapacity of organization on the part of the strikers, it was confidently predicted by not a few thinking men that labour would never be able to win in an organized fight against capital. Labour's weak point was mental apparently. Its contests were not simply against money as power, but against trained business intelligence as power. However, events came to pass which showed that the cause of labour was not nearly so hopeless as had been imagined; and that something not intellectual at all, but purely emotional, might eventually prove more than a match for business intelligence and capacity of far-reaching combination. Mr. Fletcher's article begins with the consideration of an event which seems to us the first manifestation of this fact,—the gigantic Baltimore and Ohio strike of 1877. It was suppressed by the Government with armed force,—but not until millions of property had been destroyed, and hundreds of lives lost. Other strikes followed. Meantime the arbitrary exercise of power by the railroad corporations—in matters of politics as well as in matters of commerce—had alarmed the public to a degree that brought abut the passage of laws for the regulation of interstate commerce and the appointment of commissions for the investigation of railroad troubles. The laws effected no good; the commissions, having no power to enforce any modification of existing conditions, accomplished nothing but reports. And no attempts to effect such legislation as might enforce justice to employés were made at all. But the employés were not idle in the effort to win their rights. They were organizing upon a scale so formidable that in December, 1893, the receivers of the Northern Pacific R.R., having repeatedly cut down wages, were alarmed by the possibilities of a strike, and applied to the U.S. Court for an injunction to prevent it. The order was issued by Judge Jenkins, and the strike was temporarily averted. The Union Pacific R.R., resolving to cut down wages, expected similar aid from the law; but Judge Caldwell of the U.S. Court answered that whether dividends were paid or not, fair wages *must* be paid; and this decision in favour of the railroad employés averted another strike by a decision exactly opposed to that of Judge Jenkins. On the Great Northern Railway a strike could not be averted; but the strikers won a complete victory, under the leadership of Mr. Debs,—after having "tied up the commerce of seven States, and 4,500 miles of railway."

But the enormous strike of 1894 was preparing,—a strike exceeding in magnitude anything in history,—a strike directed by the whole American Railway Union against the Pullman company. The entire railway commerce of the country was paralyzed; the losses reached a figure appalling to consider; and the movement was only put down at last, after tremendous trouble, by military force. And now the railways are endeavouring to break up the gigantic guild which would have ruined them but for the assistance of United State Courts and troops.

They will not be able to break it up. It is not a union of the old sort which they are fighting; it is not, indeed, a union which any methods can disorganize. It is simply a body of more than one million employés who will act together upon one common impulse. That impulse is emotional. Popular emotion will prove stronger than disciplined business intelligence,—given fair odds. Popular emotion makes revolutions. Besides the million employés— ever increasing—who will certainly again at some future time act as one,— there are their sympathizers, numbering a great many millions,—the vast mass of working-people now suffering more or less from the natural results of the concentration of wealth into comparatively few hands.

The conditions in America are therefore these:—On the one side are the railroads and the industrial classes, whose interests depend upon the working of the railroads. On the other hand is the army of railroad employés, backed by the popular feeling that makes revolutions. Between is the Government and the law. What is to be done?

Hitherto the Government and the law have taken part with the rich, and have put down by bayonets every serious strike. And as a strike means bloodshed and violence and destruction of property, there is no question as to whether the action of the Government, at least, was necessary or just. It was inevitable. The attitude of the Courts has been this:—Property must be protected. Strikes are directed against property. Therefore strikes are illegal.

But there is a very serious problem involved by this attitude,—a problem that touches the Constitution of the United States. Just so surely as the rights of property must be respected, the rights of the individual to cease from labour, or to refuse inadequate wage,—must also be respected. The railroad question presents the enigma, How can the law be enforced in favour of property, without infringing the liberties of the citizen? What right has a United States Court to forbid workingmen from striking? Can such an order be sustained by the Constitution?

Gigantic as they are, the labour-troubles are still young. Each year they will become huger and more menacing. There seem only three possible solutions of the question. First, that the Government takes over the railroads, (which involves awful political possibilities, such as that of placing more than a million votes at the disposal of party government); secondly, that special laws be passed to protect railroad employés against their employers; third, a revolution. If the Government cannot, the people certainly will, settle the railroad enigma.

25

THE RACE-PROBLEM IN AMERICA

It is difficult for any one who has not, by long residence in the Southern States of America, made himself familiar with the abnormal social conditions there existing, to form a fair judgment about the race-question. Even in the Northern States,—even in the cultivated New England atmosphere,—there still prevail misconceptions extraordinary of the real issues at stake in the South; and although a thinking minority of Eastern men now openly recognize that interference by the United States Government with Southern affairs could only produce immense mischief, the Northern people as a mass are still more or less influenced by those war politicians who clamour for the enforcement of those absurd laws conferring all political and social rights upon the negroes of the Black Belt. All over the civilized world these sentiments are being re-echoed; and it must be acknowledged that the conditions thus protested against are horrible enough. Rarely can one open an American newspaper without reading of lynchings and killings of negroes; and occasionally much worse things are reported,—such as that frightful case in Paris, Texas, last year, when a negro criminal was fiendishly tortured and burned alive. It would be impossible to contradict the often-reiterated assertion that the conditions in certain parts of the South are not the conditions of civilization,—that they are in every sense of the word atrocious,—and that every rational means should be used to bring about a better state of affairs.

But what rational means can be used is a problem of the most serious description. The English press,—reflecting English experience only, and the impulses natural to the most orderly and systematic of all races,—suggests the use of force. And as the use of force would involve the ugly possibility of another civil war, and bring up constitutional questions of the most troublesome kind, much needless but ingenious foreign advice has been volunteered upon the subject. Only to a few really well-informed critics of the situation has it ever occurred that the American nation might be in the condition of a patient suffering from a tumour impossible to extirpate without endangering his life.

Putting the facts in briefest form, the situation is about as follows:— Those who knew the character of the African race had nothing to do with the irrational legislation made in its behalf after the time of emancipation,—the conferring of universal suffrage upon millions ignorant as cattle, and the constitutional amendments declaring them entitled to all privileges of citizenship, and the special laws punishing refusal to acknowledge their rights to such privileges. Those who did not know, or who did not care, about the negro race made those laws, whose averred object was humane, but whose real object was the maintenance in power of the Republican party. The negro, taught to distrust his former masters, and taught that he could only escape the most frightful calamities by loyalty to the Republican party, made himself a fanatical religion out of politics, and gave himself utterly into the hands of unscrupulous advisers,—clever half-breeds and cunning white adventurers. The negro-vote was used by these to enrich themselves out of the ruin of States; and men so poor that the blacks had to buy clothes for them in order to send them to Congress, became millionaires in a few years. Warmoth of Louisiana is said to have made his father a present of a million after having been a twelve-month in office. Moses of South Carolina ended in the penitentiary. The South was squeezed until universal ruin seemed inevitable. But such a state of things could only be maintained by power of United States bayonets. That pressure once removed, after the desperate revolt of the White League, all the whites of the former slave-holding States united solidly against the Republican policy. The weapon of that policy had been the negro-vote; and it was decided that the negro-vote must be controlled. There was but one possible way of controlling it,—by terror, and the negroes of the South were terrorized and mastered. Then came the period of the Ku-Klux. Massacres and cruelties were perpetrated of which the reports afterwards obtained by a United States Commission would probably vie with the story of the horrors in Bulgaria. And long after the Ku-Klux-Klan had ceased to exist, the system of terror continued. The means were detestable; but the purpose was achieved. The blacks were mastered; the South became politically a unit; and the man who might have dared to oppose the sectional Democracy from any motive whatever, necessarily became regarded both as a social and a political enemy. But under this new order of things, the South began to recover from the effects of the war. At the present time she is richer, more industrious, more prosperous than ever before.

Nevertheless the race-problem remained unsettled. The physiological meaning of slavery to the slave race has been revealed by the results of emancipation in all countries where the system formerly existed. In the English West Indies first, in the French West Indies afterwards, in British, French, and Dutch Guiana, the black race began, immediately after obtaining its freedom, to multiply with extraordinary rapidity. Already it seems inevitable that these possessions must eventually pass out of the hands of the white race, and the white Creole populations are diminishing year by year. But the multiplication of the blacks shows no sign of decrease; and Jamaica and Barbadoes yearly send the surplus of their population to seek work on the Isthmus or in Central or South America.

And now the same race-danger menaces the Southern United States. The blacks, estimated at only between five and six millions after the war, are said to have multiplied to eight millions; and their multiplication constantly increases its rate. The original project of transporting them all to Liberia, or some other part of the African coast, is no longer talked of, since it has ceased to be feasible. The old prediction that miscegenation would settle the problem,—that the race would be "bleached out of existence"— would never be ventured to-day. A very small black element might be thus absorbed by a white race; but the immense black population of the United States to-day could not even be visibly diminished by any such natural process. Furthermore, race-hate has been developed to a degree never previously known. The black population is becoming more and more a unit,—both racial and political—within the larger racial unit of the political Solid South. Its reverence for the politics first imposed upon it,—its tendency to vote *en masse,*—its superstitious faith in Republican leaders of any description, have not been lessened in the least. And it is always growing, growing,—multiplying at an appallingly greater rate than the white population which still masters it. There would seem now to be an instinctive feeling in the South that a day must come at last when it can be no longer controlled,—when the great question shall be the question not of race-supremacy, but of race-existence. And the fierce hate of such a feeling is manifesting itself in the atrocities committed by Southern mobs,—by the lowest classes of Southern whites. Besides these evils directly due to the old folly of Republican legislators, certain indirect moral evils of a very grave nature have been developed in the South. The necessity of aggression has made aggression habitual, has savagely hardened hearts, has developed some of the most terrible types of men existing in any civilized country. All such conditions react upon character. It is impossible now to predict what evils the next twenty-five years may bring to the South. But it is sadly evident that the worst ultimate consequences of slavery are yet to come; and that the enormous error of it will furnish legislators yet unborn with a host of Sphinx-riddles to solve.

26

SOME JAPANESE IDEAS OF AMERICAN POLICY

Several of the Japanese papers, commenting upon the attitude of the United States towards Japan, have betrayed a curious misconception of American politics. They have gravely averred that the question of Chinese and Japanese immigration governs American policy in this regard,—because in America the will of the majority makes the government, and that majority is composed of working-men opposed to Chinese and Japanese immigration.

While it is quite true that on the Pacific slope, the hostility to Chinese emigration did at one period obtain in Congress a strong popular representation, it would be quite a mistake to suppose that the subsequent action of Congress in the matter was the work of that representation. It was largely the work of a very different representation, and was decided by motives of a much larger character than those which agitated the Pacific slope. The international questions involved by past and possible massacres, the ultimate consequences to trade and commerce of anarchy in California, the moral dignity of the Republic, and many other considerations,—had far more to do with Congressional decision on the Chinese question than the direct will of the working-men.

As for Japanese immigration, it has not yet become a question of national importance to America; and the few agitations it has provoked were scarcely more than reflexes from the previous great excitement about Chinese emigration. As a mass, the American working-men know very little about the Japanese, and have never been brought into serious competition with them. The troubles have been small and localized; and there is as yet no Japanese immigration-question in a national sense.

The mistake made by our Japanese contemporaries is entirely due to the supposition that American politics are the same in practice as in theory. If any general statement on the subject be possible, the facts are just the reverse. In theory, indeed, the government is the government of the people, and should represent the will of the majority,—the will of the working-masses. But as a matter of fact the government represents the will of banks, railroads, trusts, monopolies,—the will of the wealthy middle classes; and the struggles of party are not for principles, but for interests. However a society be organized with a view to equal privileges and rights, a minority will find means to rule it—first by superior intelligence, subsequently both by intelligence and money—which is force. Probably the working-classes are in ordinary years less well represented in America than they are in England, or even in Imperial Germany. And our Japanese contemporaries may rest quite assured that the will of American working-men will have nothing whatever to do with the question of treaty-revision. Should America refuse to accede to the terms which Great Britain has accepted, her decision will be made according to the supposed interests of her merchants settled in Japan, and the probable results to the volume of her Oriental commerce.

We do not wish, however, that our Japanese contemporaries should be led to infer from these remarks that the will of the majority is *never* represented in America. On the whole the American Constitution works admirably well. In spite of all abuses and corruptions, the minority, or minorities, use their power wisely. Since their interests are mostly identified with the interests of the nation—itself an industrial community,—they are the most competent to secure the public welfare under ordinary conditions. The rivalry of different interests, again, precludes the possibility of great abuses of power. But in extraordinary circumstances,—in time of national danger or national misfortune,—then the will of the nation as a whole, the will of the people as a mass, makes itself felt, and practically rules the hour. No people understand as well as the Americans the value of the national instinct in situations of peril. It is a common saying that whenever things go too far wrong, the sense of the people can be trusted to set them right.

27

Prevention of Cruelty to Women

We expressed our opinion some days ago in regard to the probable inefficacy of such laws against seduction as that which recently passed the Lower House of the Kentucky Legislature. The advocacy of the bill referred to nevertheless prompts us to the consideration of simpler and more efficacious laws to punish crimes against women—laws which we believe would have a positive and practical effect toward the improvement of public morals.

If there be any sentiment of true chivalry in these days it has not made itself manifest in the enactment of laws for the protection of women. Thousands of delicate women are yearly killed by brutal and cowardly abuse, and the husband is seldom punished. A sudden blow which kills on the instant is murder, but long years of ill-treatment and of cruelty which kills by inches, or, in other words, a systematized manner of torturing women to death, is not punished at all—unless, in the agony of despair, the unfortunate wife has the man arrested and has enough resolution to testify against him afterwards in court, which is seldom the case. Usually her affection forgives all—even the brutality which disfigures her permanently; and it has actually been claimed that some women find a strange pleasure in being beaten.

This is not true of one civilized country alone; but of nearly all; and it will perhaps be remembered that not long ago in London a man who stole a coat or some other article of small value, was transported for fourteen years; while a man who had thrown his wife out of a third-story window and killed her got off with six months' hard labor. Civilization cannot be considered very much advanced from a moral standpoint, while the primitive and savage idea of compelling woman to obedience by force continues to pervade the masses, and while the efforts of philanthropic organizations are directed rather to the prevention of cruelty to animals than to its prevention in the case of those delicate and sensitive beings whose only weapons of defense are beauty, affection, and gentleness. The old Norsemen, rough and fierce as they could be, were far more advanced in some moral respects than the people of modern times. They at least recognized in woman the divine Creator and worshiped her with a blind devotion and a noble idolatry which gave to another age the Spirit of Chivalry.

Perhaps it may sound chimerical; but we sincerely believe that a law declaring it a crime to strike or ill-treat a woman would have a most desirable effect upon present social conditions. The importance of protecting women from abuse may be best realized by considering how much of the moral and physical deformity of this generation has had its origin in the ill-treatment of women who were mothers.

As regards seduction, we have already observed that this evil is probably impossible to prevent by legislation. But, to a certain extent, judicious legislation might surely lessen it. In example, we may adduce an imaginary case, which represents the history of numbers of unfortunates.

A girl has been ruined, and lives with her seducer as his mistress—perhaps for a month, perhaps for a year. He tires of her, and feeling himself hindered by no legal obstacle, and knowing the helplessness of his victim, abandons her. After the first burst of grief, she is often compelled to listen to the advances of another who makes large promises. He treats her in the same manner. After a few more such bitter experiences, she becomes hardened, and abandons herself to degradation.

It is absurd to claim that so great a moral wrong as the above imaginary case presents, cannot be prevented by legislation. It is nonsense to claim that the law can afford women no adequate protection against such treatment as this. Let it be enacted simply that the man who lives with a woman for a certain length of time shall be legally considered, *ipso facto,* as the husband of that woman, and bound by the law to support, protect, and honor her as well as though a marriage ceremony had been performed with all ecclesiastical pomp and due formality of law.

28

RECENT AMERICAN NOVELS

⊶ ⊷

There has been what we might call a literary spurt lately among the younger school of American writers to catch up with the trans-Atlantic English literature of fiction. We refer especially to society fiction—to novels illustrating American society as British novels portray various phases of English society. We are represented, not largely, but well, in historical romance not American, but written by Americans, and European romances written by natives of the United States. But as regards novels illustrating American life proper we have had few productions of late years. At the same time there is a quantity of light American literature produced with this very aim, never attained though incessantly pursued. Some publishers have taken a good step in this direction by issuing series of anonymous novels intended to be peculiarly American. The intention was excellent, but its fulfillment has been found very difficult indeed. No fine American romance has been called into life by this new phase of enterprise. The creations it has begotten are imitations mostly of English or French novels, with nothing American about them except here and there a bit of scene painting from New England or Virginia. There is a curious similarity about all these romances; they are all the production of one particular school. Those who write have all breathed the same educational atmosphere, been guided by similar social influences, read the same literature, studied the same philosophy, traveled in the same countries, and studied art-ideas from the same standpoint. And all this study and thought and feeling and experience, is not only confined within the narrow circle of a certain preconceived Boston sentiment; but under the influence of that sentiment to such an extent everything is pedantically colored. There is much fine writing, much elegance of expression, much evidence of scholarship; but no idea whatever of studying American life from a standpoint not New English. The idea of seeking for the beautiful and the picturesque in the lower strata of society as well as in the upper, of studying agricultural home life as well as Fifth Avenue drawing-room personages, of portraying distinctly national and local characteristics, of picturing phases of existence to be found in the United States only, does not seem to enter into the mind of these novelists. And this is the reason that in spite of style and scholarship and fine taste, the finest of those productions will find no readers within a few years. They teach nothing new, reproduce nothing of striking interest, contain nothing which may not be found in European contemporary novels in a far more acceptable shape.

The characteristics of the upper class of society are similar in all highly civilized countries; and even the tone of cultured thought has a universal resemblance. Differences of nationality create only the faintest tints of variation. For strong and characteristic color and sentiment, we must study not this hothouse growth of fashionable intellectuality, which resembles a flower that may be found in the private conservatories of all climates and countries; but rather the wild plants, the natural blossoms of human life. Bret Harte did this. Elizabeth Stuart Phelps did it. Oliver Wendell Holmes did it; and Hawthorne and Irving before him. What is wanted now is something distinct and unique and truthful, which cannot be found in the factitious life of drawing-rooms, but in the workshops and factories, among the toilers on river and rail, in villages fringing the sea line or hidden among the wrinkles of the hills, in mining districts and frontier towns, in the suburbs of vast industrial centers, in old-fashioned communities about which quaint traditions cling, among men who, without culture, have made themselves representatives of an enormous financial force, and among those who, in spite of culture, have remained unable to rise above the condition of want, in the office of the merchant, and the residence of the clerk, and the home of the servant, and the rented rooms of the laborer.

29

AMERICAN MAGAZINES

‑‑ ⚌✦⚌ ‑‑

Walt Whitman, being interviewed on literary matters some time ago, stated that "there is a great underlying stratum of young men and women in America, who cannot speak, because the magazines are in the hands of old fogies like Holland or fops like Howells"—an observation which contains no little truth. There are not many magazines in the United States; and those that are successfully established and possess real influence are conducted with a rather narrow policy. Only a limited number of subjects are permitted to contributors. One magazine excludes any matter of a historical character. Another excludes antiquarianism in any shape. Others are entirely in the hands of literary rings or cliques—composed indeed of good writers, but rings for all that. *Harper's* is really better conducted in some respects than any other, articles being paid for as soon as accepted, and manuscripts examined no matter from whom they come. But *Harper's Magazine* is necessarily conducted in a lighter vein than what we should expect from a purely literary periodical. It owes its successful popularity to the fact that it is not purely literary, but largely instructive and historical. But there is no magazine in the country now to compare with the *Atlantic* of twenty years ago, when everything of real merit was gladly received from casual contributors. Its brilliancy at that period was really matchless. Latterly it has become a second-rate publication. To keep a periodical at the pitch of first class merit, it must be constantly refreshed with material from new contributors. As the literary medium of a small clique of writers it can never sustain itself above mediocrity; for the cleverest men will write heavily or uninterestingly at times, and the most imaginative minds weary of graceful invention. Perhaps it is rather a misfortune that such high prices are paid for magazine articles—as this enables a few men to live upon a periodical, and creates a system of literary office-holding which needs reformation. At all events, we know that the *Atlantic* was far superior in the days when the prices paid for contributions were far smaller, and that certain English magazines of remarkable merit pay very small prices. It were better, too, that noted authors should not be induced to seek pay from magazines, as it withdraws them from far more important fields of labor. It is the fire of youth, the first strong soaring of young imaginations, the first warmth of literary aspiration, which should nourish our magazines. For there is certainly a period in life in which young men can create such little glowing works of art as they could not in later years—when the style, indeed, becomes more correct, more precise, more polished, but when the heart has grown colder, and the beauty of things natural no longer excites that charming enthusiasm which, although never forgotten, in a maturer age can never be revived.

30

AMERICAN ART TASTES

A few years ago, except in the matter of literature, it was truly said of America, that she possessed no native art taste. The East, which led in matters of literary taste, chiseled sternly according to New England standards, gave to national thought in such matters a somber tone, a peculiar gray tint of puritanism. This puritanism has not yet wholly disappeared; it is visible in a thousand shapes. Even at a very late period when Eastern publishers reproduced the publications of European dilettanti, there was a great deal of ridiculous emasculation done, and much fig-leaf nonsense displayed. Even to-day there is much of the spirit visible among the people—the nudity of true art shocks them, the antique spirit horrifies them. Only under such conditions could an American "artist," who actually ridiculed the antique art, and spoke of the Venus di Medici as "misshapen," have imposed such an absurdity as the Greek Slave upon the public as a true work of art. The same spirit has manifested itself in the reproduction of foreign literature; nearly all American translations from the various Latin tongues being shamefully emasculated.

With the present generation, however, much has been changed. The students of art now trained in the schools of Rome, Paris, Munich, and Florence, have shaken off the conventionalities which the old-fashioned home spirit imposed upon them. They inundate their canvases with life and light and warmth; they model their plastic work unfettered by puritanical ideas. While it is true that they must first succeed in Europe—as a general rule—in order to be appreciated at home; still, it is encouraging to know that thereafter their pictures and statues do not lack generous American purchasers. Not long ago, the *Protectionist,* a very able paper, was lamenting the absence of art taste in New York, and mourning that our metropolis should not be an art center, like London, like Paris, like Rome, like Madrid. But the fact is that New York will certainly become before another half-century the art center of the Western world and well worthy to vie with any European capital. In fact the treasures of European art are gradually but surely flowing there; the capitalists of the United States are doing all that wealth can do to establish a correct standard of American art tastes. And they will assuredly succeed. Art flourishes only in those centers of civilization where wealth and leisure combine to create a class of dilettanti. The West is rich; but the West is too busy, and will be for generations to come, to produce such a class as is now forming in the East. We shall probably live to see the result; and we may dare to predict that the development of correct art taste in America will be as rapid as her industrial progress during the past century.

31

THE FRENCH IN LOUISIANA

The encouragement given by our Legislature to the French language in Louisiana has been ridiculed a great deal by persons apparently incapable of reflection and clad in the impenetrable mail of prejudice. It has been said that New Orleans is not a French city, but an American city; and that the use of the English language alone should be permitted in public affairs and public schools. It has also been said that the law was passed through Creole influence and to satisfy the selfish ends of a small clique. Finally it has been said that this maintenance of a foreign tongue by legislative complaisance is an ill-advised and ill-timed encouragement of old fashions, old manners, and old prejudices which should be abolished as soon as possible for the sake of public prosperity.

It is needless to say that these statements are wholly untrue. Even supposing that the law had been passed for the benefit of a few newspaper publishers, school teachers, and notaries, its actual importance would not be lessened one jot or tittle thereby. As far as the old-fashioned French manners and customs go, we must say that we admire and commend most of them, and are sorry to find that many are falling into disuse. The good old customs need encouragement; they ought to be maintained; and they make life in New Orleans more agreeable for strangers—especially Europeans—than may readily be described. It is really the old French population here which knows most of the philosophy of comfort and hygiene, and which lives most naturally and healthily. As to the remarks about old prejudices no sensible man can pretend for a moment that the use of any one language can keep the smouldering fire of old prejudices alive more than the use of any other language could do. In fact, we believed that the Legislature saw further than the prejudiced myopes who criticize them, and perceived that the encouragement of the French language in Louisiana was highly important from a purely commercial standpoint.

Let us explain ourselves more fully upon this subject. For years and years we have been conceiving and practicing and abandoning in despair all kinds of schemes for the encouragement of emigration. It would be a waste of time to record our failures. The old conditions are still extant; and the greater number of our real immigrants are from France and Italy. We believe that whatever may be said regarding other immigration, the French has been increasing of late years; and it is exceedingly important that we should do all in our power to encourage it. The French emigrant has almost always a good trade and is a first-class workman; he is remarkably industrious; he understands economy quite as well as the most thrifty German; and he always works with a fixed object in view. There are hundreds of thriving little businesses in this city which have been created out of nothing—one might almost say—by poor French emigrants who are now well-to-do citizens. It is true that the proportion of French immigration is not as large as we could wish, because the French—unlike the Germans—prefer to stay at home as long as any hope of comfort remains rather than go abroad to seek fortune. But there are regular periods in the life of every nation, however prosperous, which develop conditions that force emigration; and France cannot always remain exempt. We believe there will be a considerable increase in French immigration before many years; and we know that such immigrants will be only too glad to seek a French-speaking community in the United States. New Orleans, by proper management, might obtain at least four fifths of this foreign element, with immense advantage to herself, and might become the central point for America-seeking French emigrants. It is of great moment that the French language be encouraged in Louisiana in view of this fact, and the good effect of the new laws will be felt before many years.

THE ROAR OF A GREAT CITY

When Hogarth painted his story of "The Enraged Musician," whose music was drowned in the thousand cries and noises that surrounded him; when Chambers described "The Roar of a Great City," the blending of a thousand noises, it was of the city of the past they told. Since then this roar has been growing louder and louder, until now, miles away, even before you see the smoky coronet that surrounds the modern city, you can hear a wild growl like that of some enraged beast. Neither Hogarth nor Chambers dreamed of the fierce whistle of the steamboat and locomotive, of the rattle of engine and machinery, of the cannonade as a cotton float flies over the granite pavement, of the stunning noise of the New York Elevated Railroad. All these have come of late years.

The electric light, the telephone and telegraph wires have added new music to our city. When the winds blow at night one can hear a somber, melancholy music high up in the air—as mysterious as that of Ariel himself or the undiscovered music of the Pascagoula. If you want to hear it in perfection go some of these windy nights we have lately enjoyed to Delord or Dryades, or some of the streets in the neighborhood of the electric light works, where the wires are numerous and the houses low, and where there is a clean sweep for the wind from the New Basin to the river. There the music becomes wild and grand indeed. The storm whistling and shrieking around some sharp corner never equalled it. Above, around, in every direction can be heard this music, sighing, mourning like the tree-tops, with a buzzing metallic sound that almost drowns your conversation. There is something in it weird and melancholy—it is like the last wail of a dying man, or the shriek of the angel of death as he clasps his victim to him.

If such it is to-day, what have we to hope for in the future? If the city is already a monstrous spider web, a great Aeolian harp, what is its destiny with several new telegraph and telephone companies, and thousands of new poles, and millions of new wires promised us? If this aerial music increases, this shrieking and wailing and moaning will reach such a pitch that we will greet the rattle of the floats and tinkle of the street cars as tending to drown this new noise, and welcome the roar of the city as likely to muffle its meaning.

BIBLIOGRAPHY

Bisland, Elizabeth. 1906. *The Life and Letters of Lafcadio Hearn.* 2 vols. Boston: Houghton Mifflin.

Bronner, Milton, ed. 1907. *Letters from the Raven: Being the Correspondence of Lafcadio Hearn with Henry Watkin.* London: Archibald Constable.

Bronner, Simon J. 1998. *Following Tradition: Folklore in the Discourse of American Culture.* Logan: Utah State University Press.

Cott, Jonathan. 1992. *Wandering Ghost: The Odyssey of Lafcadio Hearn.* Tokyo: Kodansha International.

Cowley, Malcolm. 1949. "Lafcadio Hearn." In Goodman, *Selected Writings of Lafcadio Hearn,* 1-15.

Goodman, Henry, ed. 1949. *The Selected Writings of Lafcadio Hearn.* New York: Citadel Press.

Gould, George M. 1908. *Concerning Lafcadio Hearn.* Philadelphia: George W. Jacobs.

Gwyn, Ann S., comp. 1977. *Lafcadio Hearn: A Catalogue of the Collection at the Howard-Tilton Memorial Library, Tulane University.* New Orleans: Friends of the Tulane University Library.

Hearn, Lafcadio. 1884. *Stray Leaves from Strange Literature.* Boston: Houghton Mifflin.

———. 1885. *Ghombo Zhèbes: A Little Dictionary of Creole Proverbs.* New York: Will H. Coleman.

———. 1885. *La Cuisine Creole: A Collection of Culinary Recipes.* New York: Will H. Coleman.

———. 1887. *Some Chinese Ghosts.* Boston: Roberts Brothers.

———. 1889. *Chita: A Memory of Last Island.* New York: Harper and Brothers.

———. [1890] 2001. *Two Years in the French West Indies.* New York: Interlink Books.

———. [1890] 1969. *Youma: The Story of a West-Indian Slave.* New York: AMS Press.

———. 1904. *Japan: An Attempt at Interpretation.* New York: Macmillan.

———. [1905] 1969. *The Romance of the Milky Way and Other Studies and Stories.* Freeport, N.Y.: Books for Libraries Press.

———. 1910. *Exotics and Retrospectives.* Boston: Little, Brown.

———. 1911. *Leaves from the Diary of an Impressionist.* Boston: Houghton Mifflin.

———. 1914. *Fantastics and Other Fancies.* Ed. Charles Woodward Hutson. Boston: Little, Brown.

———. [1917] 1969. *Life and Literature.* Ed. John Erskine. Freeport, N.Y.: Books for Libraries Press.

———. [1920] 1967. *Talks to Writers.* Ed. John Erskine. Freeport, N.Y.: Books for Libraries Press.

———. [1923] 1968. *Essays in European and Oriental Literature.* Ed. Albert Mordell. Freeport, N.Y.: Books for Libraries Press.

———. 1924. *An American Miscellany.* 2 vols. Ed. Albert Mordell. New York: Dodd, Mead.

———. 1924. *Creole Sketches.* Ed. Charles Woodward Hutson. Boston: Houghton Mifflin.

———. 1925. *Occidental Gleanings.* 2 vols. Ed. Albert Mordell. New York: Dodd, Mead.

———. 1926. *Editorials.* Ed. Charles Woodward Hutson. Boston: Houghton Mifflin.

———. 1929. *Essays on American Literature.* Ed. Sanki Ichikawa. Tokyo: Hokuseido Press.

———. 1939. *Barbarous Barbers and Other Stories.* Tokyo: Hokuseido Press.

———. 1939. *Buying Christmas Toys and Other Essays.* Tokyo: Hokuseido Press.

———. 1957. *Children of the Levee.* Ed. O.W. Frost. Lexington: University of Kentucky Press.

———. 1960. *Editorials from the Kobe Chronicle.* Ed. Makoto Sangu. Tokyo: Hokuseido Press.

———. 1975. *Articles on Literature and Other Writings from the Cincinnati Enquirer 1873.* New York: AMS Press.

Hendrick, Ellwood. 1929. *Lafcadio Hearn.* New York: New York Public Library.

Hirakawa, Sukehiro, ed. 1997. *Rediscovering Lafcadio Hearn: Japanese Legends, Life and Culture.* Folkestone, Eng.: Global Books.

Hughes, Jon, ed. 1990. *Period of the Gruesome: Selected Cincinnati Journalism of Lafcadio Hearn.* Lanham, Md.: University Press of America.

Hull, Robert. 1983. *The Art of Lafcadio Hearn: An Exhibition of Books, Manuscripts, and Art from the Clifton Waller Barrett Library.* Charlottesville: Alderman Library, University of Virginia.

Ichikawa, Sanki, ed. 1925. *Some New Letters and Writings of Lafcadio Hearn.* Tokyo: Kenyusha.

Johnson, William S., ed. 1979. *Lafcadio Hearn: Selected Writings, 1872-1877.* Indianapolis: Woodruff Publications.

Jordan, Philip D. 1943. *Ohio Comes of Age: 1873-1900.* Columbus: Ohio State Archaeological and Historical Society.

Kennard, Nina H. [1912] 1967. *Lafcadio Hearn.* Port Washington, N.Y.: Kennikat Press.

Kunst, Arthur E. 1969. *Lafcadio Hearn.* New York: Twayne.

Lewis, Oscar. 1930. *Hearn and His Biographers: The Record of a Literary Controversy.* San Francisco: Westgate Press.

Marcus, Jacob Rader. 1990. *To Count a People: American Jewish Population Data, 1585-1984.* Lanham, Md.: University Press of America.

McNeil, W.K. 1978. "Lafcadio Hearn, American Folklorist." *Journal of American Folklore* 91:947-67.

McWilliams, Vera. 1946. *Lafcadio Hearn.* Boston: Houghton Mifflin.

Mordell, Albert. 1964. *Discoveries: Essays on Lafcadio Hearn.* Tokyo: Orient/West.

Murray, Paul. 1993. *A Fantastic Journey: The Life and Literature of Lafcadio Hearn.* Folkestone, Eng.: Japan Library.

Nannichi, Tsunetaro. 1927. *Catalogue of the Lafcadio Hearn Library in the Toyama High School.* Toyama, Japan: Toyama High School.

Stempel, Daniel. 1948. "Lafcadio Hearn: Interpreter of Japan." *American Literature* 20:1-19.

Stevenson, Elizabeth. 1961. *Lafcadio Hearn.* New York: Macmillan.

Temple, Jean. 1931. *Blue Ghost: A Study of Lafcadio Hearn.* London: Jonathan Cape.

Thomas, Edward. 1912. *Lafcadio Hearn.* Boston: Houghton Mifflin.

Tinker, Edward Larocque. 1924. *Lafcadio Hearn's American Days.* New York: Dodd, Mead.

————. 1943. "Cable and the Creoles." In *Old Creole Days,* by George Washington Cable, vii–xviii. New York: Heritage Press.

Trotter, Joe William, Jr. 1998. *River Jordan: African American Urban Life in the Ohio Valley.* Lexington: University Press of Kentucky.

Yu, Beongcheon. 1964. *An Ape of Gods: The Art and Thought of Lafcadio Hearn.* Detroit: Wayne State University Press.

SOURCES OF THE ESSAYS

"Levee Life," *Cincinnati Commercial,* March 17, 1876.
"Saint Malo," *Harper's Weekly,* March 3, 1883.
"Sicilians in New Orleans," *Cincinnati Commercial,* December 27, 1877.
"The Last of the New Orleans Fencing-Masters," *Southern Bivouac,* November 1886.
"A Gypsy Camp," *Cincinnati Enquirer,* April 21, 1873.
"Some Pictures of Poverty," *Cincinnati Commercial,* January 7, 1877.
"Pariah People," *Cincinnati Commercial,* August 22, 1875.
"Les Chiffonniers," *Cincinnati Enquirer,* July 26, 1874.
"Within the Bars," *Cincinnati Enquirer,* March 16, 1873.
"Cincinnati Salamanders," *Cincinnati Enquirer,* December 27, 1874.
"Steeple Climbers," *Cincinnati Commercial,* May 26, 1876.
"Cheek," *New Orleans Item,* January 10, 1881.
"The Creole Patois," *Harper's Weekly,* January 10, 17, 1885.
"The Creole Doctor," *New York Tribune,* January 3, 1886.
"The Last of the Voudoos," *Harper's Weekly,* November 7, 1885.
"New Orleans Superstitions," *Harper's Weekly,* December 25, 1886.
"The Music of the Masses," *Cincinnati Commercial,* October 21, 1877.
"Black Varieties," *Cincinnati Commercial,* April 9, 1876.
"Among the Spirits," *Cincinnati Enquirer,* January 25, 1874.
"Some Strange Experience," *Cincinnati Commercial,* September 26, 1875.
"Haceldama," *Cincinnati Commercial,* September 5, 1875.
"The Manufacture of Yellow and Rockingham Ware in Cincinnati," *Cincinnati Commercial,* September 9, 1877.
"Growth of Population in America," *Kobe Chronicle,* November 7, 1894.
"The Labour Problem in America," *Kobe Chronicle,* October 31, 1894.
"The Race-Problem in America," *Kobe Chronicle,* October 20, 1894.
"Some Japanese Ideas of American Policy," *Kobe Chronicle,* October 29, 1894.
"Prevention of Cruelty to Women," *New Orleans Item,* April 6, 1880.
"Recent American Novels," *New Orleans Item,* June 18, 1881.
"American Magazines," *New Orleans Item,* October 27, 1879.
"American Art Tastes," *New Orleans Item,* September 30, 1881.
"The French in Louisiana," *New Orleans Item,* March 2, 1880.
"The Roar of a Great City," *New Orleans Times-Democrat,* November 30, 1884.

INDEX

songs (*cont.*)

Sixty-Ninth," 160; "Gal That Danced in Baba," 162; "Ginger Blues, The," 160; "Girl at the Sewing Machine, The," 162; "Gliding Down the Stream," 161; "Goat," 162; "Good Bye, John," 159; "Goodbye, Liza Jane," 159; "Go Way Bumblebee," 162; "Hail Columbia," 158; "Hanki Panki," 162; "Hard Times Come Again No More," 159; "Her Heart Was True to Poll," 162; "Higgenbottom Sisters, The," 162; "Hildebrand Montrose," 160, 166; "Hold the Fort," 169; "Home, Sweet Home," 158; "Hoolahan Musketeers," 160; "Hypochondriac, The," 162; "I Come Down the Mountain," 42; "If Ever I Cease to Love," 162; "I'm a Twin," 162; "I'm going away to New Orleans!," 41; "In a Garden," 161; "Independence Day," 158; "It's Funny How They Do It, But They Do," 162; "It's Funny When You Feel That Way," 162; "I Wish I'd Been Born a Girl," 162; "Jamie's on the Dark Blue Sea," 157; "Jenny with the Light Brown Hair," 158, 168; "Jim Crow," 158; "John Brown's Body," 158; "Jolly Young Sophomore, The," 159; "Jordan Is a Hard Road to Travel," 158; "Just as Good as Gold," 159; "Just Before the Battle, Mother," 158; "Keep Off the Grass," 162; "Kemo Kimo," 158, 162; "Killarney," 157; "Lancashire Lass," 157; "Lannigan's (Lannagan's) Ball," 159, 160; "Lass o' Lowrie," 157; "Lazy Club," 162; "Lean Banana, A," 161; "Let de Guilty Man Escape," 162; "Letter in the Candle," 168; "Lily Dale," 158; "Limber Jim" (or "Shiloh"), 44; "Litoria," 159; "Little Fraud," 161; "Little Maud," 161; "Love Among the Roses," 168; "Mabel Waltz," 159;

"Make Doun dem Blinds," 161; "Marching Along," 159; "Marching Through Georgia," 158; "Marriage Free," 162; "Maryland, My Maryland," 158; "Massa in de Cold, Cold Ground," 158; "Matinee Brigade, The," 162; "Meeting of the Waters," 157; "Memory Bells," 168; "Mill in the Valley, The," 159; "Moet and Chandon," 162; "Molly Darling," 161; "Molly Was a Good Gal, and a Bad Gal, Too," 40; "Monkey Married the Baboon's Sister," 165; "Mountains, The," 159; "Mother, Is the Battle Over?," 158; "Mother, I've Come Home to Die," 158, 161; "Mulligan Guards," 160; "My Nose," 162; "My Old Wife and I," 168; "Nelly Bly," 158; "Nelly Was a Lady," 158; "Nobody's Child," 159; "No One to Love," 168; "Norah O'Neil," 168; "Nothing," 162; "Number Ninety-Nine," 39; "Oh, Ain't I Gone, Gone, Gone," 39; "Oh Dat Watermelon," 162; "Oh Susanna," 158; "Old Cabin Home, The," 168; "Old Dog Tray," 158; "Old Folks at Home," 158, 161; "Old Kentucky Home," 158; 168; "Old Kitchen Floor," 162; "Old Log Cabin in the Lane," 168; "Old Oaken Bucket," 158, 162; "Ole Virginny Never Tire," 158; "Olive Oil, Olive Oil," 167; "On Shiloh's Bloody Hill," 159; "On the Beach at Long Branch," 160; "One Fish Ball," 159; "Patent Rubber Bustle," 162; "Pat. Malloy," 159; "Periwinkle Man," 162; "Peter Gray," 159; "Picayune Butler," 158; "Pretty as a Picture," 160, 168; "Pretty Little Polly Perkins," 159; "Pretty Waiter Gal," 162; "Pull Back Dress," 162; "Pull Down the Blind," 161; "Pull Down Your Vest," 161; "Pulling Hard Against